VOLUME I

TROUBLE
SPOTS
OF
ENGLISH
GRAMMAR

A TEXT-WORKBOOK FOR ESL

VOLUME
I

TROUBLE
SPOTS
OF
ENGLISH
GRAMMAR

A TEXT-WORKBOOK FOR ESL

MARY JANE COOK
The University of Arizona

Harcourt Brace Jovanovich, Inc.

New York   San Diego   Chicago   San Francisco   Atlanta
London   Sydney   Toronto

Preface

Trouble Spots of English Grammar: A Text-Workbook for ESL is a remedial grammar textbook and workbook for intermediate and advanced students whose first language is not English or is not standard English. The book may be used by students of English in other countries, by foreign students in the United States, and by speakers who come from bilingual backgrounds in the United States. Although it is primarily suited for university and college students, it can also be used for remedial and review grammar at any level, including junior college and high school, as well as in institutes and other special programs. The text is basically designed for written English and should be particularly useful in advanced grammar and composition courses for ESL students. The exercises can also be used for oral work in classes.

Trouble Spots of English Grammar is presented in two volumes. Volume I contains Chapters 1 to 9, and Volume II contains Chapters 10 to 17, with appendixes and an index in both volumes. Appendixes A, B, and C are included in both volumes, but Volume II also contains an Appendix D. Volume I presents verb forms and their usage in sentence patterns, including verb + verbal combinations and phrasal verbs. Volume II discusses nouns, pronouns, adverbs, adjectives, and other grammatical structures that function as these parts of speech. Prepositions are also presented in Volume II.

The material is organized topically, each chapter containing rules, examples, and exercises on one part of speech or point of usage. The topics are presented in sequence, and in each chapter it is assumed that the student is familiar with earlier chapters. However, because of this topical organization and the frequent cross-references to places where a point is treated in detail, an instructor can use the text in another order.

The terminology throughout the text is for the most part that of traditional grammar because traditional terminology is used universally and most teachers and students at the intermediate and advanced levels are already familiar with it. On the few occasions when a term from a newer grammar is used, the term is explained with examples.

Trouble Spots of English Grammar, as its subtitle —*A Text-Workbook for ESL* — suggests, can be used as both a textbook and a workbook. In each chapter the grammatical points covered are presented in sections. At the end of each section, the student is referred to exercise material on the point. The exercises are on perforated pages and are grouped at the end of each chapter so that the student may remove them without disturbing the textual explanation at the beginning of the chapter. An answer key to the exercises is available on request to the publisher.

Because of the sheer number of the colleagues and friends who have contributed to this text, it would be impossible for me to thank them all properly. I must, however, express my particular appreciation and gratitude to the late William A. Pullin, senior editor of the College Department of Harcourt Brace Jovanovich, for all of the help and encouragement he gave me; to Albert I. Richards, senior editor of the College Department of Harcourt Brace Jovanovich, for his assistance with the manuscript in its final stages; and to a very special person in my experience, Dr. Archibald A. Hill, who introduced me to the study of linguistics and whose interest and support throughout the years have been of inexpressible value to me. Finally, I must say a few special words in praise and appreciation of the many students, some of them learning English and some of them graduate students already teaching English or planning to teach English, who have been my inspiration in writing this text and have made the whole undertaking worthwhile.

Mary Jane Cook

Contents

INTRODUCTION: A REVIEW OF BASIC WORD ORDER 1

This chapter presents a review of basic word order and grammatical terms for the various parts of English sentences. It acts only as an introduction. If a term or point of word order is not entirely clear from the discussion and examples in this chapter, the student should refer to the index (or to the index in Volume II) to find where more detailed discussion is given. Also, when a grammatical item is discussed later in the text, the student may wish to refer to this chapter for a better understanding of how the various parts of a sentence function together.

Word order is the most important feature of English grammar. The order in which the parts of a sentence occur conveys their meanings and functions. Often only one order is possible in a sentence. When word order can vary, there are usually rules for acceptable usage. The major parts of a sentence are called **sentence functions.** The functions in an English sentence are these:

Subject.

Verb.

Complements. The kinds of complements are these: subject complement (also called predicate nominative, or predicate noun); subjective complement (also called predicate adjective); direct object; indirect object; object complement; and objective complement.[1] See Table 1 for examples.

Adverbials (also called adverbial modifiers).

Absolutes.

Complements, adverbials, and absolutes following the verb are often referred to as the **remainder.**

---

[1]There is one other type of complement: object of preposition. Objects of prepositions, however, appear only in prepositional phrases — prepositions plus their objects — and not as sentence functions.

TABLE 1

| Basic Sentence Patterns: Order of Subject, Verb, and Complements |

1. *Subject*   *Verb*
   John   sings.

2. *Subject*   *Verb*   *Subject Complement*
   John   is   a lawyer.

3. *Subject*   *Verb*   *Subjective Complement*
   John   is   friendly.

4. *Subject*   *Verb*   *Direct Object*
   John   knows   a lawyer.

5. *Subject*   *Verb*   *Indirect Object*   *Direct Object*
   John   wrote   his mother   a letter.

6. *Subject*   *Verb*   *Direct Object*   *Object Complement*
   John   named   his dog   Rover.

7. *Subject*   *Verb*   *Direct Object*   *Objective Complement*
   John   considers   Rover   intelligent.

The order in which sentence functions occur is called a **sentence pattern,** or the word order of the sentence. The order of complements, adverbials, and absolutes in many kinds of sentence patterns is the same; and differences among them often occur only in the order of the subject and the verb or the subject and the auxiliary.[2]

1.1   BASIC AND NONBASIC SENTENCE PATTERNS

Basic Sentence Patterns

The **basic sentence pattern** is a positive statement whose verb is not in the passive voice. There are seven types of basic sentence patterns,[3] as shown in Table 1. Following are some comments on the patterns and grammatical terms used.

A basic kind of **subject** is a noun. In the sample sentences in Table 1, the proper noun *John* functions as the subject. Other kinds of grammatical items that can function as subjects are said to have noun or nominal functions and are often called **nominals.** Another term for "nominal" is **substantive.** Here are examples of nominals in subject function:

John is friendly. (Proper noun)

Those children are friendly. (A noun phrase consisting of the demonstrative adjective *those* + the noun *children*)

They are friendly. (Personal pronoun)

To see is to believe. (Infinitive)

Seeing is believing. (Gerund)

---

[2]See Chapter 2 for a discussion of auxiliaries and auxiliary verbs.

[3]Some grammarians recognize a different number of types of basic sentence patterns, usually ten, often putting sentences with *be* as the verb in special categories.

Nominals are discussed in detail in Volume II, Chapter 11.

The verb in a sentence pattern is called a **finite verb.** A finite verb is a verb form that shows tense when it is "tied" to a subject. A very small number of verb forms show tense when they appear without a subject, among them the third-person-singular present forms (such as *sings, is, knows,* and *considers* in Patterns 1, 2, 3, 4, and 7 in Table 1) and some past forms (such as *wrote* in Pattern 5). Most verb forms, however, do not show tense when they are not tied to a subject. For example, in Pattern 6 in the table, *named* shows past tense when tied to the subject *John.* Not tied to a subject, however, *named* does not show tense. It could be part of a perfect verb form, as in "They *have named* the baby George," or part of a passive verb form, as in "The baby *was named* George by his fond parents."

The verb in Pattern 1 is called an **intransitive verb.** Intransitive verbs are verbs that are not followed by complements. Verbs describing motion, such as *swim* and *go,* are generally intransitive.

The verb in Patterns 2 and 3 is called a **linking verb.** Linking verbs are verbs that are followed by **subject complements** and **subjective complements** and generally include *be, appear, become, look* (in the sense of "appear"), *seem, feel, smell, sound,* and *taste.* A subject complement is a noun or other nominal that refers to the same person or thing as the subject. For example, in Pattern 2 in the table, "John" and "a lawyer" are nominals that refer to the same person. A subjective complement is an adjective, such as "friendly" (or another adjectival, such as "very friendly"), that follows the verb, as in Pattern 3. The terms *subject complement* and *subjective complement* are often used interchangeably.

The verbs in Patterns 4–7 are called **transitive verbs.** Transitive verbs are verbs that are followed by **direct objects.** A direct object is a noun or other nominal that refers to a different person or thing from the subject. For example, in Pattern 4, "John" and "a lawyer" refer to two different persons. Pattern 4 includes only one complement: a direct object. Patterns 5–7 include another kind of complement in addition to the direct object.

Pattern 5 includes an **indirect object** as well as a direct object. The subject, indirect object, and direct object refer to three different persons or things. Note that the indirect object precedes the direct object. Another way of stating the idea in the sentence is: *John wrote a letter to his mother.* In the latter construction, the direct object comes before the prepositional phrase *to his mother.* Some transitive verbs, among them *write,* may take an indirect object without a stated direct object, as in *John wrote his mother.* (The concept "letter" is unstated.) Or, the notion of indirect object may be expressed in a prepositional phrase: *John wrote to his mother.*

Pattern 6 includes an **object complement,** as well as a direct object. The direct object and the object complement refer to the same person or thing; but the direct object refers to a real person or thing, and the object complement is a title or a name. The direct object precedes the object complement.

Pattern 7 includes an **objective complement,** which is an adjective rather than a noun as in Pattern 6. The adjective denotes an appraisal or an opinion. It follows the direct object. The terms *object complement* and *objective complement* are often used interchangeably.

It has been explained that all grammatical items that can function as subjects are said to have noun or nominal functions and are often called nominals. A similar statement can be made about subject complements, direct objects, indirect objects, and object complements. These are all said to be nominal functions and are filled by nominals.

Nonbasic Sentence Patterns

All sentence patterns except the basic patterns just described are called **nonbasic sentence patterns.** The principal nonbasic patterns are found in negative sentences; *yes/no* questions; information questions with *when, where, why, how,* and other adverbial interrogative expressions, all of which will be referred to as *wh*-Adv in the text; direct information questions with interrogative pronouns (*who, which,* and *what,* for example) and similar interrogative expressions, all of which will be referred to as *wh*-N forms in the text; passive sentences; imperative sentences and sentences with *let's* and *please;* expletive-*there* sentences; and relative clauses, indirect questions with *wh*-N forms, and indefinite relative clauses, all three of which generally pattern alike.[4]

1.2   ADVERBIALS AND ABSOLUTES

The examples of basic sentence patterns in Table 1 include only subjects, verbs, and complements. The other two types of sentence functions, adverbials and absolutes, may occur in all types of sentence patterns, and they generally occur in the same order, regardless of the type of sentence pattern. Adverbials and absolutes are discussed in detail in Volume II, Chapter 15.

Adverbials

An **adverb** is one word, a part of speech. Adverbs may modify verbs, or they may modify adjectives and other adverbs. Adverbs that function in sentence patterns modify verbs and generally describe place (P), manner (M), frequency (F), or time (T).

Examples

   We went *there.* (Adverb of place)

   We walked *quickly.* (Adverb of manner)

   We rang the doorbell *once.* (Adverb of frequency)

   We entered the store *then.* (Adverb of time)

Other grammatical items also can modify verbs and describe place, manner, frequency, and time, as well as have other meanings. Adverbs and other grammatical items that function in the same way as adverbs are called **adverbials.**

Examples

   We went to *Mr. Cunningham's house.* (Prepositional phrase that consists of the preposition *to* + the object, *Mr. Cunningham's house,* and describes place)

   We walked *very quickly.* (Adverb phrase consisting of an intensive adverb, *very,* and an adverb describing manner)

---

[4]See the indexes (both volumes) for the respective pages on which all of these sentence patterns are discussed.

We knocked *several times.* (Noun phrase that consists of the indefinite adjective *several* and the noun *times*, and describes frequency)

We entered *after we had knocked.* (Subordinate clause describing time)

A basic position of adverbials is final position after Subject + Verb + Complements.

If more than one adverbial occurs in this position, generally the order is (1) place or manner, (2) frequency, (3) time.

Examples

John visited his grandparents *in Florida* [P] *twice* [F] *last month.* [T]

Eileen answered questions *incorrectly* [M] *several times* [F] *during the last class period.* [T]

The order of adverbials of place and manner is sometimes P - M and sometimes M - P.

Examples

Bill sang *beautifully* [M] *in the recital* [P] *last Saturday.* [T]

Anne went *home* [P] *in a hurry* [M] *after class.* [T]

Generally if one adverbial of any kind is shorter than the others, as in the two examples just given, it precedes the longer.

Adverbials of time may generally occur initially or finally.

Examples

Frances studied Italian *in Italy* [P] *last year.* [T] OR:

Last year [T] Frances studied Italian *in Italy.* [P]

One special class of adverbs, the adverbs of indefinite time (**always-words,** including *always, never, seldom,* and *rarely*), does not pattern as other adverbials do but has its own rules of word order. Briefly, in positive statements, adverbs of indefinite time follow these rules:

(1) They follow one-word forms of *be*, as in:

   The post office *is always* open at noon on weekdays.

(2) They precede one-word forms of other verbs, as in:

   It *never closes* for the noon hour.

(3) They follow the (first) auxiliary in a compound verb form (a verb form that consists of more than one word), as in:

   It *has never been* open on Sunday.

   It *has always been closed* for holidays.

In negative statements, *always*-words follow the word *not*, as in:

   It is *not always* open.

In positive and negative questions, *always*-words follow the subject, as in:

Is $\underset{\text{Subject}}{\underline{\textit{the post office}}}$ *always* closed on Sunday?

Isn't $\underset{\text{Subject}}{\underline{\textit{the post office}}}$ *always* closed on holidays?

The types and order of adverbials are discussed in detail in Volume II, Chapter 15.

Absolutes

Absolute is a sentence function filled by various kinds of grammatical items. Absolutes include the expressions *yes* and *no*; words of direct address (for example, *Bob*, in a sentence like "Have you read the paper today, Bob?"); conjunctive adverbs (*however, moreover, nevertheless, therefore,* and other such words): parenthetic expressions (expressions such as *as a matter of fact, in fact, in my opinion,* and *of course*); absolute phrases (for example, *it being a nice day*, in a sentence like "It being a nice day, we went for a walk."); and interjections.

Some absolutes, *yes* and *no* and interjections, can occur only before a sentence pattern, as in these examples:

Would you like to go to the movies? *Yes*, I would. OR: *No*, I wouldn't.

Oh, that is a beautiful car.

The other absolutes can generally occur in initial position (before a sentence pattern), in final position, and sometimes in medial position (within the sentence pattern), as in these examples:

In fact, I support your views strongly. (Parenthetic expression in initial position)

I, *in fact*, support your views strongly. (Medial position)

I support your views strongly, *in fact*. (Final position)

It being a nice day, we drove to the beach. (Absolute phrase in initial position)

We drove to the beach, *it being a nice day*. (Final position. Absolute phrases sometimes occur in medial position, but the order is often considered awkward by native speakers.)

The types and order of absolutes are discussed in detail in Volume II, Chapter 15.

Two Rules of Thumb

Two other important basic rules of word order are these:

(1) Do not put anything between a subject and a verb except for *always*-words and adverbs that can pattern like them, and some absolutes, as explained.

(2) Do not put any kind of adverbial between a verb and a direct or indirect object. Generally do not put anything between a verb and a direct object except an indirect object.

▶ *Now do Exercise 1A at the end of the chapter.*

The term **sentence** refers to a grammatical item in the language. The term **sentence pattern** refers to the order in which sentence functions occur. A group of words containing a sentence pattern is called a **clause.** A sentence may consist of one or more clauses. One way of classifying sentences is in terms of clauses: how many clauses and what kinds of clauses the sentence consists of.

There are two major types of clauses: **main clauses,** also called **independent clauses,** which can exist as sentences; and **dependent clauses,** which normally exist only as parts of sentences. Dependent clauses generally subdivide into two types, classified according to the ways in which they pattern: subordinate clauses; and clauses marked by words like *who* and *which* (relative clauses, some dependent interrogative clauses, and indefinite relative clauses), as will be discussed in this section.

Main Clauses

A **main clause** consists of a sentence pattern that either is not preceded by a conjunction or is preceded by a **coordinate conjunction** (*and, but, for, nor, or*).

Examples

> *The telephone rang.*

> I walked in the door, and *the telephone rang.*

Subordinate Clauses

A **subordinate clause** consists of a sentence pattern introduced by a **subordinate conjunction.** Common subordinate conjunctions are these: *after, although, as, because, before, if, since, that, unless, until, when, where, whereas,* and *while.*

Examples

> *When the telephone rang,* I was walking into the house. OR:

> I was walking into the house *when the telephone rang.*

Subordinate clauses that pattern in both of the orders just given function as adverbials. For this reason, they are sometimes called **adverb clauses.**

A subordinate clause may also occur after a reporting word like *say* or *ask.*

Examples

> The person at the information desk said *that the buildings on the campus were closed on Saturdays.*

> I asked *where the administration building was.*

In the first sentence just given, the clause beginning with *that* is an indirect statement. In the second sentence, the clause beginning with *where* is an indirect question. (Indirect statements and questions are discussed in Section 7.5.) Both clauses function as direct objects, just as a noun may function. For this reason, subordinate clauses used in this way are sometimes called **noun clauses.**

NOTE: Some subordinate clauses may optionally occur without subordinate conjunctions. For example, the sentence beginning "The person . . ." may have been stated without *that,* in this way: "The person at the information desk said *the buildings on the campus were closed on Saturdays."* Also, in formal style, *if*-conditions may occur without *if* with reverse order of the subject and verb or auxiliary. For example, the sentence "*If John were here,* he would play," can also be phrased "*Were John here,* he would play." (Conditional sentences are discussed in Section 7.1.)

Relative Clauses, Dependent Interrogative Clauses Marked by *wh*-N Forms, and Indefinite Relative Clauses (*wh*-N Clauses)

Relative clauses, some **dependent interrogative clauses** (also called **indirect questions**), and **indefinite relative clauses** function differently from each other but are grouped together because (1) with a few specific exceptions, they all pattern alike, that is, follow the same rules of word order; and (2) they are marked by relative, interrogative, or indefinite relative pronouns or by relative, interrogative, or indefinite relative adjectives, all of which are similar in form.

Except for the relative pronoun *that,* all of these pronouns and adjectives begin with *wh-.* The pronouns include *who, whose, whom, which, what, that,* and forms ending in *ever,* such as *whoever* and *whichever.* The adjectives include *whose, which, what,* and forms ending in *ever,* such as *whatever* and *whichever.* Most of the pronoun and adjective forms are alike. If they are not followed by nouns, they are called *pronouns.* If they are followed by nouns, they are called *adjectives.* The combination of an adjective + a noun is one type of **noun phrase.** The noun in a noun phrase is called the **noun headword.** Here are some examples:

ADJECTIVE	PRONOUN
I asked *whose book* it was.	I asked *whose* it was.
I wondered *which movie* you had seen.	I wondered *which* you had seen.

In the examples just given, *whose book* is a noun phrase consisting of the interrogative adjective *whose* and the noun headword *book* that it modifies. *Whose,* in the question "*Whose* is that?", is an interrogative pronoun. Similarly, *which movie* is a noun phrase consisting of the interrogative adjective *which* and the noun headword *movie. Which,* in "*Which* did you see?", is an interrogative pronoun. In the text, ***wh*-N form** will be used to mean relative, interrogative, and indefinite relative pronouns and noun phrases consisting of a relative, an interrogative, or an indefinite relative adjective + a noun. A *wh*-N form always has a nominal function in the clause in which it occurs. Word order in the clause depends on the function of the *wh*-N form. Clauses marked by *wh*-N forms will be referred to as ***wh*-N clauses.**

Relative, interrogative, and indefinite relative adjectives are three types of a class of words called **determiners.** These kinds of determiners are discussed in Volume II, Sections 14.9-14.11. Other kinds of determiners are discussed in Volume II, Chapters 12 and 13.

Relative and indefinite relative forms and clauses are discussed in detail in Volume II, Sections 14.9 and 14.11. Dependent interrogative clauses (indirect questions) are discussed in detail in Section 7.5 and also in Volume II, Section 14.10. Table 2 gives some examples illustrating how these three kinds of clauses pattern.

Relative clauses always modify nouns or other nominals and thus function as adjectives do. For this reason, they are sometimes called **adjective clauses.** Indefinite relative clauses and indirect questions generally function as nouns do (as subjects, subject complements, direct objects, indirect objects, object complements, and objects of prepositions) and so are sometimes called **noun clauses.**

TABLE 2

Some patterns in Clauses with *wh*-N Forms: Relative Clauses, Dependent Interrogative Clauses (Indirect Questions), and Indefinite Relative Clauses

***wh-N form as subject* (the subject is underscored):**

	Pronoun	*Adjective + Noun*
Relative clause	The person *who answered the telephone* was very polite.	The person *whose mother* answered the telephone was out.
Dependent interrogative clause	I wondered *what was on* television.	I wondered *what program* was on television.
Indefinite relative clause	Give your message to *whoever answers the telephone.*	Give your message to *whatever attendant answers the telephone.*

***wh-N form as direct object* (the direct object is underscored):**

	Pronoun	*Adjective + Noun*
Relative clause	The book *that I borrowed* is now out of print.	The book *whose title I mentioned* is now out in paperback.
Dependent interrogative clause	I wonder *who(m) John visited.*	I wonder *whose friends* John met.
Indefinite relative clause	Take *whatever you like.*	Take *whatever book you like.*

***wh-N form as object of preposition* (the object of the preposition is underscored):**

	Pronoun	*Adjective + Noun*
Relative clause	The person *who(m) I spoke to* took my message.	The person *whose secretary I spoke to* took my message.
Dependent interrogative clause	I wonder *who(m) you spoke to.*	I wonder *which attendant you spoke to.*
Indefinite relative clause	*Who(m)ever I spoke to* was very helpful.	*Whatever person I spoke to* was very helpful.

1.4 SENTENCE TYPES

As noted in Section 1.3, one way in which sentences are classified is according to how many clauses and what kinds of clauses they consist of. According to this kind of classification, there are four sentence types: simple, compound, complex, and compound-complex.

Simple Sentences

A sentence that consists of one main clause is called a **simple sentence.** For example:

The telephone rang.

Simple sentences may contain **compound elements,** as in these examples:

The telephone and the doorbell rang at the same time. (Compound subject: two parts)

Someone *shouted and knocked* at the same time. (Compound verb: two parts)

We looked out the window and saw *a man, a woman, and three small children.* (Compound direct object: three parts)

Compound Sentences

A sentence that consists of more than one main clause and no dependent clauses is called a **compound sentence.** Clauses in a compound sentence may be connected by a comma and a coordinate conjunction. For example:

I walked in the door, *and* the telephone rang.

Or they may be connected in other ways, principally by a semicolon. If a semicolon is used, a conjunctive adverb (a word like *however* or *therefore*) is also generally used.

Examples

We had hoped to be home before dark; *however,* the plane was late. OR:
We had hoped to be home before dark; the plane, *however,* was late.

Occasionally a conjunctive adverb appears in final position (as in, for example, "the plane was late, *however*"), but the order is not as common as the orders in the two examples just given.

Conjunctive adverbs are generally set off (preceded and followed) by punctuation, as in the examples.

Complex Sentences

A sentence that consists of a main clause and one or more dependent clauses is called a **complex sentence.** Here are examples of main clause + subordinate adverbial clause:

> I was walking into the house *when the telephone rang.* OR:
>
> *When the telephone rang,* I was walking into the house.

Note that when the main clause precedes, as in the first example just given, a comma is generally not used between the clauses. When the subordinate clause precedes, as in the second example, a comma is used.

Here is an example of main clause + clause marked by a *wh*-N form:

> The person *who answered the telephone* was helpful.

This example contains a relative clause. Relative clauses may or may not be set off with commas, depending on whether they are *restrictive* or *nonrestrictive*. Restrictive and nonrestrictive relative clauses and punctuation are discussed in Volume II, Section 14.9. Sentences in which clauses with *wh*-N forms function in nominal functions, as subjects and complements of various kinds, normally are not separated from the rest of the sentence by commas.

Examples

> *Who(m)ever I spoke to* was very helpful. (The indefinite relative clause functions as a subject. It is not separated from the predicate by a comma.)
>
> I wonder *who(m) Alice visited.* (The indirect question functions as a direct object. It is not separated from the verb *wonder* by a comma.)

Compound-Complex Sentences

A sentence that consists of more than one main clause and at least one dependent clause is called a **compound-complex sentence.** For example:

> When I walked in the door, the telephone rang, and the person who answered gave me your message.

The main clauses are *the telephone rang* and *the person gave me your message.* The dependent clauses are *when I walked in the door* (subordinate clause) and *who answered* (relative clause).

Punctuation in a compound-complex sentence depends on the specific elements and their order in the sentence: whether they are adverbial, restrictive or nonrestrictive, and so on. Often a semicolon rather than a comma is used with a coordinate conjunction when there are other commas in the sentence, as in the sentence just given. It could also have been punctuated in this way:

> When I walked in the door, the telephone rang; and the person who answered gave me your message.

Now do Exercise 1B at the end of the chapter. ◀

1.5 LEVELS OF USAGE IN THE TEXT

Throughout the text, the usage described and contained in the examples is generally **standard,** that is, accepted on both the written and spoken levels by educated speakers of English according to current handbooks of usage and current dictionaries. This kind of usage is generally not labeled. Where appropriate in the text, reference is made to usage accepted on the spoken but not the standard written level by educated speakers. This kind of usage is labeled **informal** in this text, as it generally is in current handbooks and dictionaries. Informal usage is also accepted in such writing as letters to family and friends, in reproduced conversation, and so on. In this text, the term **formal** generally refers to usage that conforms to the most traditional rules. In some instances, standard and formal usage may coincide.

Here are examples that illustrate the three levels in the same kind of structure: a relative clause in which the relative pronoun, *whom* or *who,* is the object of a preposition, *with.*

FORMAL AND STANDARD: The person *with whom I spoke* gave me excellent directions.

In this example, the traditional rule requiring that a preposition — in this case, *with* — precede its object, *whom,* has been followed.

STANDARD: The person *whom I spoke with* gave me excellent directions.

In this example, the preposition, *with,* occurs at the end of the relative clause. This is acceptable order in current English.

INFORMAL: The person *who I spoke with* gave me excellent directions.

In this example, the subjective form *who* is used for the object of the preposition. The use of *who* instead of *whom* for objects in initial position in a clause is not accepted in standard written English.

The term **stylistic** is occasionally used in the text in referring to usage. *Stylistic* refers to special usage suitable to a specific style or situation, such as poetry, emphatic style, and so on. For example, adjectives usually precede the nouns that they modify, as in this example:

An *old, weatherbeaten* cottage stood among the dunes.

For literary effect or for emphasis, the adjectives might have been placed after the noun and joined with *and,* in this manner:

A cottage, *old and weatherbeaten,* stood among the dunes.

Finally, a word needs to be said about contractions. This text is primarily concerned with written English. Partly for this reason and partly for the sake of simplicity, examples throughout generally do not include contractions. However, a table of contractions is given in Chapter 2, Section 2.4, and contracted forms are used in examples of tag questions and other constructions where full forms are generally not used.

Sentence Functions   1A

For this exercise, refer to pages 1–2 and Sections 1.1 and 1.2, pages 3–4. For each sentence below, give the name of the sentence function of the word(s) underlined.

Example

_____ Our city is very beautiful.

Answer:

___Subjective complement___ Our city is very beautiful.

1. _____ Edward just telephoned.

2. _____ An old friend wrote him a letter.

3. _____ She is planning a visit to our city.

4. _____ She has never visited our city before.

5. _____ She has never even been in this area.

6. _____ Visiting here will be a new experience.

7. _____ Our city is a very beautiful city.

8. _____ It is not large.

9. _____ It is very quiet, and life here seems very leisurely.

10. _____ Some people call our city "the garden spot of the state."

11. _____ They also call it "the city of parks."

12. _____ When we show visitors around the city, we always take them to our largest park.

13. _____ We also take them to our historical museum if we have enough time.

14. _____ We have lunch in an outdoor restaurant.

15. _____ Sometimes we pack a picnic lunch instead.

16. _____ In fact, we enjoy bringing our own lunch even more than eating in a restaurant.

17. _____ We will try to have lunch outdoors at least once while Edward's friend is here.

18. _____ Both activities, however, are very pleasant ways of passing the time.

19. _____ We often show visitors a view of the city from the nearby mountains.

20. _____ It being a beautiful drive, we try to take them to the mountains as well.

Exercises

21. _____ We like to give them snapshots to remember their
experiences by.

22. _____ We think that our city is well worth seeing.

23. _____ We always like to hear what people say about it.

24. _____ Whoever sees our city is sure to want to come
back.

25. _____ We always invite them to visit us again.

1B   Sentence Types

For this exercise, refer to Sections 1.3 and 1.4, pages 7–11. Give the sentence type
of each of the following sentences. Underline each main clause once and each
dependent clause twice. Mark each dependent clause either S for subordinate or
wh-N for clauses marked by *wh*-N forms.

Example

When I went to the door, the person who had rung the doorbell introduced herself.

Answer:

Complex	<u>When I went to the door,</u> the person <u>who had</u> <u>rung the doorbell</u> introduced herself.

1. _____ The newspaper was just delivered.

2. _____ The mail and the newspaper were both left at the
same time.

3. _____ Someone just rang the bell and knocked on the
door.

4. _____ I see a car and some people in the driveway.

5. _____ I think that I have seen them before.

6. _____ They may be members of the Parent-Teacher Association that is meeting later today.

7. _____ I will answer the door, and you can put some
water on for tea.

8. _____ We can serve them some of the cake that I just
baked.

9. _____ The cake should be delicious; however, you had
better try a slice first.

10. _____ When you have seated our visitors in the living
room, I will bring in the tea and cake.

11. _____ I wonder what they are visiting us for.

12. _____ I wonder what business brings them here.

13. _____ I think that I know the woman who is wearing the green sweater.

14. _____ Whoever she is, she is dressed very attractively.

15. _____ I think that I have already met the man who is wearing the leather jacket.

16. _____ If you know those people, you can introduce us to each other.

17. _____ Strangers usually do not come to our house when they have not telephoned first.

18. _____ If they are members of the Parent-Teacher Association who have matters to discuss, perhaps I know either their children or their children's teachers.

19. _____ I see another car and seven people altogether; nevertheless, I think that we will have enough tea and cake for everyone.

20. _____ It should be interesting to meet these people, to learn their names, to find out the reason for their visit, and to talk with them a little.

LEXICAL VERBS AND AUXILIARIES IN SENTENCE PATTERNS 2

Throughout this chapter, examples of verb forms are given to illustrate the order of Subject + Verb in the various kinds of sentence and clause patterns. Detailed discussion and examples are given in Chapter 5 ("Independent Usage of Verb Forms"), Chapter 6 ("Nonindependent Verb Forms"), and Chapter 7 ("Sentence Patterns That Require Special Usage of Verb Forms").

INTRODUCTION: LEXICAL VERBS AND AUXILIARIES 2.1

With specific exceptions, the order, or pattern, of complements and adverbials in all types of sentences and clauses is the same, and only the order of Subject + Verb or Subject + Auxiliary differs. The important verb classifications from the point of view of word order are (1) lexical verbs and (2) auxiliaries. **Lexical verbs** carry the base meaning of verb forms and may occur with or without auxiliaries. Examples of lexical verb forms that do not have auxiliaries are these:

Mr. Woodward *plays* tennis. (*Plays* is the present form of the lexical verb *play*.)

Mr. Woodward *played* tennis this morning. (*Played* is the past form of the lexical verb *play*.)

Examples of the lexical verb forms that have auxiliaries are these:

Mr. Woodward *has* often *played* tennis. (*Has played* is the present perfect form[1] of the lexical verb *play* and includes the auxiliary *has*.)

---

[1]The present perfect form is discussed on pages 94–96.

17

Mr. Woodward *will play* tennis tomorrow. (*Will play* is the future form of the lexical verb *play* and includes the auxiliary *will*.)

The lexical verb in a verb form may be stated, as in the examples just given, or it may be implied in an elliptical construction, such as the reply to the question in this example:

Has Mr. Woodward often *played* tennis? Yes, he *has*. (The form *has* in the question is the auxiliary in the stated lexical verb form *has played*. *Has* in the reply is the auxiliary in the implied lexical verb form *has played*.)

Throughout the text, the term **form** (as in "present continuous form" or "past form") rather than **tense** (as in "present continuous tense" or "past tense") will generally be used in referring to verbs. The reason is that verb forms commonly referred to as "tenses" always include grammatical features besides tense. For example, in a sentence like "John *is reading* the newspaper," the verb form "is reading" — often called "present continuous tense" — includes not only present tense but also continuous *aspect*, or kind of activity, to be discussed in this chapter. Also, in a sentence like "If I *had* time, I would go for a walk," the verb form "had," sometimes called "past subjunctive tense," or more often simply "past tense" because it contains no subjunctive marker, includes not only past tense but also subjunctive *mood*, to be discussed in this chapter. Thus "form," being the more general and inclusive term, will be preferred to "tense."

2.2 PRINCIPAL PARTS OF LEXICAL VERBS

The table below gives examples of the principal parts of lexical verbs. Note that the **base form** is also called the **infinitive form.** It may occur with *to* or without *to*. In the text, the infinitive with *to* will be referred to as ***to* + Verb.** The infinitive without *to* is often called the **bare infinitive.** The present participle will be referred to as **Verb-*ing*.**

	BASE	PAST	PAST PARTICIPLE	PRESENT PARTICIPLE	*s*-FORM[2]
REGULAR	walk	walked	walked	walking	walks
IRREGULAR	ride	rode	ridden	riding	rides

A list of common irregular verbs and their principal parts is given in Appendix B. An outline of verb forms is given in Appendix C.

2.3 SPELLING RULES FOR ADDING *d, ing,* AND *s*

Adding *d* for Past and Past-Participle Forms of Regular Verbs

Add *ed* to the base form with these exceptions:

(1) If the base form ends in *e*, add *d: hope, hoped; tie, tied.*

(2) If the base form ends in consonant + *y*, change the *y* to *i* and add *ed: study, studied; try, tried; hurry, hurried.* But: *employ, employed; stay, stayed.*

---

[2]The *s*-form is the third-person-singular present form.

(3) If the base form ends in a single consonant preceded by a single vowel and the base-form final syllable is stressed when *ed* is added, double the final consonant. With words of one syllable in this category, always double the final consonant. An exception to the rule is that final *h, w, x,* and *y* are never doubled (Verbs ending Vowel +*h* are extremely rare.)

Here are some examples, with the symbol ´ indicating strong stress on a syllable.

NOT DOUBLED		DOUBLED	
wéed	wéeded	wéd	wédded
gléam	gléamed	hém	hémmed
bénefit	bénefited	fít	fítted
		permít	permítted
díffer	díffered	refér	reférred
rów	rówed		
stáy	stáyed		
fíx	fíxed		

With words ending in the spelling *u* pronounced as *w* + Vowel + Consonant, *u* counts as a consonant, not as a vowel, when endings are added. Examples are: *équal, équaled; equíp, equípped; quíz, quízzed.*

Adding *ing*

Add *ing* to the base form with these exceptions:

(1) If the base form ends in *e* preceded by a consonant, drop the *e* and add *ing*: *ride, riding; mine, mining.* But: *see, seeing.*

(2) With verbs ending in *ie*, replace the *ie* with a *y* and add *ing*, as follows: *die, dying; lie, lying; tie, tying.*

(3) If the base form ends in a single consonant preceded by a single vowel and the base-form final syllable is stressed when *ing* is added, double the final consonant. With words of one syllable of this type, always double the final consonant. An exception to the rule is that final *h, w, x,* and *y* are never doubled. Here are some examples, with the symbol ´ indicating strong stress on a syllable:

NOT DOUBLED		DOUBLED	
wéed	wéeding	wéd	wédding
gléam	gléaming	hém	hémming
bénefit	bénefiting	fít	fítting
		permít	permítting
díffer	díffering	refér	reférring
rów	rówing		
stáy	stáying		
fíx	fíxing		

With words ending in the spelling *u* pronounced as *w* + Vowel + Consonant, *u* counts as a consonant, not as a vowel, when endings are added. Examples are: *équal, équaling; equíp, equípping; quíz, quízzing.*

NOTE 1: In British English the final *l* is always doubled except in words derived from *parallel (paralleled, paralleling).*

American English: *tráveled, tráveling, tráveler*
British English: *trávelled, trávelling, tráveller*

NOTE 2: A small number of verbs have two acceptable spellings of derivative words, among them the following:

diagram	diagramed/diagrammed	diagraming/diagramming
program	programed/programmed	programing/programming
kidnap	kidnaped/kidnapped	kidnaping/kidnapping
worship	worshiped/worshipped	worshiping/worshipping

The spellings with doubled final consonants are more common in British English than in American English.

Adding *s* for Third-Person-Singular Present Form

Add *s* to the base form with these exceptions:

(1) Add *es* to base forms ending in *s, x, z, ch,* and *sh: miss, misses; relax, relaxes; watch, watches; wash, washes.* Words ending in *z* preceded by a single consonant follow the rule for doubling the final consonant when adding *es,* as in *quiz, quizzes; whiz, whizzes.*

(2) If the base form ends in consonant + *y,* change the *y* to *i* and add *es: study, studies; hurry, hurries.* But: *employ, employs; stay, stays.*

▶ *Now do Exercise 2A at the end of the chapter.*

2.4   VERB FORMS AND AUXILIARIES[3]

There are two kinds of auxiliaries: **form auxiliaries** and **modals,** also called **modal auxiliaries.** Form auxiliaries combine with lexical verbs to describe tense, aspect, voice, and mood in the verb system. These four properties will be discussed shortly. Modals combine with lexical verbs to convey different kinds of meaning.

FORM AUXILIARIES   *be, do, have, will/shall, would/should*

MODALS   *can, could; may, might; must; ought to; will, would; shall, should*

---

[3]The basic verb forms are presented briefly in this section. Chapters 3–7 explore these forms and their usage more thoroughly.

Will, shall, would, and *should* occur as both form auxiliaries and modals.[4] All auxiliaries follow the same patterns in relation to their subjects.

NOTE: All form auxiliaries occur as both lexical verbs and auxiliaries. Some examples:

Lexical verb *be:*	Anne *is* in her office now.
Auxiliary *be:*	Anne *is reading* the paper now.
Lexical verb *do:*	Mr. Woodward *does* some chores at home.
Auxiliary *do:*	Mr. Woodward *does* not *drive* to work.
Lexical verb *have:*	Paul *has* a new car.
Auxiliary *have:*	Paul *has bought* a new car.
Lexical verb *will:*	Mr. Anderson *willed* his estate to his children.
Auxiliary *will:*	Mr. Johnson *will leave* everything to his children.

Verb forms have the properties of tense (present, past, and future); aspect (generally continuous and perfect); voice (active and passive); and mood (indicative, subjunctive, and imperative). Verb forms and their properties are discussed in this section.

Simple Verb Forms
and Their Accompanying Auxiliaries

There are three basic verb forms, or tenses, in English: present, past, and future forms. They are often called the *simple forms,* or *simple tenses.* The present and past forms of *be* (*am, is, are, was,* and *were*) in all sentence patterns have no auxiliaries.

Examples

Positive statement	Mr. Woodward *is* a tennis player.
Negative statement	He *is* not a golf player.
Yes/no question	*Is* he a squash player?

The past form *was* would pattern in the same way as the present form *is* in these examples.

The present and past forms of other verbs in positive statements in which the verb is not passive also have no auxiliaries.

Examples

Present John *sings.*

Past   John *sang.*

---

[4]*Will* and *shall* act as form auxiliaries for the future forms, and *would* and *should* for the conditional forms, as explained in this chapter. However, they may also act with modal meanings such as volition, obligation, and so on. Modals are discussed in Chapter 4.

Auxiliaries *do/does, did*

In negative and interrogative sentence patterns, *do* and *does* are used in the present form and *did* in the past form of all verbs except *be*.

Examples

Present	*do/does (not)* + Verb	John *does not sing*.
		Does John *sing?*
Past	*did (not)* + Verb	John *did not sing*.
		Did John *sing?*

NOTE: In British English the present and past forms of *have*, as well as *be*, pattern without an auxiliary, as in "Have you an appointment?" and "I haven't an appointment."

Future Form: Auxiliary *will* + Verb

The **future form** for all subjects in present-day English is *will* + Verb. The traditional rules requiring *shall* + Verb for first persons and *will* + Verb for second and third persons to describe future time (as well as *will* + Verb for first persons and *shall* + Verb for second and third persons to express determination) are no longer common usage.

Examples

We *will sing*.

Jane *will accompany*.

I *will start* first.

Aspect

Aspect is a term that has only recently begun to appear in English grammar. The term *aspect* means generally "kind of activity or condition." The simple verb forms just discussed — present, past, and future — are usually not described in terms of aspect. If they are, they are often said to have punctual aspect.

Punctual Aspect

Punctual aspect basically describes an activity or condition taking place at one point in time, or repeated at several points in time. ("Punctual" is derived from Latin *punctum*, meaning "point.") There is no auxiliary marking punctual forms.

Examples

John *takes* a walk every day. (Describes an activity repeated at points in time in the present.)

John *took* a walk yesterday. (Describes an activity at one point in time in the past.)

John *will take* a walk this afternoon. (Describes an activity at a point in time in the future.)

Two other kinds of verb forms that describe aspect are the continuous forms and the perfect forms, which are discussed next.

Continuous Forms: Auxiliary *be* + Verb-*ing*

Continuous forms, often called continuous tenses, basically describe an activity or a condition continuing at the time of speaking. (The term *progressive* is a synonym for *continuous* in describing verb forms.) Continuous forms are said to have **continuous aspect.** The general form is *be* + Verb-*ing*.

Examples

Carolyn *is eating* dinner now. (Present continuous: present of *be* + Verb-*ing*. Describes an activity continuing in the present.)

Carolyn *will be eating* breakfast when we arrive. (Future continuous: future of *be* + Verb-*ing*. Describes an activity continuing in the future.)

Perfect Forms: Auxiliary *have* + Past Participle

Perfect aspect forms, often called perfect tenses, basically describe an activity, a condition, or a series of repeated activities or conditions *perfected*, or *completed*, at the time of speaking — which may be present, past, or future. Perfect forms are said to have **perfect aspect.** The general form is *have* + past participle.

Present Perfect: present of *have* + past participle.

Example

John *has eaten* dinner. (*Has eaten* describes an activity completed from the point of view of *present* time.)

Past Perfect: past of *have* + past participle.

Example

John *had eaten* dinner before we arrived. (*Had eaten* describes an activity completed from the point of view of *past* time, before another activity in the past.)

Future Perfect: future of *have* + past participle.

Example

John *will have eaten* dinner before we arrive. (*Will have eaten* describes an activity completed from the point of view of *future* time, before another activity in the future.)

NOTE: Shades of meaning besides basic aspect (perfect, continuous, or punctual) may also be expressed in verb forms.

Example

> I *was reading* when you telephoned. (The past continuous form *was reading* not only describes an activity continuing in past time but also implies an interruption of the activity.)

Also, verb forms are not the only means by which aspect is expressed in English. Aspect may be expressed semantically, in the meanings of verbs and other kinds of expressions.

Example

> John *studied* all afternoon. (*Studied* is a simple past, or punctual, form; but it expresses continuous aspect through the meanings of *study* and *all afternoon.*)

Voice and Passive Voice Auxiliary: *be* + Past Participle

Voice is a verb property that indicates the relationship between a subject — that is, a grammatical subject — and a verb. A **grammatical subject** is the subject in a sentence pattern. When the grammatical subject of a verb is the **agent,** sometimes explained as the person or thing that "causes" the activity or condition, the verb is in the **active voice.** When the grammatical subject of a verb is not the agent, the verb is normally in the **passive voice.** The general form of the passive voice is *be* + past participle.

Examples

Active   *Everyone will see* the new play.
              (*Everyone* is both the grammatical subject and the agent. The verb form *will see* is in the active voice.)

Passive   *The play will be seen* by everyone.
              (*The play* is the grammatical subject but not the agent. The verb form *will be seen* is in the passive voice.)

NOTE: English is generally described as having two voices: active and passive. Actually only transitive verbs — verbs that take direct objects — can have active and passive voice. In the examples just given, the verb *see* is transitive. Intransitive verbs (such as *going* in a sentence like "Everyone *is going* to the new play") and linking verbs (such as *is* in a sentence like "The new play *is* excellent") do not have direct objects and cannot occur in passive forms. Such verbs are sometimes said to have "**middle voice.**" More often, they are not described in terms of voice at all. In this text, the term **nonpassive** will sometimes be used to describe intransitive and linking verbs.

Mood is a verb property that indicates whether the notion expressed is to be understood as fact, or as contrary to fact or of a doubtful or only possible nature. There are three moods in English: **indicative, subjunctive,** and **imperative.** There are no auxiliaries of mood, as such. Auxiliaries are in the indicative, subjunctive, or imperative mood according to notions that they are expressing.

Indicative and Subjunctive Moods

Generally indicative mood indicates that the notion expressed is to be understood as fact; subjunctive mood indicates that the notion expressed is to be understood as contrary to fact or of a doubtful or only possible nature. In an earlier stage of English, there were complete sets of corresponding indicative and subjunctive forms, generally recognizable from one another. In present-day English, most indicative and subjunctive forms are the same, and there remain only a few subjunctive forms that are different from the indicative forms.

NOTE: We principally know verb forms to be subjunctive because of the specific sentence patterns in which they still occur: conditional sentences, clauses following the verb *wish*, and clauses following such expressions as *demand* and *be necessary.* All of these patterns describe "subjunctive situations," situations understood to be contrary to fact, doubtful, or only possible. These sentence patterns are discussed in Chapter 7.

Another clue to subjunctive usage is that a subjunctive form, even when identical with an indicative form, often indicates a *time* different from that of its *tense.* To understand the subjunctive mood, it is important to distinguish between tense and time. **Tense** refers to a grammatical feature used to describe time in the verb systems of English and many other languages; **time** refers to the nonlinguistic notion of a succession of events divided into present, past, and future. Some languages do not have tense but describe time in other ways, such as through adverbs.

Examples

I *had* time to visit some friends yesterday. (*Had* is *past indicative:* it expresses fact. The tense and the time are both past.)

If I *had* time (but I do not), I would visit some friends this afternoon. (*Had* is *past subjunctive:* here it expresses a notion contrary to fact. The tense is past, but the time is present.)

Generally, in present-day English, verb forms that are not clearly subjunctive or imperative, as discussed in this section, are not described in terms of mood. Subjunctive forms continue to disappear from the English language.

The only subjunctive forms that are different from indicative forms today are these:

(1) The present subjunctive of all lexical verbs and auxiliaries is the same as the base form.

Example

The president demanded that every club member *vote*. (Clause following *demand/be necessary* expression. Meaning: Even though the vote is demanded, every member still may or may not vote.)

(2) The past subjunctive of *be* is *were* for all subjects. Compare:

Past indicative of *be:*   I, he, she, it *was*
                                  we, you, they *were*

Past subjunctive of *be:*   I, you, he, she, it, we, they *were*

Example

If John *were* here, he would surely help you. (Past subjunctive in a present contrary-to-fact condition. Many grammarians now accept "if John [or I, he, she, it] was" in informal usage.)

(3) The present conditional (*would* + Verb) and the past conditional (*would have* + past participle) generally occur as subjunctive forms, that is, in one of the sentence patterns describing a "subjunctive" situation.

Examples

I wish that Anne *would come* with us. (Clause following *wish*. Meaning of doubt or possibility rather than fact: Probably Anne will not come with us, but she may.)

If I had known your flight number, I *would have met* your plane. (Past contrary-to-fact condition. Meaning: I did not meet your plane.)

Imperative Mood

The **imperative mood form,** and imperative sentence pattern, express a command. The imperative form of a verb is the same as the base form, and the subject (*you*) is generally not expressed.

Examples

Be quiet.

Give me back my pencil.

NOTE: The subject *you* may be expressed if the meaning is highly emphatic: "You be quiet" or "You give me back my pencil."

The imperative form and pattern may appear with *let's* and *please* in what are often called "polite imperatives," as in these examples:

Let's be quiet. (May mean a polite command or suggestion.)

Please be quiet. (Command.)

Combinations of Properties of Verb Forms

Verb forms usually include more than one of the properties of tense, aspect, voice, and mood.

Examples

Everyone *saw* the play. (Past tense, active voice)

The play *was seen* by everyone. (Past tense, passive voice)

The play *was being seen* by everyone last week. (Past tense, passive voice, continuous aspect)

If the play *were being seen* by everyone, there would be no tickets available. (Past tense, subjunctive mood, passive voice, continuous aspect.)

Now do Exercise 2B at the end of the chapter. ◀

Contractions of Form Auxiliaries, Modals, and *not*

Contractions occur frequently in spoken English and in informal written English, such as reproduced conversation, personal letters, and so on. Contractions are becoming increasingly acceptable in written English and are found in newspapers, magazines, and many books, including textbooks. Common contractions are listed in Table 1.

TABLE 1

Forms of Contractions	
be	I'm; you're, we're, they're; he's, she's, it's; who's, what's, how's
have/has	I've, you've, we've, they've; he's, she's, it's; who've, who's, what's
had/would	I'd, you'd, we'd, they'd, he'd, she'd, it'd; who'd
will/shall	I'll, you'll, we'll, they'll, he'll, she'll, it'll; who'll, what'll
modal + *have*	could've, might've, must've, should've, would've
be + *not*	I'm not; you're not, you aren't; we're not, we aren't; they're not, they aren't; he's not, he isn't; she's not, she isn't; it's not, it isn't; who's not, who isn't; what's not, what isn't
do + *not*	I don't, we don't, you don't, they don't, he doesn't, she doesn't, it doesn't
modal + *not*	can't, couldn't; mustn't; shouldn't; won't, wouldn't*
Noun subjects	Noun subjects may occur with contractions, as in *John's here, John's not at home, The Browns're here, The dog'll bark,* and so on.
Indefinite pronoun subjects	Indefinite pronouns may occur with contractions, as in *Everybody's here, No one's arrived yet,* and so on. (For a list of indefinite pronouns, see Volume II, Section 14.7.)
Questions	-n't forms appear in questions, as in *Aren't you coming with us? Don't you like movies? Can't you come with us?*

*The forms *mayn't, mightn't, shan't,* and *oughtn't* are rare in American English. They are more common in British English.

2.5 PATTERNS IN POSITIVE AND NEGATIVE STATEMENTS, *yes/no* QUESTIONS, AND SHORT-FORM *yes/no* ANSWERS

This section deals with sentence patterns in positive and negative statements, *yes/no* questions, and short-form *yes/no* answers. For sentences with the basic positive pattern Subject + Verb ± Complement(s) ± Adverbial(s), differences occur only in connection with the subject and verb auxiliary (or first auxiliary, if there is more than one auxiliary). The order of complements and adverbials is generally the same. In negative statements and questions, *not* follows one-word forms of *be* or the (first) auxiliary. In *yes/no* questions, the order of Subject + Verb or Subject + (First) Auxiliary is inverted.

Patterns with One-Word Forms of *be:* No Auxiliary

Sentences with one-word forms of *be* (the present forms *am*, *is*, and *are* and the past forms *was* and *were*) pattern as in these examples. There is no form auxiliary.

POSITIVE STATEMENT	*The library is* open now.
NEGATIVE STATEMENT	*The library is not* open now.
POSITIVE YES/NO QUESTION	*Is the library* open now?
SHORT-FORM POSITIVE ANSWER	Yes, it is.
SHORT-FORM NEGATIVE ANSWER	No, it is not. OR: No, it isn't. OR: No, it's not.

Present and Past Forms of Verbs Other than *be*

In positive statements, verbs other than *be* take no form auxiliary in the simple present and past forms. In American English, however, all verbs other than *be* take the auxiliary *do/does* in the present and *did* in the past for negative statements and all *yes/no* questions.

PRESENT FORMS

Positive statement:	Anne *drives* to school every day.
	Her friends *drive* to school every day.
Negative statement:	Anne *does not drive* to school every day.
	Her friends *do not drive* to school every day.
Positive *yes/no* question:	*Does* Anne *drive* to school every day?
	Do her friends drive to school every day?
Short-form positive answer:	Yes, she does.
Short-form negative answer:	No, she does not. OR: No, she doesn't.
Short-form positive answer:	Yes, they do.
Short-form negative answer:	No, they do not. OR: No, they don't.

PAST FORMS

Positive statement:	George *drove* to school last year.
Negative statement:	George *did not drive* to school last year.
Positive *yes/no* question:	*Did* George *drive* to school last year?
Short-form positive answer:	Yes, he did.
Short-form negative answer:	No, he did not. OR: No, he didn't.

NOTE: These forms of *do* are also used for emphasis, especially in oral English. Some grammarians classify *do* in this function as a type of modal, calling it the "emphatic *do*." An example of this usage may be seen in the second item below.

Speaker 1: I understand that you *don't* like movies. (Present negative auxiliary *do*.)

Speaker 2: On the contrary! I *do* like movies very much. (Present auxiliary *do*, stressed when used for emphasis in oral English.)

Patterns with All Other Verb Forms: One Auxiliary and More than One Auxiliary

In these patterns, other forms have at least one auxiliary. No matter what the specific all other verb forms contain at least one auxiliary. Regardless of what the specific verb form may be, the subject and the (first) auxiliary in positive and negative statements and *yes/no* questions pattern as in the examples below. Examples of other verb forms in patterns are given in Chapters 5–7.

ONE AUXILIARY

Positive statement:	John *has gone* to class. (Present perfect form: auxiliary *has* + past participle.)
Negative statement:	John *has not gone* to class.
Positive *yes/no* question:	*Has* John *gone* to class?
Short-form positive answer:	Yes, he *has*.
Short-form negative answer:	No, he *has not*. OR: No, he *hasn't*.
Positive statement:	Anne *is going* with us. (Present continuous form: auxiliary *is* + Verb-*ing*.)
Negative statement:	Anne *is not going* with us.
Positive *yes/no* question:	*Is* Anne *going* with us?
Short-form positive answer:	Yes, she *is*.
Short-form negative answer:	No, she *is not*. OR: No, she *isn't*. OR: *No, she's not.*

MORE THAN ONE AUXILIARY

Positive statement:	John *has been studying* all day. (Present perfect continuous form: two auxiliaries, *has* and *been* + Verb-*ing*.)
Negative statement:	John *has not been studying*.
Positive *yes/no* question:	*Has* John *been studying*?
Short-form positive answer:	Yes, he *has*.
Short-form negative answer:	No, he *has not*. OR: No, he *hasn't*.
Positive statement:	Paul *will have finished* his work by noon. (Future perfect form: two auxiliaries, *will* and *have* +past participle.)
Negative statement:	Paul *will not have finished* his work by noon.
Positive *yes/no* question:	*Will* Paul *have finished* his work by noon?
Short-form positive answer:	Yes, he *will*.
Short-form negative answer:	No, he *will not*. OR: No, he *won't*.

▶ *Now do Exercise 2C at the end of the chapter.*

Negative *yes/no* Questions, with Expected Answer Suggested

The positive *yes/no* question is a request for information. The negative *yes/no* question suggests the answer *yes*. It may also have an admonitory implication that the answer should be yes.

Examples

Positive *yes/no* question:

Is the library open now?
(The answer provides the information "Yes, it is open," or "No, it is not open.")

Negative *yes/no* question:

Isn't the library open now? (The expected answer is "Yes, it is." The question may also imply, "It certainly ought to be open. Why isn't it?")

NOTE: The form "Is the library not open?" — as well as equivalent forms in the examples that follow — is very formal and is probably more common in British English than in American English.

Tag questions are short-form questions attached to statements. Positive state-ments take negative short-form questions, and negative statements take positive short-form questions. Tag questions are rarely seen in print except for reported speech. Here are the basic forms they take.

Tag questions with present and past forms of *be (am, is, are, was, were):*

Your car *is* new, *isn't* it? Yes, it *is.*

Your car *isn't* new, *is* it? No, it *is not.* OR: No, it's *not.* OR: No, it *isn't.*

You *were* in Europe last summer, *weren't* you? Yes, I *was.*

You *weren't* in Europe last summer, *were* you? No, I *was not.* OR: No, I *wasn't.*

Tag questions with present and past forms of verbs other than *be:*

Anne *plays* the piano, *doesn't* she? Yes, she *does.*

Anne *doesn't play* the piano, *does* she? No, she *does not.* OR: No, she *doesn't.*

The students *held* a picnic last week, *didn't* they? Yes, they *did.*

The students *didn't hold* a picnic last week, *did* they? No, they *did not.* OR: No, they *didn't.*

With all other verb forms, the same auxiliary is used in the tag question as was used in the statement. For example:

You *have been* on vacation, *haven't* you? Yes, I *have.*

You *haven't* been on vacation, *have* you? No, I *have not.* OR: No, I *haven't.*

John *will be* at home, *won't* he? Yes, he *will.*

John *won't be* at home, *will* he? No, he *will not.* OR: No, he *won't.*

Anne *can play* the piano, *can't* she? Yes, she *can.*

Anne *can't play* the piano, *can* she? No, she *cannot.* OR: No, she *can't.*

Now do Exercise 2D at the end of the chapter. ◀

DIRECT QUESTIONS WITH *when, where, why, how,*   2.7
AND OTHER ADVERBIAL EXPRESSIONS

Questions other than *yes/no* questions are called **information questions.** Some information questions are introduced by the adverbial interrogative words *when, where, why,* and *how* and by expressions such as *at what time* and *for what reason.*

Keep in mind that the symbol **wh-Adv** is used to mean adverbial interrogative words and expressions. Other information questions, discussed in the next section, are marked by interrogative pronouns, such as *who* and *which*, and similar interrogative expressions, referred to as *wh*-N forms in this text. Information questions with *wh*-Adv and those with *wh*-N forms follow different rules of word order. In *wh*-Adv questions, the subject and verb, or subject and (first) auxiliary, follow the same order as in *yes/no* questions. Here are some examples:

YES/NO QUESTIONS	*wh*-ADV QUESTIONS
Is John at home now?	*When is John* at home?
Does Jane drive to school?	*At what time does Jane drive* to school?
Is John having lunch?	*Where is John having* lunch?
Isn't John at school?	*Why isn't John* at school?
Will John be traveling to New York next week?	*How will John be traveling* to New York next week?

▶ *New do Exercise 2E at the end of the chapter.*

2.8 DIRECT QUESTIONS WITH INTERROGATIVE PRONOUNS AND INTERROGATIVE ADJECTIVES

This type of information question is marked by an interrogative pronoun or an interrogative adjective. The interrogative pronouns are: *who, whose, whom, which, what,* and some forms with *ever*, such as *whoever* and *whatever*. The interrogative adjectives are: *whose, what, which,* and some forms with *ever,* such as *whatever.* Some of the pronoun and adjective forms are alike. If the word is not followed by a noun, it is a pronoun, such as *who(m), what,* and *which* in Table 2. If the word is followed by a noun, it is an adjective; the combination of adjective + noun, such as *whose children, what book,* and *which book* in Table 2, is one type of noun phrase. Interrogative adjectives are also sometimes referred to as determiners because they are one type of a class of words called determiners.[5] Interrogative pronouns and noun phrases consisting of an interrogative adjective + a noun will both be referred to as *wh*-N forms. *Wh*-N forms occur in various nominal func-

---

[5]Interrogative adjectives and other determiners are discussed in Volume II, Sections 12.3–12.5 and Chapter 13.

tions. Patterns in information questions with *wh*-N forms depend on the function of the *wh*-N form. Examples of some of the different patterns are shown in Table 2. Further examples are given in Volume II, Section 14.10.

TABLE 2

Some different Patterns of *wh*-N Forms in Information Questions

The following symbols are used in this table:

S = Subject	Prep = Preposition	V = Verb	Remainder = Complements and adverbials following the verb
DO = Direct object	OP = Object of preposition	Aux = Auxiliary	

Function	Interrogative pronoun	Interrogative adjective + noun
wh-N form as subject: order is Subject + Verb	$\overset{S}{\underline{Who}}\ \overset{V}{\underline{was}}$ at the party?	$\overset{S}{\underline{Whose\ children}}\ \overset{V}{\underline{were}}$ at the party?
	$\overset{S}{\underline{What}}\ \overset{V}{\underline{is}}$ the news today?	$\overset{S}{\underline{What\ news}}\ \overset{V}{\underline{is}}$ there today?
wh-N form as direct object: order is Direct Object + Aux + S + V	$\overset{DO}{\underline{Who(m)}}\ \overset{Aux}{\underline{did}}\ \overset{S}{\underline{you}}\ \overset{V}{\underline{see}}$ at the party?	$\overset{DO}{\underline{Whose\ children}}\ \overset{Aux}{\underline{did}}\ \overset{S}{\underline{you}}\ \overset{V}{\underline{see}}$ at the party?
	$\overset{DO}{\underline{What}}\ \overset{Aux}{\underline{have}}\ \overset{S}{\underline{you}}\ \overset{V}{\underline{read}}$ lately?	$\overset{DO}{\underline{What\ books}}\ \overset{Aux}{\underline{have}}\ \overset{S}{\underline{you}}\ \overset{V}{\underline{read}}$ lately?
wh-N form as object of preposition: order is	$\overset{OP}{\underline{Who(m)}}\ \overset{Aux}{\underline{did}}\ \overset{S}{\underline{you}}\ \overset{V}{\underline{speak}}\ \overset{Prep}{\underline{with}}$?	$\overset{OP}{\underline{Whose\ children}}\ \overset{Aux}{\underline{did}}\ \overset{S}{\underline{you}}\ \overset{V}{\underline{speak}}\ \overset{Prep}{\underline{with}}$?
	$\overset{Prep}{\underline{With}}\ \overset{OP}{\underline{whom}}\ \overset{Aux}{\underline{did}}\ \overset{S}{\underline{you}}\ \overset{V}{\underline{speak}}$? (formal)	$\overset{Prep}{\underline{With}}\ \overset{OP}{\underline{whose\ children}}\ \overset{Aux}{\underline{did}}\ \overset{S}{\underline{you}}\ \overset{V}{\underline{speak}}$? (formal)
OP + Aux + S + V ± Remainder + Prep, OR Prep + OP + Aux + S + V ± Remainder (formal order)	$\overset{OP}{\underline{Which}}\ \overset{Aux}{\underline{did}}\ \overset{S}{\underline{you}}\ \overset{V}{\underline{decide}}\ \overset{Prep}{\underline{on}}$?	$\overset{OP}{\underline{Which\ book}}\ \overset{Aux}{\underline{did}}\ \overset{S}{\underline{you}}\ \overset{V}{\underline{decide}}\ \overset{Prep}{\underline{on}}$?
	$\overset{Prep}{\underline{On}}\ \overset{OP}{\underline{which}}\ \overset{Aux}{\underline{did}}\ \overset{S}{\underline{you}}\ \overset{V}{\underline{decide}}$? (formal)	$\overset{Prep}{\underline{On}}\ \overset{OP}{\underline{which\ book}}\ \overset{Aux}{\underline{did}}\ \overset{S}{\underline{you}}\ \overset{V}{\underline{decide}}$? (formal)

---

*In object functions, the forms *whom* and *who* both occur in initial position, as do *whomever* and *whoever*. *Who* and *whoever* are both accepted in informal usage (generally, spoken English), but *whom* and *whomever* are generally required in written English. Interrogative pronouns and their case forms are discussed in detail in Volume II, Section 14.10.

Now do Exercise 2F at the end of the chapter. ◀

2.9 EXPLETIVE-*there* SENTENCE PATTERNS

Expletive-*there* sentence patterns have inverted word order of Subject and Verb or Subject and (First) Auxiliary, as in these examples:

          V S
There *is time* to go to the library before dinner.

        V Neg S
There *is not enough time* to go to the post office.

V   S
Is there *enough time* to pick up a few groceries?

Replies: Yes, there is.

          No, there is not. OR: No, there isn't. OR: No, there's not.

Expletive sentences are discussed in further detail in Volume II, Section 14.5.

Spelling the Principal Parts of Regular Verbs   2A

For this section, refer to Section 2.3, pages 19–20. Give the principal parts of the regular verbs listed below.

BASE	PAST	PAST PARTICIPLE	PRESENT PARTICIPLE	s-FORM
Example				
walk	walked	walked	walking	walks
1. annoy				
2. play				
3. study				
4. hurry				
5. carry				
6. defy				
7. die				
8. lie				
9. tie				
10. advise				
11. agree				
12. argue				
13. change				
14. hope				
15. mine				
16. leak				
17. seem				
18. drop				
19. plan				
20. wed				
21. fix				
22. row				
23. control				
24. permit				
25. refer				
26. differ				
27. allow				

28. develop   _____

29. travel   _____

30. total   _____

31. diagram   _____

32. program   _____

33. miss   _____

34. relax   _____

35. buzz   _____

36. reach   _____

37. wash   _____

38. ditto   _____

39. radio   _____

40. solo   _____

2B   Verb Forms

For this section, refer to Section 2.4, pages 21–27. Describe each italicized verb form in terms of:

Tense

Perfect aspect or continuous aspect (if applicable)

Voice (active or passive)

Mood (indicative or subjunctive)

In your description, follow the order given in the list above.

Examples

John *works* hard.
Answer:
_____ present active indicative _____

John *will have been studying* the piano for ten years next May.
Answer:
_____ future perfect continuous active indicative _____

John *has been invited* to play in Latin America.
Answer:
_____ present perfect passive indicative _____

1. The neighbors *are* at home.

_____

2. Our city *accomplishes* a great deal of good each year.

_____

3. Much good *was accomplished* by our city last year.

_____

4. The city *built* a new bridge last year.

_____

5. A new bridge *was built* by the city last year.

_____

6. Tourists *will spend* a great deal of money this summer.

_____

7. A great deal of money *will be spent* by tourists.

_____

8. Our city *is accomplishing* a great deal.

_____

9. A great deal *is being accomplished* by our city.

_____

10. The secretary *was typing* the end of the report an hour ago.

_____

11. The end of the report *was being typed* an hour ago.

_____

12. The students *have learned* a lot this year.

_____

13. Much *has been covered* in this course since September.

_____

14. The workers *had* nearly *finished* the new library before school started.

_____

15. The new library *had* nearly *been finished* before school started.

_____

16. We *will have paid* for our house by September.

_____

17. Our house *will have been paid* for by September.

_____

18. Our neighbors *have been repainting* their house this fall.

_____

19. The house next door *has been being repainted* this fall.

_____

20. The painters *will be finishing* their work this week.

_____

21. John's doctor recommended that he *take* a rest.

_____

22. A club member moved that the meeting *be adjourned.*

_____

23. If John *were* here, he would help us with our project.

_____

24. If John were here, he *would help* us with our project.

_____

25. If I *were studying* Spanish, I would spend the summer in Mexico.

_____

26. If I were in your place, I *would be spending* the summer in Mexico.

_____

27. If I *had finished* my work on time, I would have gone to the play.

_____

28. If I had finished my work on time, I *would have gone* to the play.

_____

29. If I *had been asked* in time, I would have been happy to babysit for you.

_____

30. If I had finished my work on time, I *would have been sitting* in the theater at this very moment.

_____

2C   Supplying a Negative Statement, Positive *yes/no* Question, and Short-Form Answers

For this section, refer to Table I and Section 2.5, pages 22–30. For each of the following positive statements, give (a) the negative statement form, (b) the positive *yes/no* question form, and (c) the short-form *yes* and *no* answers.

Example

The plane is on schedule.
Answer:
a. The plane is not on schedule.
b. Is the plane on schedule?
c. Yes, it is. No, it is not. OR: No, it's not. OR: No, it isn't.

1. The dog next door is a German shepherd.

   a. _____

   b. _____

   c. _____

2. The tickets for the play were sold out.

   a. _____

   b. _____

   c. _____

3. The committee planning for the new library meets every Wednesday.

   a. _____
      _____

   b. _____
      _____

   c. _____
      _____

4. The roses in my neighbor's garden bloomed last week.

   a. _____
      _____

   b. _____
      _____

   c. _____
      _____

5. The bus will leave for downtown soon.

   a. _____

   b. _____

   c. _____

6. John has bought a new car.

   a. _____

   b. _____

   c. _____

7. The library had closed before Anne arrived.

   a. _____

   b. _____

   c. _____

8. The cleaning woman in our building will have finished by five.

   a. _____
      _____

   b. _____
      _____

   c. _____
      _____

9. A famous baritone is singing tonight.

   a. _____

   b. _____

   c. _____

10. John was asked to sing at our annual community festival.

    a. _____
    _____

    b. _____
    _____

    c. _____
    _____

2D   Tag Questions with Answers

For this exercise, refer to Section 2.6, pages 31–32. Add a tag question to each of the following statements, and give a short-form response, using pronouns and a contraction wherever appropriate.

Example

   The plane is late.
   Answer:
   _____ The plane is late, isn't it? Yes, it is. _____

1. Business is slow this fall.

   _____
   _____

2. The students are not having a picnic.

   _____
   _____

3. The students were on time this morning.

   _____
   _____

4. Jane does not look happy.

   _____
   _____

5. The Watsons bought a new car last year.

   _____
   _____

6. The dog got out of the yard last night.

_____

_____

7. Our neighbors will not be at home.

_____

_____

8. Anne and Helen have not gone shopping.

_____

_____

9. John will finish his paper this afternoon.

_____

_____

10. Dr. Watson will not be leaving soon.

_____

_____

Direct Questions with *when, where, why* and *how* (*wh*-Adv)   2E

For this section, refer to Section 2.9, page 32. Form an information question from each of the following statements using the *wh*-Adv in parentheses.

Example

The plane is late. (why)
Answer:
_____ Why is the plane late? _____

1. Business is slow this fall. (why)

_____

2. The students are having a picnic. (where)

_____

3. Only four students were in class this morning (why)

_____

4. Jane looks happy. (why)

_____

5. The Watsons bought a new car. (when)

_____

6. The dog got out of the yard last night. (how)

_____

7. Our neighbors will be at home. (when)

_____

8. Anne and Helen have gone shopping. (why)

_____

9. John will finish his paper this afternoon. (how)

_____

10. Dr. Watson will be leaving soon. (why)

_____

2F   Direct Questions with Interrogative Pronouns and Adjectives (*wh*-N Forms)

For this section, refer to Section 2.8, pages 32–33. Form a question from each of the following statements, substituting the expression in parentheses for the italicized expression and making any necessary changes in word order.

Example

Someone knocked at the door. (who)
Answer:
Who knocked at the door?

_____

If *who* and *whom* are both possible, give both forms.

1. *Paul* was at the party. (who)

_____

2. Anne saw *Paul* at the party. (whom/who)

_____

3. Anne spoke *with Paul* at the party. (with, whom/who; two orders)

_____

_____

4. *John's car* was in the driveway. (whose car)

_____

5. Anne bought *Paul's car*. (whose car)

_____

6. Paul got a ride *in John's car*. (in, whose car; two orders)

_____

_____

7. *Something* is bothering Jane. (what)

_____

8. She needs to buy *a present.* (what)

_____

9. Jane knows *that salesperson.* (which salesperson)

_____

10. Jane is going to speak *with that salesperson.* (with, which salesperson; two orders)

_____

_____

PASSIVE VOICE: FORMS AND PATTERNS 3

BASIC FORMS OF THE PASSIVE VOICE   3.1

Passive and active voices were briefly explained in Chapter 2, Section 2.4. The general form of the passive voice is Auxiliary *be* + past participle. Table 1 shows examples of active and passive forms.

TABLE I

Tense	Active Voice	Passive Voice
Present	ask/asks	am/is/are asked
Past	asked	was/were asked
Future	will ask	will be asked
Present continuous	am/is/are asking	am/is/are being asked
Past continuous	was/were asking	was/were being asked
Present perfect	have/has asked	have/has been asked
Past perfect	had asked	had been asked

PATTERNS OF SUBJECT AND PASSIVE AUXILIARY *be*   3.2

In sentences with verbs in the passive voice, subjects and auxiliaries pattern in the same way as other subjects and auxiliaries.[1]

POSITIVE STATEMENT	*Dogs are* loved by many people.
NEGATIVE STATEMENT	*Dogs are not* loved by many people.
POSITIVE *yes/no* QUESTION	*Are dogs* loved by many people?

---

[1] For use of passive forms with modals, see Chapter 4, Section 4.11.

Yes, *they are.*
                              No, *they are* not. OR: No, *they aren't.*
                              OR: No, *they're* not.

INFORMATION QUESTIONS   When *is* your dog *fed?*
                              Who *will be invited* to speak?

3.3   ACTIVE AND PASSIVE VOICES COMPARED

Sentences with verbs in the passive voice are generally associated with sentences with verbs in the active voice having the same meanings, as in these examples.

ACTIVE VOICE

(1) Many people *love* dogs all over the world. (*Love:* active voice, present form)

(2) The parcel service *did* not *leave* your package here. (*Did leave:* active voice, past form)

(3) I suggest that our directors *invite* Dr. Mosley to speak at our banquet. (*Invite:* active voice, present subjunctive form)

PASSIVE VOICE

Dogs *are loved* by many people all over the world. (*Are loved:* passive voice, present form of *be* + past participle)

Your package *was* not *left* here by the parcel service. (*Was left:* passive voice, past form of *be* + past participle)

I suggest that Dr. Mosley *be invited* by our directors to speak at our banquet. (*Be invited:* passive voice, present subjunctive form of *be* + past participle)

▶ *Now do Exercise 3A at the end of the chapter.*

3.4   PREPOSITIONS USED FOR AGENT, MEANS, AND INSTRUMENT

The passive pattern may be expressed with or without an agent. An agent, as noted in Chapter 2, is the grammatical item that occurs as the subject (that is, the grammatical subject) of a verb form that is not passive and as the object of a preposition with a verb form that is passive.

Examples

Active voice   *Many people* love dogs. (*Many people* is both the grammatical subject and the agent.)

Passive voice   Dogs are loved *by many people*. (*Dogs* is the grammatical subject but not the agent. The agent is *many people*, the object of the preposition *by*.)

Prepositional phrases expressing agent, such as *by many people* in the example just given, are a type of adverbial called an **adverbial of agent.**

The examples given in Section 3.3 all include agents. In each of those examples, the agent might not have been stated, as here:

(1) Dogs *are loved* all over the world.

(2) Your package *was* not *left* here.

(3) I suggest that Dr. Mosley *be invited* to speak at our annual banquet.

When an agent is expressed, the prepositions generally used are *by* and *with*. *By* is used for most agents other than instruments and for means; *with* is used for instruments.

(1) *By* is used for personal and other animate agents.

Examples

My favorite book was written *by a friend of mine.* (Personal agent.)

The child next door was bitten *by a rabid dog*. (Animate agent other than a person.)

Mr. Adams was struck *by a car* while crossing the street. (Suggestion of a personal agent.)

(2) *By* is also used for natural forces.

Example

A whole town on the east coast of Florida was demolished *by a hurricane.*

NOTE: *through* is sometimes used for intangible agents other than natural forces, as in this example:

John was injured *through his own carelessness.*

(3) *By* is used for means.

Examples

This table was made *by hand.*
That one was made *by machine.*

(4) *With* is used for instruments.

Example

This examination must have been written *with a ballpoint pen.*

Order of Prepositional Phrases Expressing Agent

Prepositional phrases expressing agent are a kind of adverbial. There is no absolute rule for the order of Preposition + Agent and other adverbials (place, manner, frequency, time). Preposition + Agent does not usually occur initially except for extreme emphasis. As a rule, Preposition + Agent immediately follows the verb, and other adverbials follow Preposition + Agent.

Examples

>Dogs are loved *by many people* *all over the world.*

>Our fence was damaged *by a storm* *early yesterday morning.*

In both of these sentences, however, the reverse order of the adverbials would have been acceptable:

>Dogs are loved *all over the world* *by many people.*

>Our fence was damaged *early yesterday morning* *by a storm.*

▶ *Now do Exercises 3B, 3C, and 3D at the end of the chapter.*

3.5 USE OF THE PASSIVE VOICE

Generally use the active voice unless there is one of these specific reasons for using the passive voice:

(1) The speaker does not wish to identify the agent, as in this example:

>It *was rumored* that the presidential candidates have chosen their running mates.

(2) The speaker does not know the identity of the agent and /or feels that the identity of the agent is not important, as in this example:

>The wheel *was invented* many thousands of years ago.

The passive voice is also widely used in the jargon of some professions, among them a number of the sciences.

NOTE: The pattern Aux *(be)* + past participle may occur without describing activity, but rather a *state* or *condition.* Such sentences do not generally have corresponding active forms. This usage is called the **statal passive.** Here are some examples:

Passive: The library *is closed* by the custodian promptly at ten every evening.

Active: The custodian *closes* the library promptly at ten every evening.

Statal passive: This library *is closed* for the summer.

▶ *Now do Exercise 3E at the end of the chapter.*

For this exercise, refer to Sections 3.1–3.2, pages 45–46. Fill in the blank in each of the following sentences with the passive form of the verb in parentheses. Use the specified tense and the word *not*, if given.

Example

Television _____ by thousands of
people every day. (present; watch)
Answer:
Television _____ is watched _____ by thousands of
people every day.

1. Our local newspapers _____ by thousands of city
   residents every day. (present; read)

   In many cities, news _____ by television stations between
   one o'clock and six o'clock in the morning. (present; not, broadcast)

2. A new play _____ by our drama department just now.
   (present continuous; produce)

   The public _____ to rehearsals of the new play for the
   time being. (present continuous; not, invite)

3. Next month holiday parades _____ by millions of
   television viewers. (future; watch)

   Unfortunately, complete coverage of the next Olympic competitions _____

   _____ by all local television stations. (future; not, give)

4. The fireworks display at the local fair last night _____ by
   residents several miles away. (past; see)

   The sound of the fireworks display _____ by residents
   more than a few blocks away. (past; not, hear)

5. Earthquakes in this area _____ on a seismograph.
   (present perfect; record)

   Ground motion _____ by local residents recently.
   (present perfect; not, report)

3B The Use of *by*, *with*, and *through* in Expressing Agent with Passive Forms

For exercises 3B–3D, refer to Sections 3.1–3.4, pages 45–48. Complete each sentence below by filling in the blank with *by*, *with*, or *through*.

Example

All of the oak trees here were planted ＿＿＿＿＿＿ settlers.
Answer:
All of the oak trees here were planted ＿＿＿by＿＿＿ settlers.

1. Our graduation address will be given ＿＿＿＿＿＿ the governor.

2. Have you ever been thrown ＿＿＿＿＿＿ a horse?

3. Many plants were damaged ＿＿＿＿＿＿ early frosts this year.

4. Does anyone know who this statue was carved ＿＿＿＿＿＿?

5. This statue was carved ＿＿＿＿＿＿ an unknown artist long ago.

6. This wall must have been painted ＿＿＿＿＿＿ a roller.

7. Angel food cake should not be cut ＿＿＿＿＿＿ a knife.

8. Anne was injured ＿＿＿＿＿＿ her own thoughtlessness.

9. Was the embroidery in this tablecloth done ＿＿＿＿＿＿ hand?

10. The embroidery in that tablecloth was done ＿＿＿＿＿＿ machine.

3C Changing Active to Passive Patterns.

Change the following sentences from active to passive pattern. Rewrite the complete sentence.

Example

Many people all over the world love dogs.
Answer:
Dogs are loved by many people all over the world.

1. The postal service handles millions of letters each week.

＿＿＿＿＿＿＿＿＿＿＿＿＿＿＿＿＿＿＿＿＿＿＿＿＿＿

The postal service does not deliver mail on Sunday.

＿＿＿＿＿＿＿＿＿＿＿＿＿＿＿＿＿＿＿＿＿＿＿＿＿＿

Does the postal service collect mail on Sunday?

＿＿＿＿＿＿＿＿＿＿＿＿＿＿＿＿＿＿＿＿＿＿＿＿＿＿

2. Millions of people saw the last eclipse of the sun.

_____

Everyone did not understand the phenomenon.

_____

Have scientists predicted the date of the next eclipse of the sun?

_____

_____

3. Next week the president of our university will announce plans for a new stadium.

_____

_____

The builders will not begin construction before spring.

_____

Will the graduates pay for the new stadium?

_____

4. Recently heavy rains have caused a great deal of damage.

_____

Fortunately floods have not destroyed homes.

_____

Have heavy frosts damaged the fruit trees?

_____

5. Patient effort accomplishes much.

_____

Careless effort did not produce John's success.

_____

Did carelessness cause Alan's accident?

_____

Changing Passive to Active Patterns   3D

Change the following sentences from passive to active pattern. Rewrite the complete sentence.

Example

A newspaper is read by many people every day.
Answer:

Many people read a newspaper every day.
_____

1. Exercise is needed by most people.

   _____

   Regular exercise is not taken by many people.

   _____

   Is too much exercise taken by many people?

   _____

2. This morning's local paper will be read by thousands of people.

   _____

   _____

   Its editorial views will not be appreciated by all of its readers.

   _____

   _____

   Will the editorial page be read by many people?

   _____

3. All of the food supplies for our camp were eaten by a brown bear.

   _____

   Our tents were not destroyed by the bear.

   _____

   Was the bear seen by the forest rangers?

   _____

4. Many facts have been brought to light through research.

   _____

   The lecturer's presentation was made more meaningful through the use of colored slides.

   _____

   _____

   Have many discoveries been brought to light through accidents?

   _____

Use *someone* as a subject in these sentences, as in this example:

Passive: This bread was cut with a dull knife.

Active: Someone cut this bread with a dull knife.

5. This table was dusted with a clean cloth this morning.

_____

This floor was not cleaned with a wet mop this morning.

_____

Has this sink been scrubbed with scouring powder today?

_____

Directed Writing   3E

1. In a paragraph of 100–150 words, describe the procedure for something that you have done or seen done, such as painting a room or performing a laboratory experiment. Write in present time, using the passive voice. You may begin your paragraph with a sentence like this, for example: "When a room is to be painted, the first thing that must be done is . . ."

2. In a paragraph of 200–250 words, describe the procedure for something that you have done or seen done, such as preparing for a parade or a fair, preparing a stage for a play, or planting a crop or a garden. Describe the procedure in past time, using the passive voice. You may begin your paragraph with a sentence like this, for example: "Early on the morning of the parade, bleachers were put up for the judges to sit on."

MODALS: 4
FORMS AND PATTERNS

FORMS OF MODALS   4.1

The forms of the modals, or modal auxiliaries, are presented in the table below:[1]

PRESENT TENSE	PAST TENSE	PRESENT TENSE + *have* + PAST PARTICIPLE	PAST TENSE + *have* + PAST PARTICIPLE
can	could	can have	could have
may	might	may have	might have
must	—	must have	—
ought (to)	—	ought to have	—
shall	should	shall have	should have
will	would	will have	would have

Tenses and Times Expressed by Modals

Modals are used to express various meanings, as presented in the following sections. One of the most important features of modal meanings, however, is that the *tense* forms of modals, as shown in the table, often do not correspond with the *times* that they describe. For example, the present tense forms of all of the modals, not only *will* and *shall*, can express future meaning, as in this example:

I *can (may, must, ought to) leave* tomorrow.

---

[1] *Will, shall, would,* and *should* function as both form auxiliaries and as modals. *Will* and *shall* are the future form auxiliaries, and *would* and *should* are the conditional form auxiliaries (see Chapter 2, Section 2.4). These words are also classified as modals, partly because they can also function with modal meanings, and partly because they share the structural features of modals, as explained in this chapter.

So, however, can the past tense forms *could, might, should,* and *would,* as in these examples:

> I *could (might, should) leave* tomorrow.

> I *would leave* tomorrow if I were you.

Could also sometimes describes past time, as in this example:

> George *could speak* Spanish when he was a child.

Thus the meanings of modals might sometimes be best learned almost as formulas without regard to tense.

Characteristic Features of Modals

Modals share the following features:

(1) They have the same form for all subjects in the present form (unlike other verb forms, which have an *s*-ending in the third-person-singular present form).

(2) They have only present and past forms and the perfect forms with *have* listed in the table.

(3) They cannot occur without lexical verbs, which may be either stated or implied in elliptical constructions.

Examples

> Lexical verb *(sing)* stated:

>> John can *sing.* Can John *sing?*

> Lexical verb *(sing)* implied in an elliptical construction:

>> Can John sing? Yes, he *can.*

>>> No, he *can*not. OR: No, he *can't.*

(4) They are followed by the bare infinitive: "I should *leave.*" The only exception is *ought:* "I ought to *leave.*"

(5) They have first position before other auxiliaries, if any: "John *could have been singing* when you passed the practice room." (The modal, *could,* comes before the form auxiliaries, *have* and *been.*)

The remainder of this chapter deals with the usage of modals.

4.2   WILLINGNESS AND VOLITION

Will is generally used as a future form auxiliary, and *would,* its past form, as a conditional form auxiliary. Both forms are also used with the modal meaning of *be willing to.* Compare the use of *will* in these two sentences:

I think that I *will go* shopping this afternoon. (In this sentence, *will* functions as a future tense auxiliary in the future form *will go*, simply describing future activity.)

Some people either cannot or *will* not *learn* to dance. (In this sentence, *will* functions as a modal in the form *will learn*, meaning "are [not] willing [to]".)

Some other examples of the modal use of *will* and its past form *would* are these:

If you *will help* me with my chores, I can go to the movies with you.

If you *will not help me*, I will have to stay home.

(In both of these sentences, *will help* expresses not only future time, but also the notion of willingness to do something.)

If the children *would* just *be* quiet, I could finish my work.

If they *would not be* so noisy, I could finish my work.

(In both of these sentences, *would* expresses the notion of willingness to do something.)

Generally the subject is animate, but the usage pertains to forces of nature and other nonhuman subjects as well.

Examples

If only it *would stop raining*, we could go for a walk. OR: If only it *would stop* raining!

If only this car *would go* faster!

Will and *would* also occur in certain conventionally polite expressions, such as the following:

If it *would be* convenient, I would like to see you for a few minutes this afternoon.

If it *would not be* too much trouble, I would like to look up something in your atlas.

(*Will* might have occurred in both of these sentences, as in "If it *will be* convenient," but appears less commonly than *would*.)

NOTE: A general rule in present-day English is that *will* and *would* are not used after *if* in conditional sentences. This rule holds true for the future and conditional forms of verbs in general. The rule does not apply when the modal meanings of *will* and *would* are expressed as in the examples given in this section.

PERMISSION: *may, might, can,* AND *could*   4.3

May, might, can, and *could* + Verb are used in expressing notions of permission.

Requests for Permission

May, *might*, *can*, and *could* are all used in asking permission.[2] With all forms, it is customary to use *please*, and *could* is especially likely to sound blunt without it. *Might* is more commonly used in British English than in American English.

Examples

> *May* I please *use* your telephone?
>
> *Can* I please *use* your telephone?
>
> *Could* I please *use* your telephone?
>
> *Might* I please *use* your telephone?

Generally only *may* and *can* are used in replies to requests for permission.

Examples

> *May (can, could, might)* I please *use* your telephone?
>
> Yes, you *may.* OR: Yes, you *can.*
>
> No, I'm sorry. You *may (can)* not just at this moment.

Requests for Information About Whether or Not an Activity Is Permitted

Only *may* and *can* are used in requests for information about whether or not an activity is permitted.

Examples

> *May* library users *borrow* tapes and records?
>
> *Can* library users *borrow* tapes and records?
>
>> (Meaning: Is it permitted for library users to borrow tapes and records?)

May and *can* are used in replies.

Examples

> *May (can)* library users *borrow* tapes and records?
>
> Yes, they *may.* OR: Yes, they *can.*
>
> Sorry, no, they *may* not. OR: Sorry, no, they *can*not.

NOTE: Common replies to both kinds of question, in addition to the structured replies above, are these: "Certainly"; "Of course"; "By all means"; "Sorry. I'm afraid not at the moment [OR: today, OR: just now]."

---

[2] A conservative rule requires that *may* be used in asking permission and that *can* be used only in describing ability. Current usage is as stated in this section.

Statement of Information About Whether or Not an Activity Is Permitted

May and *can* are generally used in statements of information about whether or not an activity is permitted. *Might* is also used in statements about past time, but more commonly in British English than in American English.

Examples

Present time:

Only employees *may use* this door.

Trucks over 14' high *cannot use* this underpass.

Past time:

One hundred years ago anyone *could stake* a claim here.

Ten years ago the general public *could* not *drive* through this park. Now it is open to all.

Offers of Assistance

All four of the forms *may, can, could,* and *might* are used in offering assistance.[3] *Might* is more common in British English than in American English.

Examples

May I *help* you? (Common offer of assistance by a clerk in a store or in a similar situation)

May I *help* you put away these books?

Can (could, might) I *help* you put away these books?

The modal used in the offer of assistance may be used in the reply, as in "Yes, you *may*." Commonly, however, other conventionally polite responses are used, such as "Yes, please," "Yes, thanks," "That would be kind of you," "No, thank you, I've just about finished," and so on.

Requests in Indirect Discourse

All four modals can be used in indirect discourse, but rules for usage of verb forms must be observed. See Chapter 7, Section 7.5, for rules for usage of verb forms in indirect discourse.

Examples

Let's ask whether or not we *may (can) use* the telephone.

I asked whether I *could (might) use* the telephone.

---

[3]As with requests for permission, a conservative rule requires *may.*

I will ask whether library users *may (can) borrow* tapes and records.

I asked whether library users *could (might) borrow* tapes and records.

Let's ask whether we *may (can) help* put away the books.

I asked whether I *could (might) help* put away the books.

Note that *could* is more commonly used in American English than *might*.

▶ *Now do Exercise 4A at the end of the chapter.*

4.4   ABILITY: *can, could,* AND *could have*

Can + Verb is used to express ability in present and future time. *Could* + Verb and *could have* + past participle are used to express ability in past time and in sentence patterns where special rules of usage require the past and past perfect forms.[4] (Examples are given below.) In the meaning of ability, the lexical verb phrase *be able to* is synonomous with *can* and is used where the appropriate form of *can* does not exist, as well as in the present and past forms.

Examples

Present time:

George *can speak* Spanish. OR:

George *is able to speak* Spanish.

Past time:

He *could speak* Chinese when he was a child. OR:

He *was able to speak* Chinese when he was a child.

Present form to express future time:

Can you *come* with us tomorrow? OR:

Will you *be able to come* with us tomorrow?

Past form required in contrary-to-fact condition but expresses present time:

If Dr. Duncan *could hear* us [but he cannot], he would know that we have profited from his teaching. OR:

If Dr. Duncan *were able to hear us* . . .

Past perfect form required in contrary-to-fact condition to express past time:

If Dr. Duncan *could have heard* us yesterday [but he could not], he would have known that we had profited from his teaching. OR:

If Dr. Duncan *had been able to hear* us . . .

Past form required in indirect statement after the past form *told* but expresses future time:

---

[4]See Chapter 7, Section 7.1, pages 123–31, and Section 7.5, pages 136–43.

Paul told us that he *could drive* us to the picnic tomorrow. OR:

Paul told us that he *would be able to drive* us to the picnic tomorrow.

Present perfect of *be able to* required (there is no present perfect form of *can* to express the idea):

John *has* not *been able to walk* without crutches since his skiing accident last spring but hopes to do without them soon.

Now do Exercises 4B and 4C at the end of the chapter. ◀

POSSIBILITY: *may (have)*, *might (have)*, *can* 4.5 *(have)*, AND *could (have)*

All of these forms can be used to express possibility in positive statements. In negative statements and in questions, they sometimes have different meanings, or their use is restricted for some other reason.

Possibility in **present time** and **future time** is generally expressed with *may*, *might*, *can*, and *could* + Verb.

Examples — Present Time

Positive statement:

Tom *may be* at home now. OR: He *might be* at home now. OR: He *could be* at home now. OR, less commonly: He *can be* at home now. (All of these sentences have approximately the same meaning: "It is possible that Tom is at home now.")

Negative statement:

Tom *may (might) not be* at home now. (Meaning: "It is possible that Tom is not at home now." *Cannot* and *could not* would suggest fact or strong disbelief rather than simple possibility: "Tom *cannot (could not) be* at home now" implies "It is not possible that he is at home now.")

Question:

Do you think that Tom *might (could) be* at home now? OR, less commonly: Do you think that he *may be* at home now?

Examples — Future Time

Positive statement:

It *may rain* later today. OR: It *might (could) rain* later today.

Negative statement:

The sky is cloudy, but it *may (might)* not *rain* here. (*Cannot* and *could not* would suggest strong disbelief rather than simple possibility.)

Question:

Do you think that Paul *may (might) get* here tomorrow? (*Can* and *could* would suggest ability rather than possibility in this question. "Do you think that Paul *can (could) get* here tomorrow?" would imply the meaning, "Do you think that Paul will be able to get here tomorrow?")

NOTE: The use of *can* to express possibility in present time seems rare, but its use to express future possibility is common in such instances as these:

Both teams playing tomorrow are so excellent that anything *can happen* in that game. OR: Anything *may (might, could) happen.* (Meaning: It is possible that anything will happen.)

Nothing *can go* wrong.

Can anything *go* wrong?

    Past time is expressed with *may have, might have, can have,* and *could have* + past participle.

Examples

Positive statement:

Our speaker is not yet here. Her plane *may have arrived* late. OR: Her plane *might have arrived* late. OR: Her plane *could have arrived* late. OR, less commonly: Her plane *can have arrived* late.

Negative statement:

Her plane *may (might)* not *have arrived* on time. ("Her plane *can (could)* not *have arrived* on time" would suggest fact rather than possibility.)

Question:

May (might/can/could) her plane *have arrived* late?

The adverb *possibly* is often used to emphasize the notion of possibility, as in "Tom may *possibly* be at home now," "It may *possibly* rain today," and so on.

▶ *Now do Exercise 4D at the end of the chapter.*

4.6   NECESSITY, COMPULSION: *must* AND *have to*

In the sense of necessity or compulsion, *must* + Verb has only a present form. A synonym for *must* is *have to. Have to* + Verb is used whenever verb forms expressing other times are required. (An exception is the present negative form, as will be seen.)

Examples — Present Time

Positive statement:

Visitors *must use* the visitors' entrance. OR:

Visitors *have to use* the visitors' entrance.

Question:

Must visitors *use* the visitors' entrance? OR:

Do visitors *have to use* the visitors' entrance?

Negative statement:

Visitors *must not use* the employees' entrance.

NOTE: A negative statement containing *must* is not synonymous with a negative statement containing *have to*.

Visitors *must not use* the employees' entrance.	MEANS	Visitors *are not permitted to use* the employees' entrance.
Visitors *do not have to use* the employees' entrance.	MEANS	Visitors *are not required to use* the employees' entrance but may if they wish.

Here are examples of other instances where a form of *have to* is needed to express compulsion.

I *had to leave* the office early yesterday.

George *has had to work* hard since the beginning of the school year.

He said that he *had* already *had* to write three term papers this year.

The modal *must* is also used in some social formulas that express polite requests and suggestions.

Examples

You *must keep in touch* with us. (Meaning: Please keep in touch with us.)

You *must come to see* us soon. (Meaning: Please come to see us soon.)

You *must* not *wait* so long to visit us again. (Meaning: Please do not wait so long to visit us again.)

Must can also be used in recommendations for activities.

Examples

Washington is a beautiful city. You *must see* it. (Meaning: I suggest that you see it.)

You *must* not *miss seeing* Washington. (Meaning is equivalent to that of the statement above: I suggest that you see Washington.)

Now do Exercise 4E at the end of the chapter. ◀

4.7   SUPPOSITION: *must (have)*

The notion of supposition may be expressed by *must* + Verb for present time and *must have* + past participle for past time. The usage occurs only in positive and negative statements.

Present time is expressed by *must* + Verb.

Examples

Jane has not called recently. She *must be* busy. (Meaning: I suppose that she is busy.)

John's car is not in his garage. He *must not be* at home. (Meaning: I suppose that he is not at home.)

Past time is expressed by *must have* + past participle.

Examples

Some students did not come to the meeting yesterday. They *must have forgotten* about it. (Meaning: I suppose that they forgot about it.)

Alan has not called. He *must not have received* my message. (Meaning: I suppose that he did not receive it.)

Questions related to these situations are not expressed with *must* and *must have.* They may be expressed with the same modals as those used for possibility — *can, could,* and *might* for present time, as in this example:

Can (could, might) Jane *be* busy?

Can have, could have, and *might have* may be used for past time, as in this example:

Can (could, might) the students *have forgotten* about the meeting?

(Questions like these occur with *may* and *may have* but are rare and very formal.)

4.8   LOGICAL NECESSITY: *must (have)*

Must to express "logical necessity" (strong supposition based on facts) occurs only in positive statements. *Can* is used in negative statements. *Can* and *could* (or, more formally, *might*) are used in questions.

Examples

What John said *must be* a rumor.

It *cannot be* true.

Can (could, might) what John said *be* a rumor?

That strange noise *must have been* a dog barking.

It *cannot have been* a bear.

Can (could, might) it *have been* a bear?

Now do Exercise 4F at the end of the chapter. ◀

OBLIGATION, ADVISABILITY, AND EXPECTATION: *should (have)* AND *ought to (have)*   4.9

The forms *should (have)* and *ought to (have)* + past participle are synonymous and are used to express several different meanings: obligation, advisability, and expectation.

Positive Statements

In positive statements, *should* + Verb and *ought to* + Verb are interchangeable and describe present or future time. *Should have* + past participle and *ought to have* + past participle are interchangeable and describe past time.

Present Time

Should + Verb and *ought to* + Verb describe a condition or an activity that is obligatory, advisable, or expected at the present time but that may or may not occur.

Example

    John *should be (ought to be)* at home now.

This sentence may have any of the following meanings:

(1) It is John's obligation or duty to be at home now. Perhaps he is at home, perhaps he is not.

(2) It would be advisable for John to be at home now. Perhaps he is at home, perhaps he is not.

(3) I expect John to be at home now. Perhaps he is, perhaps he is not.

Future Time

Should + Verb and *ought to* + Verb suggest a condition or an activity in the future that may or may not occur.

Example

    Dr. Richards *should arrive (ought to arrive)* at his office before nine o'clock.

This sentence may have any of the following meanings:

(1) It is Dr. Richards' obligation or duty to arrive at his office before nine o'clock. Perhaps he will, perhaps he will not.

(2) It would be advisable for Dr. Richards to arrive at his office before nine o'clock. Perhaps he will, perhaps he will not.

(3) I expect Dr. Richards to arrive at his office before nine o'clock. Perhaps he will, perhaps he will not.

Past Time

Should have + past participle and *ought to have* + past participle describe a condition or an activity that was obligatory, advisable, or expected in the past but that did not occur.

Example

> Anne *should have written (ought to have written)* to her parents last week. But she did not.

This sentence may have any of the following meanings:

(1) It was Anne's obligation or duty to write to her parents last week, but she did not.

(2) It would have been advisable for Anne to write to her parents last week, but she did not.

(3) I expected Anne to write to her parents last week, but she did not.

Forms in Negative Statements and in Questions

In negative statements and in questions, *should* + Verb and *ought to* + Verb are synonymous, as are *should have* + past participle and *ought to have* + past participle. However, the negative and question forms of *ought to* and *ought to have* are more common in British English than in American English. These forms are likely to sound excessively formal in American English, and for this reason *should* and *should have* are preferable in American English. The negative and interrogative forms express the same meanings of obligation, advisability, and expectation as the positive forms.

Negative Sentences

should not + Verb and *ought not to* + Verb

These forms can describe either present or future time.

Example — Present Time

> Parents *should not be (ought not to be)* away from home at this hour.

This sentence may have any of the following meanings:

(1) It is the parents' obligation or duty not to be away from home at this hour. Perhaps they are, perhaps they are not.

(2) It is advisable for parents not to be away from home at this hour. Perhaps they are, perhaps they are not.

(3) I expect parents not to be away from home at this hour. Perhaps they are, perhaps they are not.

Example — Future Time

> We *should not miss (ought not to miss)* the meeting tomorrow.

This sentence may have the following meanings:

(1) It is our obligation or duty not to miss the meeting tomorrow. Perhaps we will, perhaps we will not.

(2) It would be advisable for us not to miss the meeting tomorrow. Perhaps we will, perhaps we will not.

(3) We are expected not to miss the meeting tomorrow. Perhaps we will, perhaps we will not.

should not have + Past Participle and *ought not to have* + Past Participle

These forms describe past time.

Example

> Eileen *should not have been (ought not to have been)* late for our meeting.

This sentence may have the following meanings:

(1) It was Eileen's obligation or duty not to have been late for our meeting. But she was.

(2) It would have been advisable for Eileen not to be late for our meeting. But she was.

(3) I did not expect Eileen to be late for our meeting. She left home in plenty of time. (But she was late.)

Questions

should + Verb and *ought to* + Verb

These forms can describe either present or future time.

Example — Present Time

> *Should* we *have (ought* we *to have)* someone at the desk during the noon hour?

This sentence may have the following meanings:

(1) Is it our obligation or duty to have someone at the desk during the noon hour?

(2) Is it advisable for us to have someone at the desk during the noon hour?

(3) Are we expected to have someone at the desk during the noon hour?

Example — Future Time

> *Should* I or the secretary *complete* (*ought* I or the secretary *to complete*) this report?

This sentence may be interpreted in ways similar to those in the preceding examples.

should have +Past Participle and *ought to have* +Past Participle

These forms describe past time.

Example

> *Should* I *have answered* (*ought* I *to have answered*) the telephone when it rang?

This sentence may also be interpreted in ways similar to those in the preceding examples.

▶ *Now do Exercise 4G at the end of the chapter.*

4.10 EXPRESSIONS RELATED TO MODALS

Some expressions that are related to modals in meaning and form are *had better (have)* and *would* (or *had*) *rather (have)*. These expressions are sometimes confused with each other, probably because they often occur in contracted forms in spoken English and sound alike, as in this example: "I'd better leave now, but I'd rather stay." The two *I'd* forms have different meanings. The first *I'd*, a contraction of *I had* with *better*, expresses advisability; the second, a contraction of *I would* or *I had* with *rather*, expresses preference.

had better +Verb and *had better have* +Past Participle

The form *had better* + Verb implies a suggestion and may be expressed as "It would be a good idea to do what is suggested." The meaning is future.

Examples

> You *had better carry* an umbrella. It looks as though it might rain today. (Meaning: It would be a good idea for you to carry an umbrella.)

You *had better not be* late for class. (Meaning: It would be a good idea for you not to be late for class.)

The question form is usually in the negative:

Hadn't you *better carry* an umbrella?

Hadn't you *better be* on time for class? OR: *Hadn't* you *better not be late* for class?

The form *had better have* + past participle expresses past time.

Examples

You *had* (*You'd*) *better have finished* your homework by the time I get back from the movies.

NOTE: The expression also occurs in the superlative: *had best* + Verb. This usage is more common in British English than in American English. For example:

It is late. I *had best be going.*

would rather +Verb and *would rather have* + Past Participle

These forms express preference. The forms *had rather* + Verb and *had rather have* + past participle also occur but less commonly than the forms with *would.*

would rather + Verb

This form describes present and future time.

Examples

Would you *rather stay* at home or *go* to the movies this evening? (Meaning: Would you prefer to stay at home or go to the movies this evening? Future time.)

I *would rather* not *go* to the movies this evening. (Future time.)

I *would rather be* here at home than out in that storm. (Present time.)

would rather have + Past Participle

This form describes past time and implies a situation that occurred contrary to a person's preferences.

Examples

Would you *rather have walked* to school than ridden? (Meaning: You rode to school. Would you have preferred to walk to school rather than ride?)

I *would rather have walked* to school than ridden. (Meaning: I rode to school. I would have preferred to walk rather than ride.)

4.10 Expressions Related to Modals

69

▶ *Now do Exercise 4H at the end of the chapter.*

NOTE: In their present-tense forms, *need (to)* and *dare (to)* occur both as lexical verbs, with an *s*-ending in the third-person-singular form, followed by a *to*-infinitive; and as modals, without the *s*-ending, followed by the base form, also called the bare infinitive. Here are examples. The usages marked with an asterisk (*) are more common in British English than in American English.

	PRESENT POSITIVE STATEMENT	PRESENT NEGATIVE STATEMENT
LEXICAL VERBS	Tom *needs to answer* this letter.	Bob *does not need to answer* this letter.
	Tom *dares to do* almost anything when challenged.	Bob *does not* often *dare (to) do* anything dangerous.
MODALS	*Tom *need* only *ask* in order to get what he wants.	*Bob *need not climb* the mountain.
	(The form "He *dare ask*" is uncommon, although it may occur in question form: "How *dare* he *ask*?")	*He *dare not ask* how high the mountain is.

In present-tense questions, *need* and *dare* behave as in negative statements. They commonly occur as lexical verbs in both American and British English, as in "*Does* he really *need to answer* the letter?" and "*Does* he *dare to keep going*?" Questions with modal forms, such as "*Need* he *climb* the mountain?" and "*Dare* she *leave* him there?", are more common in British English than in American English.

Other forms of *need* and *dare* pattern as lexical verbs, as in these examples: "Ruth *will* never *need to* or *dare to* ride that horse" (future form); and "*Has* anyone ever *needed to* or *dared to* ride that horse?" (present perfect).

4.11   PASSIVE FORMS OF LEXICAL VERBS WITH MODALS

The passive forms of lexical verbs following modals are the simple form, *be* + past participle, and the perfect form, *have been* + past participle.

Examples — Simple Form

Active: Anyone *may visit* the Capitol Building.

Passive: The Capitol Building *may be visited* by anyone.

Active: A child *could solve* this puzzle.

Passive: This puzzle *could be solved* by a child.

70   Modals: Forms and Patterns

Examples — Perfect Form

Active: A neighbor *may have accepted* your package during your absence.

Passive: Your package *may have been accepted* by a neighbor during your absence.

Active: A local craftsman *could have designed* this beautiful old desk.

Passive: This beautiful old desk *could have been designed* by a local craftsman.

Now do Exercise 4I at the end of the chapter. ◀

Permission: *may, might, can,* and *could*   4A

For this exercise, refer to Section 4.3, pages 57-60. Fill in the blank in each sentence below with *may, might, can,* or *could*. If more than one form is possible, give all of the alternatives on the line below the sentence.

Example

_____ I please use your pen for a moment?
Answer:
_____May_____ I please use your pen for a moment?
Can, Could, Might
_____

Yes, you _____.
Answer:
Yes, you ____may____ .
can
_____

1. _____ I please leave class early today?

_____

   Yes, you _____.

_____

2. _____ I please borrow your lawn mower?

_____

   I'm sorry, but you _____ not. I must use it for an hour or so.

_____

3. _____ I please use your telephone for a few minutes?

_____

   Yes, of course you _____.

_____

4. _____ anyone vote in the election next week?

_____

   Anyone who registered at the proper time _____ vote.

_____

5. _____ anyone who wishes attend the lecture tonight?

_____

   No, I'm sorry. Persons without reserved seats _____ not attend.

_____

6. _____ my children use this pool?

_____

Yes, they _____, until six in the evening.

_____

7. _____ children use this pool?

_____

Children under sixteen _____ not use this pool after six in the evening.

_____

8. _____ I hold the door for you?

_____

Yes, please.

9. _____ I help you carry those groceries?

_____

No, thank you. I've got them.

10. Do you need me for anything else?

No, thank you. You _____ run along now.

_____

11. Several students asked whether they _____ practice in the auditorium last week.

_____

The person in charge told them that they _____.

_____

12. Let's ask if we _____ see the special exhibits this morning.

_____

The receptionist told us yesterday afternoon that we _____ not see the special exhibits so late in the day.

_____

13. John arrived early for the party and asked whether he _____ help us in any way.

_____

We told him that indeed he _____.

_____

14. In the early days of automobiles, anyone _____ drive without a license.

_____

15. Until recently, the general public _____ not use this road. Now it has been opened as a public road.

_____

For this exercise, refer to Section 4.4, pages 60–61. Fill in the blank in each sentence below with *can, could,* or *could have* + the correct form of the verb given in the parentheses and *not,* if given.

Examples

Anne _____ . (present; sing)
Answer:
Anne _____ can sing _____ .

She _____ . (present; dance, not)
Answer:
She _____ cannot dance _____ .

1. John _____ the piano. (present; play)

2. He _____ the violin. (present; not, play)

3. _____ you _____ ready to leave in
   an hour? (present; be)

   Yes, I _____ .

4. I _____ to school in this weather. (present; walk)

5. How _____ you possibly _____
   with the noise of the band practicing under your window? (present;
   concentrate)

   Sometimes I _____ . (not)

6. When he was studying in Italy, George _____ Italian
   fluently. (speak)

7. Last year Jane _____ more than fifty yards without rest-
   ing. (not, swim)

8. _____ you _____ a letter in Spanish
   if you had to? (write)

   Yes, I think that I _____ .

9. Our next-door neighbor told me that he _____ us a ride
   to the meeting next Monday. (give)

10. Jane told me that she _____ with us next Monday. (not,
    come)

11. If Walter _____ us last week, he would have done so.
    (help)

12. The speaker last night spoke so softly that I _____ him.
    (not, hear)

Exercises

4C   Ability: *be able to*

For this exercise, refer to Section 4.4, pages 60-61. Fill in the blank in each sentence below with the proper form of *be able to* + the verb given in parentheses and *not* if given.

Example

Anne _____ Spanish when it is
necessary. (speak)
Answer:
Anne _____ is able to speak _____ Spanish when it is
necessary.

1. Bob says that he _____ with us
   tomorrow. (come)

2. He _____ any guests tomorrow. (not, bring)

3. The door stuck, and I _____ it. (not, open)

4. Helen _____ French since childhood. (speak)

5. George _____ golf since his accident. (not, play)

4D   Possibility: *may (have), might (have), can (have),* and *could (have)*

For this exercise, refer to Section 4.5, pages 61-62. Complete the sentences below to express possibility. Fill in the blank in each sentence with *may, may have, might, might have, can, can have, could,* or *could have* + the proper form of the verb given in parentheses and *not*, if given. If more than one form is possible, give all of the alternatives on the line below the sentence.

Example

I _____ home late today. (future; get)
Answer:
I _____ may get _____ home late today.
_____ might, could _____

1. John _____ in his office now. (be)

   _____

2. John _____ at home now. (not, be)

   _____

3. It _____ this afternoon. (future; rain)

   _____

4. I _____ home in time for dinner.
   (future; not, get)

   _____

5. John _____ for a drive. (past; go)

_____

He _____ for a drive because his car
is in the garage. (past; not, go)

_____

_____ he _____ for a walk? (past;
go)

_____

6. This cake has fallen flat. You _____
the recipe exactly. (past; not, follow)

_____

7. I _____ by to see you tomorrow morning. (drop)

_____

8. I was expecting a telephone call. _____ the telephone
_____ without your hearing it? (past; ring)

_____

Yes, it is possible that I _____ it. (past;
not, hear)

_____

9. I have missed my bus. _____ you possibly
_____ me a ride home? (give)

_____

10. John can't find his car keys. Where _____ he possibly
_____ them? (past; leave)

_____

Necessity, Compulsion: *must* and *have to*   4E

For this exercise, refer to Section 4.6, pages 62-63. Fill in the blank in each sentence below with *must* if possible, and with the appropriate form of *have to* if
must is not possible, + the correct form of the verb given in parentheses and *not*,
if given. Use the tense that the sentence demands or, if more than one tense is
possible, the tense given in parentheses.

Examples

I _____ for New York tomorrow.
(present; leave)
Answer:
I _____ must leave _____ for New York tomorrow.

I _____ to the library yesterday.
(not, go)
Answer:
I _____ did not have to go _____ to the library yesterday.

1. I _____ this letter before I go home today. (write)

2. Unauthorized personnel _____ this entrance. (present; not, use)

3. _____ you _____ those bandages on? (present; keep)

4. You _____ in the library. (present; not, talk)

5. County residents _____ if they wish to vote. (present; register)

6. Anne _____ to the supermarket an hour ago. (go)

7. Students _____ to class yesterday. (not, go)

8. _____ you

   _____ a test last week? (take)

9. You _____ to see us again soon. (come)

10. You _____ not

    _____ to write to us. (forget)

11. You really _____ New Orleans some-time. (see)

12. You _____ not

    _____ dining at some of our famous restaurants. (miss)

4F   Supposition and Logical Necessity: *must (have)*

For this exercise, refer to Sections 4.7—4.8, pages 64—65.

A. Fill in the blank in each sentence below with *must* or *must have* + the correct form of the verb given in parentheses and *not*, if given. When applicable, use the tense indicated.

Examples

Bill looks good. He _____ his new job. (like)
Answer:
Bill looks good. He _____ must like _____ his new job.

Joan did not telephone last night.

She _____ time. (not, have)
Answer:
Joan did not telephone last night.
She _____ must not have had _____ time.

1. Paul is not at home now. He _____ at his office. (be)

2. No one is answering the Morgans' telephone. They _____ at home. (not, be)

3. I hear the doorbell. It _____ the cleaning woman. (be)

4. Helen looks pale. She _____ well. (not, feel)

5. I sent my cousins a package two weeks ago. It _____ by now. (arrive)

6. Anne is not carrying any packages. She _____ anything on her shopping trip. (not, buy)

7. You seem so relaxed. You _____ a wonderful vacation. (past, have)

8. The auditorium is dark. The meeting _____ long. (past; not, last)

9. The Picketts have a beautiful house. It _____ very expensive. (past; be)

10. Their house _____ easy to find. (past; not, be)

B. Fill in the blank in each sentence below with *must (have)*, *can (have)*, *might (have)*, or *could (have)* + the appropriate form of the verb given in parentheses and *not*, if given. Keep in mind that *must* and *must have* cannot be used to express logical necessity (strong supposition based on fact) in negative statements and in questions.

1. The rumor you heard _____ false. (present; be)

2. The rumor _____ true. (present; not, be)

3. _____ the rumor _____ true? (present; be)

4. The newspaper report we read _____ errors. (past; contain)

5. The newspaper report _____ correct. (past; not, be)

Obligation, Advisability, and Expectation: 4G
should (have) and *ought to (have)*

For this exercise, refer to Section 4.9, pages 65–68. Fill in the blank in each sentence below with an appropriate form of either *should* or *ought to*, or *should have* or *ought to have*, + the correct form of the verb given in parentheses and *not*, if given. Keep in mind the preferences in negative and question forms in American and British English. Be prepared to explain your choices.

Examples

I _____ some letters tomorrow, but I am going to go shopping instead. (write)

Answer:

I _____ should write _____ some letters tomorrow, but I am going to go shopping instead.

OR: I _____ ought to write _____ some letters tomorrow. . .

I _____ so much time yesterday. (not, waste)

Answer:

I _____ should not have wasted _____ so much time yesterday. (More formal or British English: I _____ ought not to have wasted _____ so much time yesterday.)

1. I _____ shopping later today, but I think that I will postpone the trip until tomorrow. (go)

2. You _____ shopping now when you still have studying to do. (not, go)

3. I must be leaving. I _____ home an hour ago. (be)

4. You _____ me such an extravagant present for my birthday last week. (not, give)

5. _____ I _____ this bill now before I am satisfied with the merchandise? (pay)

6. _____ I _____ to the store now before I pay the bill? (not, complain)

7. _____ you _____ your spring flowers last week? It seems very early to have done so. (plant)

8. _____ you _____ your roses last month? (not, prune)

9. I think that you _____ an appointment with your dentist now before your toothache gets any worse. (make)

10. I think that you _____ an appointment with your dentist last week before your tooth began to bother you so much. (make)

11. It is almost seven-thirty. We _____ the plane soon. (see)

12. John has been working all afternoon. He _____ his work soon. (finish)

13. I have not heard about my hotel reservation, but I _____ pretty soon. (hear)

14. The afternoon paper is not here yet. It _____ a half-hour ago. (arrive)

15. I wonder what is keeping our speaker. He _____ here fifteen minutes ago. (be)

had better (have) and *would rather (have)*   4H

For this exercise, refer to Section 4.10, pages 68–70. Fill in the blank in each sentence below with the appropriate form of *had better (have)* or *would rather (have)*. Choose your answer according to whether preference or advisability is specified, using the correct form of the verb given in parentheses and *not*, if given.

Example

You _____ or you will be late. (advisability; future; hurry)
Answer:
You _____ had better hurry _____ or you will be late.

1. The class _____ their test tomorrow than wait for another week. (preference; take)

2. You _____ warmly if you do not want to catch cold. (advisability; dress)

3. I _____ to the movies tonight because I have a great deal of work to do. (preference; future; not, go)

4. You _____ late to the theater, or the usher may not seat you. (advisability; not, be)

5. _____ you _____ lemon or milk in your tea? (preference; future; have)

6. _____ you _____ around before you buy a car? (advisability; not, look)

7. John said that he _____ home from the game last night than to have missed your visit. (preference; past, stay)

8. Our neighbors _____ their vacation at the seashore, but their son wanted them to, and they did. (preference; past; not, spend)

9. Travelers _____ with the highway patrol to see what the weather is like before heading north today. (advisability; check)

10. I think that we _____ on swimming today because the water is very cold. (advisability; not, plan)

Passive Forms of Lexical Verbs with Modals   4I

For this exercise, refer to Section 4.11, pages 70–71.
A. Fill in the blank in each of the following sentences with *be* + past participle, using the lexical verb given in parentheses and *not*, if given.

Examples

The moon may _____ in the morning at certain times of the year. (see)
Answer:
The moon may _____ be seen _____ in the morning at certain times of the year.

The moon may _____ in the morning at some times.
(not, see)
Answer:
The moon may _____ not be seen _____ in the morning at some times.

1. May I please _____ near the entrance? (seat)

2. This seat might _____. (not, reserve)

3. Can this glue _____ for mending broken china? (use)

4. Your package could _____ yesterday. (not, deliver)

5. Library books must _____ by the due date, or a fine is charged. (return)

6. Should John _____ in advance about the surprise party we are planning for him? (tell)

7. Winners of the contest will _____ in the paper. (announce)

8. The newspaper said that the new film would _____ on television. (not, show)

9. All of our instructors ought to _____ to our picnic. (invite)

10. Last year players did not have to _____ to take part in the tennis matches. (invite)

B. Fill in the blank in each of the following sentences with *have been* + past participle, using the lexical verb given in parentheses and *not*, if given.

Examples

The dog should _____ by now. (fed)
Answer:
The dog should _____ have been fed _____ by now.

The dog should _____ outside so long. (not, leave)
Answer:
The dog should _____ not have been left _____ outside so long.

1. The house you liked may _____ by this time. (sell)

2. The damage to your tree might _____ by lightning. (not, cause)

3. The dog's barking last night must _____ for miles. (hear)

4. The noise we heard could _____ by a jet plane. (not, make)

5. Winners of the contest should _____ by now. (notify)

6. The mailman can _____ until this hour. (not, delay)

7. The mail will _____ up by now. (pick)

8. If Richard had telephoned his parents today, they would
_____. (not, surprise)

9. John's parents ought to _____ about his accident. (tell)

10. My car will not run. It must _____ properly at the
garage. (not, fix)

INDEPENDENT USAGE OF VERB FORMS 5

Some verb forms can occur independently with consistent meanings of their own. One example of a verb form that can occur independently is the present form. The present form can describe repeated or habitual activity in the present time, as in this example:

Mr. Bradley *plays* tennis every Saturday.

Or it can describe ability, as in this example:

Anne *plays* the piano. (Meaning: Anne can play, or knows how to play, the piano.)

Both of these sentences express ideas independently. No other idea need be expressed to complete the meaning of either sentence. Verb forms that can occur independently are discussed in this chapter.

One way in which verb forms will be discussed is in terms of the kinds of meaning they convey. Among other meanings, such as time, verbs can describe an activity or a condition at one point of time (in sentences like "The play *started* promptly" and "Dr. Alexander *was* in his office at nine o'clock"); an activity or a condition continuing over a period of time (in sentences like "We *waited* for three hours" and "Bob *was* unconscious for several hours after his accident"); or activities or conditions repeated over a period of time (in such sentences as "Al *has read* your book three times" and "Our instructor *has been* sick several times this year").

In the text, the phrase **an activity, a condition, or a series of repeated activities or conditions** will be used to include all of these meanings. The shorter phrase **activities or conditions** will be used synonymously. When appropriate, a specific term, such as "continuing activity," may be used in describing the usage of a specific verb form (such as the present continuous form "is studying" in the sentence "Jane is studying now").

Some verb forms cannot occur independently, but require that another activity be expressed or implied. One example of a verb form that cannot occur independently is the past perfect form (*had* + past participle — for example, *had studied*). The past perfect form can describe only an activity or condition in the past that took place before another activity or condition in the past. The latter must be stated, usually with a past form, or implied. One cannot say only, for instance, "The members of class *had studied* the play." One must also say what happened after the members of class had studied the play, as in this example:

> The members of the class *had studied* the play before they *saw* it performed. (Meaning: First the members of the class studied the play, and then they saw it performed.)

Had studied in this sentence occurs in the main clause. It could have occurred in a subordinate clause, as in this example:

> The members of the class *saw* the play performed *after they had studied it.* (The meaning of the sentence is equivalent to that of the sentence above: First the members of the class studied the play, and then they saw it performed.)

Verb forms of this kind are discussed in Chapter 6, "Nonindependent Verb Forms."

Another kind of nonindependent usage of verb forms occurs in some sentence patterns. These patterns all contain a main clause and a subordinate clause. Specific verb forms occur in the main clause, and other specific verb forms occur in the subordinate clause. An example of a sentence pattern in which specific verb forms must be used is the present contrary-to-fact condition, as in this example:

> If I *were* you, I *would register* for a course in computer techniques.

This kind of sentence requires a past subjunctive form, such as *were*, in the *if*-clause, and a present conditional form, such as *would register*, in the main clause. Often a verb form required in such a sentence pattern expresses a time different from that of its tense. In this example, the past subjunctive form *were* is required even though the time expressed is present. The meaning of the *if*-clause is, "If I *were* you, but I *am* not." Verb forms that occur in such sentence patterns are said to occur in "sequence," that is, in a special order in relation to each other. The sentence patterns are said to require **sequence of tenses** (verb forms). Such patterns are discussed in Chapter 7, "Sentence Patterns That Require Special Usage of Verb Forms."

5.1 PRESENT AND PRESENT CONTINUOUS FORMS

Present Form

The regular **present form** of the verb is the base form for all subjects except the third-person singular, which is formed by adding an *s* ending according to certain spelling rules.[1]

---

[1]See Chapter 2, Section 2.3, for spelling rules on adding *s*. See Appendix A for pronunciation of *s* endings.

Example

> I, we, you, they *work*
> he, she, it *works*

The irregular present forms are these:

> *be:*   I *am*; you, we, they *are*; he, she, it *is*
> *have:* I, you, we, they *have*; he, she, it *has*
> *do:*   I, you, we, they *do*; he, she, it *does*
> *go:*   I, you, we, they *go*; he, she, it *goes*

Modals, as discussed in Chapter 4, have the same form for all subjects.

Present Continuous Form

The **present continuous form** is the present of *be (am, is, are)* + Verb-*ing* (present participle).[2]

Example

> I am *working*
> you, we, they *are working*
> he, she, it *is working*

Usage of the Present and Present Continuous Forms

The present and present continuous forms both describe present time, but they describe different kinds of activity.

Repeated or Habitual Activity vs. Continuing Activity

The present form is used to describe repeated or habitual activity, usually over an unlimited period of time. Adverbials often used with the present form include *always*-words (*always, never, rarely, seldom,* and so on); *often, sometimes, usually*; and expressions like *every day*. The present continuous form is used to describe continuing activity, usually within a limited period of time. Adverbials often used with the present continuous form include *now, just now, right now, at this moment, at this time,* and so on.

Here are examples of the two forms:

> (a) John *reads* the newspaper every day.
> (b) John *is reading* the newspaper right now.
>
> (a) The sun *rises* in the morning.
> (b) The sun *is rising* now.

---

[2]See Chapter 2, Section 2.3, for spelling rules on adding *ing* to form the present participle.

(a) Dr. Wilson *does* not *work* in his office every day.

(b) Dr. Wilson *is* not *working* in his office this afternoon.

(a) *Does* the radio *broadcast* the news every evening?

(b) *Is* the radio *broadcasting* the news right now?

In this list, the sentences labeled (a) are in the present form. They describe a repeated, habitual activity over an unlimited period of time. The activity began at an indefinite time in the past and has continued through the present to an indefinite time in the future. The sentences labeled (b) are in the present continuous form. They describe continuing activity within a limited period of time. The period of time is often indicated by an adverbial, as it is in all of the (b) sentences.

Professional or Characteristic Activity vs. Continuing Activity

The present form is used to describe professional or characteristic activity. In each of the following pairs of sentences, sentence (a) describes professional or characteristic activity. Sentence (b) describes activity continuing at the present time, the activity to be completed within a limited period of time.

(a) Dr. Wilson *teaches* Spanish. (Teaching Spanish is Dr. Wilson's profession.)

(b) Dr. Wilson *is teaching* Spanish. (Limited time. Possible meanings: "Dr. Wilson is teaching Spanish during this class period"; "Dr. Wilson is teaching Spanish this semester"; and so on.)

(a) Dogs *bark*. (Dogs bark as a characteristic activity of dogs.)

(b) Some dogs *are barking*. (Limited time. Possible meaning: "Some dogs are barking right now.")

(a) John *does* not *fish*. (John does not fish as a habitual activity.)

(b) John *is* not *fishing*. (Limited time. Possible meaning: "John is not fishing at this moment.")

(a) *Does* it often *rain* here? (Is it characteristic?)

(b) *Is* it *raining* now? (Limited time. It will stop raining.)

Ability

The Present Form of a Verb May Be Used to Express the Meaning of Ability.

Examples

The baby *walks*. (Meaning: "The baby can [knows how to] walk.")

Dr. Williams *does* not *speak* German. (Meaning: "Dr. Williams cannot [does not know how to] speak German.")

Does your cousin *play* the violin? (Meaning: "Can your cousin play [does he know how to play] the violin?")

NOTE: The present continuous form is sometimes used informally to describe habitual activity. The usage includes an adverb such as *always*, *continually*, or *forever*, usually pronounced with strong stress on the adverb.

Ellen *is forever buying* new dresses.

Jane *is* not *always going* to parties. She spends three evenings a week as a Red Cross volunteer worker.

Compare this with the equivalent usage in the past continuous form (see note on p. 111).

Verbs That Do Not Usually Occur in Continuous Forms

All of the verbs in the preceding examples occur in both the present and present continuous forms. They also occur in all other noncontinuous and continuous forms. Certain verbs, however, do not usually occur in present continuous or in any other continuous forms, among them the following:

(1) *be, appear, look* (in the sense of "appear"), *seem*

(2) These "verbs of sensation" when followed by adjectives: *feel, smell, sound, taste*

(3) *Agree, believe, dislike, have* (in the sense of "possess"), *know, like, miss, prefer, think, understand,* and others of this type (Some grammarians call verbs in this category "personal verbs" because only the subject performing the activity knows whether or not the idea expressed is fact.)

NOTE: Verbs that regularly occur in both the noncontinuous and the continuous forms are sometimes called **process verbs** because they describe a process, an activity, or a changing condition. The verbs just listed, which do not usually occur in continuous forms, are sometimes called **status verbs** because they generally describe a status, or an unchanging condition.

Examples

Process: John *practices* the piano every day.

John *is practicing* the piano now.

Status: John *is* a pianist.

In some cases, *status verbs* may be used with *process* meanings and occur in continuous forms. In these instances, the time of the "process" is limited.

Examples

Bobby *is* rude to me. (Status verb implying that a condition is unchanging and the time is unlimited. Meaning: "Bobby is always rude to me.")

Bobby *is being* rude to me. (Status verb implying that a process or activity is occurring and the time is limited. Meaning: "Bobby is being rude to me at this moment.")

Now do Exercises 5A and 5B at the end of the chapter. ◀

5.2 VERB FORMS EXPRESSING FUTURE TIME

The verb forms most commonly used to express simple future time are these:

(1) **Future form:** *will* + Verb

I, we, you, they, he, she, it *will work*

(2) Present form of *be (am, is, are)* + *going to* + Verb

I *am going to work*
we, you, they *are going to work*
he, she, it *is going to work*

Comparison of Future Form with *am/is/are* + *going to* + Verb

The two sentences in each of the following pairs mean approximately the same thing and are used in approximately the same way:

John *will leave* for Europe tomorrow.

John *is going to leave* for Europe tomorrow.

He *will not leave* until tomorrow.

He *is not going to leave* until tomorrow.

Will John *leave* for Europe tomorrow?

Is John *going to leave* for Europe tomorrow?

NOTE: Traditional usage prescribed the future forms as *shall* for first person, *will* for second and third persons, to express simple future time; and *will* for first person, *shall* for second and third persons, to express determination. Present-day usage is *will* + Verb for all subjects to express simple future time and, especially in formal usage, *shall* + Verb for all subjects to express determination ("I *shall* finish on time"). *Shall* remains in certain conventionally polite expressions, such as in offers of assistance like "Shall I open the door for you?" and "Shall I hold those packages for you?" (Compare usage of *would* and *should* in the conditional forms, as discussed in note (2) on p. 128.)

Use of Present or Present Continuous Form to Express Future Time

The present and present continuous forms may also be used to express future time but usually require an adverbial such as *tomorrow* or *next week* to make the meaning of future time clear. The following pairs of sentences have approximately the same meanings as the pairs of sentences just given.

John *leaves* for Europe tomorrow.
John *is leaving* for Europe tomorrow.

John *does not leave* for Europe until tomorrow.

John *is not leaving* for Europe until tomorrow.

Does John *leave* for Europe tomorrow?

Is John *leaving* for Europe tomorrow?

Other Ways of Expressing Future Time

Expressions of Command

Various expressions of command imply future time:

Close the door before you leave.

Please close the door before you leave.

Don't forget to return the book before the library closes.

Let's go to the movies.

Verbs with Future Meaning

Some verbs have meanings that can imply the future, such as the following:

I *plan* to study in the library until it closes.

Other such verbs are *intend, want, wish,* and so on.

Modal Auxiliaries

Modal auxiliaries may have a future meaning:

You *may (can)* borrow my car if you want to.

I *must* leave soon.

I *should (ought to)* leave soon.

Be about to + Verb and *be* + *to* + Verb

Be about to + Verb and *be* + *to* + Verb may describe future time, but they also convey special meanings and are not interchangeable with other future forms.

Be about to + Verb

This form conveys the special meaning "be on the point of doing" something. The sentences below mean approximately the same thing:

I *am about to leave* for the airport.

I *am on the point of leaving* for the airport.

When the expression occurs with the past form of *be*, it usually means that something happened to delay or prevent the activity, as in this example:

> I *was about to leave* for the airport when the telephone rang. Then I did not leave.

When the expression occurs in the negative, it conveys strong opposition. The usage is informal, and in spoken language there is usually strong stress on the second syllable of *about*. These sentences mean approximately the same thing:

> I *am not about to sign* any petitions.

> I *do not intend to sign* any petitions.

Be + to + Verb

The expression *be + to +* Verb conveys the meaning of expectation or obligation. The following pairs of sentences mean approximately the same thing:

> I *am to pick* up my new car this afternoon.

> I *am supposed to pick* up my new car this afternoon.

> Each instructor *was to proctor* his own examinations.

> Each instructor *was supposed to proctor* his own examinations.

The expression *be + to +* Verb occurs only with the present and past forms of *be*.

▶ *Now do Exercises 5C and 5D at the end of the chapter.*

5.3   PAST FORM AND PRESENT PERFECT FORM

Past Form

Verb forms in English are either regular or irregular. The past and past participles of **regular verbs** are formed by adding a *d* ending according to certain spelling rules.[3] **Irregular** past and past participle forms must be memorized.[4] Both regular and irregular past forms are the same for all subjects, with the exception of the past forms of *be*.

Examples

> Regular: I, you, we, they, he she, it *worked*
> Irregular: I, you, we, they, he, she, it *took*
> *be*:   I, he, she, it *was*; we, you, they *were*

The **past form** of a verb is used to describe an activity, a condition, or a series of repeated activities or conditions completed at a definite time in the past. The

---

[3]See Chapter 2, Section 2.3, for spelling rules on adding *d*. See Appendix A for pronunciation of *d* endings.

[4]See Appendix B for a list of common irregular verbs and their principal parts.

Independent Usage of Verb Forms

time may be explicitly stated or implied. Common adverbials used with the past form are these: *last week* (or *month*, *January* or other name of month, *year*, *spring* or other season, *Monday* or other name of day, *night*, *evening*, and so on); *yesterday*; *the day before yesterday*; *an hour ago* (or *a week ago*, *two months ago*, *three years ago*, and so on).

Examples

An activity completed in past time:

Our class *went* to the theater last night.

Our instructor *did* not *hold* his seminar yesterday.

Did John *study* the piano when he *was* a child?

A series of activities completed in past time:

Our class *went* to the theater three times last semester.

Our instructor *did* not *hold* his seminar twice last month.

Did John often *attend* concerts when he was a student?

A condition completed in past time:

The weather *was* beautiful last week.

Alice *did* not *seem* worried about her test yesterday.

Was Dr. Williams a French major when she *was* an undergraduate?

Other Forms That Describe Definite Past Time

The forms *used to* + Verb and *would* + Verb may also be used to describe repeated or habitual activity completed at a definite time in the past. Both forms convey approximately the same meaning as the simple past used to describe repeated or habitual activity.

Examples — *used to* + Verb

Our family *used to go* on picnics when I was a child.
Our family *went* on picnics when I was a child.

Arthur Walters *used to be* the mayor of this city.
Arthur Walters *was* the mayor of this city (at some time in the past).

My family *did* not *use to go* to the movies very often when I was a child.
My family *did* not *go* to the movies very often when I was a child.

Arthur Walters *did* not *use to be* merely a private citizen.
Arthur Walters *was* not merely a private citizen (at some time in the past).

Did your family *use to go* on picnics when you were a child?
Did your family *go* on picnics when you were a child?

Did Arthur Walters *use to be* the mayor of this city?
Was Arthur Walters the mayor of this city (at some time in the past)?

Example — *would* + Verb

Our family *would* often *go* on picnics when I was a child.
We *would* never *stay* indoors when the weather was good.

This usage of *would* + Verb is considered to be informal.

Present Perfect Form

The form of the **present perfect** is: present of *have* + past participle.

Example

I, we, you, they *have worked*
he, she, it *has worked*

The past participle of regular verbs is formed by adding a *d* ending to the base form according to certain spelling rules.[5] Irregular past forms and past participles must be memorized.

The present perfect form is used to describe an activity, a condition, or a series of repeated activities or conditions that are completed as of the present time, or the moment of speaking.[6] Like the past form, the present perfect form is used to describe activities or conditions in past time. The past form, however, describes activities or conditions completed at a definite time in the past. The present perfect form describes activities or conditions begun in the past and continuing to the present, or completed at an indefinite time in the past. Compare these examples:

Ellen *has studied* Spanish *for six months.* (Present perfect form. Meaning: She started to study Spanish six months ago. The period of time, *six months*, extends to the present. The activity of studying may or may not continue.)

James *studied* Spanish *for six months.* (Past form. Meaning: The period of time, *six months*, ended at some definite time in the past.)

The present perfect form is used to describe the following situations.

Past Activities or Conditions Continuing to the Present Time

The present perfect form is used to describe activities or conditions begun in the past time and continuing to the present time, or the moment of speaking. The activities or conditions may or may not continue beyond the present time. Such situations include the following:

(1) An activity.

Ellen *has studied* Spanish for six months (OR since August 1, OR since she returned from Mexico).

---

[5] See Chapter 2, Section 2.3, for spelling rules on adding *d.* See Appendix A for the pronunciation of *d* endings.

[6] Like other perfect forms, the present form is said to have perfect aspect. It describes activities or conditions that are completed, or *perfected,* at the moment of the speaking. See note in Chapter 2, Section 2.4, pages 23–24, for discussion and examples.

Ellen *has* not *studied* anything but Spanish for six months (OR since August 1, OR since she returned from Mexico).

Has Ellen *done* anything else for the past six months (OR since August 1, OR since she returned from Mexico)?

NOTE: The time expressions in the above sentences — *for six months, since August 1,* and *since she returned from Mexico* — all describe the same period of time. *For* is used with a word or phrase describing a period of time (durative time) such as *six months. Since* is used with a word, phrase, or clause describing a point in time (punctual time), such as *August 1* or the point in time described by the clause *since she returned from Mexico.*

(2) A condition.

Emily *has been* ill for several days (OR since last Sunday, OR since she came back from her vacation).

Her brother *has* never *been* ill.

(3) A series of repeated activities or conditions.

Our Arabic instructor *has visited* the Middle East five times since he started to teach Arabic. (A series of repeated activities that may or may not continue.)

He *has been* a visiting professor three of those times.

Activities or Conditions Completed at an Indefinite Time in the Past

The present perfect form may describe activities or conditions completed at an indefinite time in the past.

Examples

Alan *has visited* England. (Meaning: At some indefinite time in the past, Alan visited England.)

Irene *has been* a Red Cross volunteer. (Meaning: Irene served as a Red Cross volunteer and then stopped serving as one at some indefinite time in the past.)

Also compare these sentences:

Ellen *has studied* Spanish *for six months.* (Meaning: She started to study Spanish six months ago and has continued to study Spanish to the present time.)

Ellen *has studied* Portuguese. (Meaning: Ellen studied Portuguese and then stopped studying Portuguese at some indefinite time in the past.)

The present perfect form may also be used to describe activities or conditions completed at an indefinite time in the past which, *from the speaker's point of view,* is immediate or very recent. The adverb *just* frequently occurs with this usage.

Examples

Alice *has (just) finished* typing her term paper. (She finished typing it ten minutes ago.)

Our French instructor *has (just) been* in Mexico. (He returned yesterday.)

John *has (just) bought* a new car. (He bought it last week.)

Activities or Conditions in Clauses Following the Superlative Form of an Adjective or Adverb

The present perfect form often appears in a clause following a present verb form and the superlative form of an adjective or adverb.

Examples

That is the *best* book that *has appeared* this year. (*Best* as adjective.)

I like it the *best* of any that I *have* ever *read*. (*Best* as adverb.)

The adverb *ever* often occurs with this usage (as in "That is the best book that I have *ever* read"), but not when there is another adverbial of time, such as *this year* in the first sentence above.

NOTE 1: The forms of the adjective and adverb are the positive degree, the comparative degree, and the superlative degree. Here are examples:

	POSITIVE	COMPARATIVE	SUPERLATIVE
ADJECTIVE	nice	nicer	nicest
ADVERB	nicely	more nicely	most nicely

Some forms are irregular, including *good, better, best*. Comparison forms of adjectives and adverbs are presented in Volume II, Chapter 16.

NOTE 2: Like the present perfect form, the present perfect continuous form (*have/has been* + Verb-*ing*) may be used to describe activities or conditions that either (1) began in past time and have continued to present time, or (2) took place in the immediate past. There is only a fine shade of difference in meaning between the two forms. Both sentences in these pairs mean approximately the same thing:

John *has read* all afternoon. (Present perfect.)

John *has been reading* all afternoon. (Present perfect continuous.)

I *have* just *taken* a final examination. (Present perfect.)

I *have* just *been taking* a final examination. (Present perfect continuous.)

Generally the present perfect is acceptable whereas the present perfect continuous is sometimes not acceptable. Therefore it is best to avoid the continuous form unless you have fully mastered the difference between the two forms.

▶ *Now do Exercises 5E and 5F at the end of the chapter.*

Present and Present Continuous Forms **5A**

For this exercise, refer to Section 5.1, pages 86–89.
A. Fill in the blank in each sentence below with the present continuous form of the verb and any adverbial given in parentheses. In doing this exercise, keep in mind the word-order rules for *always*-words (which were given in Chapter 1, Section 1).

Examples

John ＿＿＿＿＿＿＿＿＿＿ to school every day. (walk)
Answer:
John ＿＿＿＿ walks ＿＿＿＿ to school every day.

John ＿＿＿＿＿＿＿＿＿＿ to school now. (walk)
Answer:
John ＿＿＿＿ is walking ＿＿＿＿ to school now.

1. My cousin ＿＿＿＿＿＿＿＿＿＿ to school every day. (drive)

2. My cousin ＿＿＿＿＿＿＿＿＿＿ to school at this moment. (drive)

3. Some students ＿＿＿＿＿＿＿＿＿＿ lunch out of doors. (often, have)

4. Some students ＿＿＿＿＿＿＿＿＿＿ lunch out of doors this noon. (have)

5. Anne ＿＿＿＿＿＿＿＿＿＿ breakfast with her roommate. (usually, eat)

6. Anne ＿＿＿＿＿＿＿＿＿＿ breakfast right now. (eat)

7. Dr. Adams ＿＿＿＿＿＿＿＿＿＿ at home before she leaves for class. (sometimes, work)

8. Dr. Adams ＿＿＿＿＿＿＿＿＿＿ at home this afternoon. (work)

9. The class ＿＿＿＿＿＿＿＿＿＿ ten minutes for a coffee break in the middle of our seminar. (usually, take)

10. The class ＿＿＿＿＿＿＿＿＿＿ a coffee break now but must return to the seminar room in ten minutes. (take)

11. It ＿＿＿＿＿＿＿＿＿＿ in the mountains this afternoon. (rain)

12. It ＿＿＿＿＿＿＿＿＿＿ in this area in the spring. (frequently, rain)

13. The Allens ＿＿＿＿＿＿＿＿＿＿ at the beach every summer but sometimes go to the mountains instead. (not, stay)

14. The Allens ＿＿＿＿＿＿＿＿＿＿ at the beach this summer. (not, stay)

15. John ＿＿＿＿＿＿＿＿＿＿ in his room this evening. (not, study)

16. John ＿＿＿＿＿＿＿＿＿＿ in his room when the library is open. (not, often, study)

17. The sun ＿＿＿＿＿＿＿＿＿＿ every evening. (set)

18. The sun _____ right now. (set)

19. Lions _____. (often, roar)

20. Some lions _____ now. (roar)

21. The bus _____ for those people waiting on the corner. (not, stop)

22. The bus _____ at our corner on Sundays and holidays. (not, stop)

23. Some people _____ coffee to tea. (prefer)

24. The material in this scarf _____ like silk. (feel)

25. Some people _____ driving. (not, like)

26. I _____ that David Jones is a born teacher. (believe)

27. This variety of rose _____ they way one expects roses to smell. (not, smell)

28. Many students on our campus _____ their own cars. (have)

29. What does Mr. Williams do? He _____ law. (practice)

30. What is your sister doing now? She _____ law. (practice)

B. Rewrite each sentence below, substituting the adverbial in parentheses for the italicized adverbial in the sentence and using the present or the present continuous form of the verb.

Example

John *often* plays the piano.   (now)
Answer:
_____ John *is playing* the piano *now*. _____

1. Ellen is working in the library *now*. (every afternoon)

_____

2. The little girl next door watches Sesame Street *each morning*. (now)

_____

3. It does not *usually* snow in the desert.   (now)

_____

4. Dr. Webster is taking a vacation in Mexico *now*. (twice a year)

_____

5. Our Easter Lily cactus blooms *about six times a year*. (today)

_____

6. Our poetry discussion group does not meet *regularly*. (right now)

_____

Independent Usage of Verb Forms

7. Students in many schools have final examinations *at the end of each semester.* (right now)

_____

8. It is raining in the desert *today.* (seldom)

_____

9. Dr. Amory *frequently* does not eat lunch. (at this moment)

_____

10. It gets dark *early during the winter months.* (already)

_____

11. The children are walking to school *now.* (every day)

_____

12. I am not speaking Spanish *now.* (often)

_____

13. My favorite television program begins *at six o'clock every weekday.* (right now)

_____

14. Dr. Matthews is working in his office *during this hour.* (rarely)

_____

15. Dorothy does not take courses *every summer.* (now)

_____

16. Mr. Adams *puts* the cat out every evening. (now)

_____

17. Paula *often* telephones her parents. (right now)

_____

18. Mrs. Adams lies down for a short nap *after lunch every day.* (at the present moment)

_____

19. Carl swims in the university pool *every morning.* (right now)

_____

20. Philip is going to the beach *this weekend.* (often)

_____

C. Rewrite each of the following sentences by changing the verb form to express the idea of ability in two other ways.

Example

Ellen knows how to swim.
Answer:
_____
Ellen swims.
_____
Ellen can swim.

Exercises

1. John knows how to type.

   _____

   _____

2. Dr. Maynard can speak Italian.

   _____

   _____

3. Alice Andrews drives.

   _____

   _____

4. Some people cannot read maps.

   _____

   _____

5. Jane does not play bridge.

   _____

   _____

5B Directed Writing

For this exercise, refer to Section 5.1, pages 86–90.

A. Write a paragraph of 100-150 words according to the following instructions:

1. Describe how you prepare for an examination. Use such expressions as *first, next, then,* and *finally*.

2. Write on the topic: "Why ——— Is My Favorite Television Program." Use such expressions as *like, prefer,* and *think*.

3. Write on the topic: "My Morning Routine." Begin with, "I wake up at . . . ." Use such expressions as *always, never, often, sometimes,* and *usually*.

4. Write on the topic: "My Physical Fitness Program."

5. Write a paragraph beginning, "When I get back to my room (or apartment) after class, my friends are all doing different things." Use such expressions as "Some are . . . .," "Others are . . . .," and so on.

B. Write a short composition of 200–250 words according to the following instructions:

1. Describe a current problem on the campus (or the in city where you live), such as difficulties with parking, housing, or size of classes.

2. Describe a typical day in the life of a person in a profession. For example, you might begin with: "Every day a doctor . . ." or "A professional tennis player's life is very busy."

3. Describe a typical wedding ceremony (or other ceremony or custom) in your country or area.

4. Give your views on the women's liberation movement.

5. In many places in the world, people are fighting pollution. Write a paragraph describing what you, your friends or relatives, or your government agencies are doing to fight pollution.

Verb Forms Expressing Future Time   5C

For this exercise, refer to Section 5.2, pages 90–92.

A. In each of the following sentences, a verb form or phrase (sometimes negative) that describes future time is italicized. For each, give three other verb forms or phrases that express the same idea.

Example

   Our ship *will leave* port promptly at five-thirty.
   Answer:
   a. _____ is going to leave _____   b. _____ leaves _____   c. _____ is leaving _____

1. Some students *are leaving* on vacation tomorrow.

   a. _____   b. _____   c. _____

2. The library *will not reopen* this week.

   a. _____   b. _____   c. _____

3. Our new director *arrives* next month.

   a. _____   b. _____   c. _____

4. The Los Angeles Symphony *is not going to perform* at the Municipal Auditorium this coming season.

   a. _____   b. _____   c. _____

5. The author of the play that our class is producing *will speak* to us next Friday.

   a. _____   b. _____   c. _____

6. The post office *is closing* in half an hour.

   a. _____   b. _____   c. _____

7. Classes *do not begin* in September this year.

   a. _____   b. _____   c. _____

8. I *am going to plant* spring bulbs tomorrow.

   a. _____   b. _____   c. _____

9. My brother's plane *is arriving* at 11:20 a.m.

   a. _____   b. _____   c. _____

10. Our mayor *opens* the horse show this year.

   a. _____   b. _____   c. _____

B. Rewrite each of the following sentences using a phrase that means approximately the same thing as the italicized expression.

Examples

   I *am on the point of leaving* my office for the day.
   Answer:
                I am about to leave my office for the day.
   _____

It will be the secretary's duty to answer all telephone calls.
Answer:

The secretary is to answer all telephone calls.

1. *It will be Jane's duty to water* the house plants.

_____

2. The plane *is on the point of departing.*

_____

3. Dr. Wilson *expects to leave* for Mexico City in the morning.

_____

4. The play *is not expected to begin* until eight-thirty.

_____

5. I *do not intend to walk* five miles a day.

_____

C. Write a complete sentence in answer to each of the questions below. (If you are not planning a trip, think of one you would like to take.) Be sure to use the same verb form in your answer as is used in the question.

Example

What are you going to do next summer?
Possible answer:

I am going to take a trip to Europe next summer.

1. What are you going to do next summer?

_____

2. When will you leave on your vacation?

_____

3. Who is going to go with you?

_____

4. When will you make reservations for your trip?

_____

5. Where are you going to buy your tickets?

_____

6. How much money will your trip cost?

_____

7. How are you going to travel?

_____

8. Where will you go first?

_____

Independent Usage of Verb Forms

9. What other places are you going to see?

   _____

10. When will you return from your trip?

   _____

Directed Writing   5D

For this exercise, refer to Section 5.2, pages 90–92.

A. Write a paragraph of 100-150 words according to the following instructions:

1. Begin your paragraph with: "Tomorrow I am finally going to [+ Verb] . . ."

2. List some of your New Year's resolutions. Include some things that you are not going to do.

B. Write a short composition of 200-250 words according to the following instructions:

1. Describe plans for a celebration or parade to be held. Use such expressions as "First everyone will . . . ," "After that there will be . . . ," "Then the mayor [president, coach, or other] is going to . . ."

2. Describe what will happen during an eclipse, the spouting of a geyser, or some other natural phenomenon.

Past Form and Present Perfect Form   5E

For this exercise, refer to Section 5.3, pages 92–96.

A. Fill in the blank in each sentence below, using either the past or the present perfect form of the verb given in parentheses. The first sentence in each item establishes the topic.

1. Emily is now a student here at the university.

   a. Last summer Emily _____ in Mexico. (study)

   b. She _____ back here for six months. (be)

   c. She _____ from Mexico six months ago. (return)

   d. She _____ here since August. (live)

   e. She _____ in Spain. (never, be)

   f. She _____ her comprehensive examinations a week ago. (take)

   g. She _____ for them after she came back from Mexico. (prepare)

   h. She _____ one of the best students in her present class. (always, be)

   i. Her instructor is the best one that she _____. (ever, have)

   j. Her instructor _____ her on her Spanish last week. (compliment)

2. Our instructor is the author of a best-selling novel.

    a. He _____ the novel several years ago. (write)

    b. It is the first novel that he _____. (ever, publish)

    c. He _____ to write another. (just, begin)

    d. The novel _____ a prize last month. (win)

    e. A film producer _____ to him about making a film based on the novel. (already, speak)

    f. I _____ acquainted with a famous author up to now. (never, be)

    g. _____ our instructor? (you, ever, meet)

    h. He is one of the most interesting people who _____ on this campus. (ever, teach)

    i. He _____ a lumberjack before he became an instructor. (be)

    j. He _____ in Alaska for most of his childhood, and he hopes to go back there next summer. (live)

3. This is the most beautiful season of the year in this part of the country.

    a. There _____ little rain for the past few weeks. (be)

    b. The sun _____ every day during the last few days. (shine)

    c. Last month it _____ almost every day. (rain)

    d. The water _____ away a bridge a month ago. (wash)

    e. The traffic _____ to take a detour ever since then. (have)

    f. It _____ in the mountains last month. (snow)

    g. The snow _____ before the day was over. (melt)

    h. Some plants _____. (already, blossom)

    i. We _____ a few birds a week ago. (see)

    j. Many small animals _____. (just now, reappear)

4. I am in the middle of the book about interplanetary travel that you lent me last week.

    a. I _____ all yesterday afternoon reading it, but I have not yet finished it. (spend)

    b. It is one of the most interesting books on interplanetary travel that I _____ across. (ever, run)

    c. The author _____ her research thoroughly before she wrote the book. (do)

    d. I _____ a television special on the subject last week. (see)

    e. An astronomer from Chicago _____ as narrator for the program. (act)

                                        Independent Usage of Verb Forms

f. He _____ some very interesting theories about the events described on the program. (present)

g. Until last week, I _____ skeptical about the possibility of interplanetary travel. (be)

h. However, the program last week _____ a strong impression on me. (make)

i. My friends and I _____ to firm conclusions on our views of the possibility of interplanetary travel. (not, yet, come)

j. Just now, after reading the book and seeing the television special, we _____ to keep open minds on the subject. (decide)

B. For each item, write a sentence that combines the complete sentence with the expressions in parentheses, using either the past form or the present perfect form of the verb given. Be sure to follow the rules of word order for adverbials.

Example

John plays the piano.
Answers:
1. (since he was a child)

              He has played the piano since he was a child. OR:

              Since he was a child, he has played the piano.

2. (frequently, perform in public, since his debut)

              He has frequently performed in public since his debut. OR:

              Since his debut he has frequently performed in public.

3. (a week ago, give a concert)

              He gave a concert a week ago. OR: A week ago he gave a concert.

A. Paul is now working in Washington.

1. (after he graduated from college, take a trip to Europe)

2. (since September, be in Washington)

3. (for six months, be there)

4. (last month, buy a new car)

5. (during the past few weekends, take several trips)

    _____

    _____

    _____

B. Our Spanish instructor spent his most recent vacation in Venezuela.

1. (go there by plane)

    _____

    _____

2. (often, travel in Venezuela)

    _____

    _____

3. (last summer, explore some Indian villages by mule)

    _____

    _____

    _____

4. (when he visited the villages, take many slides)

    _____

    _____

    _____

5. (never, be in Spain)

    _____

    _____

C. Jane is a student at medical school.

1. (ever since she was a child, want to be a doctor)

    _____

    _____

    _____

2. (when she was five years old, make bandages)

    _____

    _____

    _____

3. (in high school, become a volunteer hospital worker)

    _____

    _____

    _____

4. (one year ago, enter medical school)

_____

_____

5. (never, change her mind about her goal)

_____

_____

Directed Writing   5F

For this exercise, refer to Section 5.3, pages 92 – 96.

A. Write a paragraph of 100-150 words according to the following instructions:

1. Write on the topic: "Why I Bought a [name of car: Volkswagen, Ford, Cadillac, or other].

2. Tell why you decided to study at [name of your college or university].

3. Describe your experiences in studying English.

4. Write on the topic: "The Best Present That I Have Ever Received [or Given]."

B. Write a short composition of 200–250 words according to the following instructions:

1. Modern transportation and communication media have caused many changes in society. Describe one important change in the United States, another country, or the world.

2. Describe how a custom, either in the United States or in another country, has changed in the last [give number of] years.

3. Explain how your first impressions of the United States [or your school, college, or university] have, or have not, changed since you first began to study here.

4. Tell what you have done to aid the cause of women's rights, world peace, the fight against pollution, or another area of interest to you.

5. Write on the topic: "The Best [or Worst] Game/Play/Movie That I Have Ever Seen," or "The Best [or Worst] Book That I Have Ever Read."

NONINDEPENDENT VERB FORMS 6

Some verb forms do not occur independently. When they are used, the occurrence of another activity or condition must also be described or be implied, usually by a date or a specific time. These forms include the past continuous, the past perfect, the future continuous, and the future perfect.

THE PAST CONTINUOUS FORM   6.1

The **past continuous form** is the past of *be (was/were)* + Verb-*ing* (present participle).[1]

Example

> I, he, she, it *was working*
> we, you, they *were working*

The past continuous form describes a continuing activity or condition in past time, but may be used to describe only the following kinds of activities.[2]

The Past Continuous Form with Another Activity or Condition Expressed

The past continuous form is used to describe an activity or condition (Activity 1) continuing over a period of time in the past and interrupted by another activity

---

[1]See Chapter 2, Section 2.3, for spelling rules on adding *d, ing,* and *s.*

[2]Like other continuous forms, past continuous is said to have continuous aspect. See Chapter 2, Section 2.4, for a discussion of aspect.

(Activity 2), which is usually described by the past form. *In this usage the past continuous form may not occur independently; Activity 2 must always be expressed.* Activity 1 may occur in either a main clause or a subordinate clause.

Examples

John *was studying*⁽¹⁾ when the telephone *rang*⁽²⁾. (Past continuous in main clause)

While John *was studying*⁽¹⁾, the telephone *rang*⁽²⁾. (Past continuous in subordinate clause)

Activity 1 and Activity 2 may also both occur in main clauses.

Examples

The Allens *were planning*⁽¹⁾ to visit Canada this summer, but a family emergency *prevented*⁽²⁾ their doing so.

I *was* not *thinking*⁽¹⁾ of going to the movies this evening, but you *have persuaded*⁽²⁾ me to change my mind.

Note that Activity 1 may occur in an elliptical construction, as in conversation:

What *was*⁽¹⁾ John *doing* when you *called*⁽²⁾?

He *was studying*⁽¹⁾.

The Past Continuous Form with a Time Expression

The past continuous form may also be used to describe a continuing activity that took place within a limited period of time expressed by an adverbial. The period of time is significant and is generally related to an activity that took place during the period of time expressed by the adverbial.

Examples

I *was vacationing* in Hawaii *during May*. (Possible other activities: "when you visited my home town"; "while you were taking your examinations"; and so on.)

John *was* not *traveling* in Canada *in July*. (Possible other activity: "when you thought you saw him there.")

Past Continuous Forms Used to Describe Activities Continuing Simultaneously in Past Time

The past continuous may be used to describe activities that continued simultaneously in past time.

Example

While you *were watching* television, John *was studying* for his final exams.

NOTE: Like present continuous, past continuous may be used informally to describe habitual or characteristic activity. The usage occurs with an adverb such as *always, continually,* or *forever,* usually with strong stress on the adverb in spoken English.

Examples

John *was* always *practicing* the piano. (Possible implied meanings: "when he was a boy"; "when he visited us"; and so on.)

Janet *was* not *continually going* to parties at school. She worked hard and earned good grades.

Keep in mind that the following verbs do not usually occur in any of the continuous forms: *be; feel, smell, sound,* and *taste* when followed by adjectives; *agree, believe, dislike, have* (in the sense of *possess*), *know, like, miss, prefer, think,* and *understand.*

Now do Exercises 6A and 6B at the end of the chapter. ◀

PAST PERFECT FORM   6.2

The **past perfect form** is the past of *have* (*had*) + past participle.[3]

Example

I, you, we, they, he, she, it *had worked.*

The past perfect form is used in the following instances.

The Past Perfect Form with Another Activity or Condition Expressed

The past perfect form is used to describe an activity, a condition, or a series of repeated activities or conditions in past time (Activity 1) that took place before another activity or condition in past time (Activity 2), expressed with past form.[4] In this usage, Activity 2 *must be expressed.* Activity 1 may occur in either a main or subordinate clause, as illustrated here:

---

[3] Regular verbs form the past participle by adding a *d* ending to the base form. See Chapter 2, Section 2.3, "Spelling Rules for Adding, *d, ing,* and *s.*" See also Appendix B for a list of common irregular verbs and their principal parts.

[4] Like other perfect forms, past perfect is said to have perfect aspect. See Chapter 2, Section 2.4, for a discussion of aspect. For examples of the past perfect form in indirect discourse and past unreal conditions, see Chapter 7, Section 7.1, pages 129 – 30, and Section 7.5, pages 140 – 41.

Examples — Activity 1 (Past Perfect Form) in Main Clause

The class members *had studied*$^{(1)}$ the play before they *saw*$^{(2)}$ it. (A single activity)

Paul *had visited*$^{(1)}$ Washington several times before he *met*$^{(2)}$ a single member of congress. (A series of repeated activities)

Congressman Adams *had*$^{(1)}$ not *been* in politics before he *ran*$^{(2)}$ for his present office. (A condition)

Examples — Activity 1 (Past Perfect Form) in Subordinate Clause

(a) After the speaker *had presented*$^{(1)}$ her views, she *presided*$^{(2)}$ over a lively question-and-answer period. (A single activity)

(b) Although the class *had*$^{(1)}$ not *met* often, the members already *seemed*$^{(2)}$ to know one another quite well. (A series of activities)

(c) Before Bill *had been*$^{(1)}$ in the infirmary for a day, he *wanted*$^{(2)}$ to get back to his classes. (A condition)

NOTE: In cases like those above, in which a time expression such as a subordinate conjunction makes the time relationship clear, common practice now is to use the simple past rather than the past perfect. Compare these sentences with sentences (a) and (c) above:

(a) *After* the speaker *presented* her views, she presided over a lively question-and-answer period.

(c) *Before* Bill *was* in the infirmary for a day, he wanted to get back to his classes.

In sentence (b), *although* is not a time expression. For this reason, the past perfect form is required.

Examples — Activity 1 and Activity 2 Both in Main Clauses

We *had* already *seen*$^{}$ the film, but we *enjoyed*$^{}$ it anyway.

Other Ways of Expressing Activity 1 [5]

A **perfect participle** form, such as *having* + past participle, may also be used to express Activity 1, as in this example:

Having presented$^{(1)}$ her views, the speaker *sat*$^{(2)}$ down.

Or a **prepositional phrase** (Preposition + Object) containing a preposition such as *after* or *before* and a **perfect gerund,** which has the same form as the perfect participle, may be used, as in this example:

After having presented$^{(1)}$ her views, the speaker *sat*$^{(2)}$ down.

---

[5] See Chapter 8, Section 8.1, for examples of all of the participle and gerund forms.

NOTE: When a preposition such as *after* or *before* makes the time relationship between Activity 1 and Activity 2 clear, it is now common practice to use the present gerund form, as well as the perfect gerund form, as in this example:

$\overset{(1)}{\underline{\textit{After presenting}}}$ her views, the speaker $\overset{(2)}{\underline{\textit{sat}}}$ down.

The Past Perfect Form with a Time Expression

The past perfect form may also describe activities or conditions completed before a time in the past indicated by a time expression, as in these examples:

Before the age of nineteen, George *had graduated* from college. *By the following September* he *had begun* his career as a computer technician.

This usage is particularly common in narrative.

NOTE: Like the past perfect form, the past perfect continuous form (*had been* + Verb-*ing*) may be used to describe an activity in past time that occurred before another activity or a condition in past time. The past perfect continuous emphasizes more the notion that the second activity interrupted the first activity than the past perfect does. The difference in meaning, however, is often very slight, and usually the past perfect form expresses approximately the same meaning as the past perfect continuous. For example, these two sentences have nearly the same meanings:

After the telephone *had been ringing* for five minutes, someone answered.

After the telephone *had rung* for five minutes, someone answered it.

Since the past perfect is usually acceptable and the past perfect continuous is sometimes not acceptable, it is best to avoid the continuous form unless you have fully mastered the two usages.

Now do Exercises 6C and 6D at the end of the chapter. ◀

THE FUTURE CONTINUOUS AND FUTURE PERFECT FORMS   6.3

The **future continuous form** (*will be* + Verb-*ing*) describes an activity continuing in the future, with one of these conditions: (a) the activity is to be interrupted, or (b) a time in the future is stated.

Examples

I *will be practicing* when you *arrive.*
I *will be studying* in the library *at three o'clock.*

(Compare with the usage of the past continuous form, this chapter, Section 6.1.)
The **future perfect form** (*will have* + past participle) describes an activity, a

condition, or a series of repeated activities or conditions to be completed before a specific time or before another activity or a condition in future time. *By* is the preposition generally used in the time expression.

Usually the future form may be used in the same way as the future perfect. These two sentences mean approximately the same thing:

John *will finish* his work *by June.*

John *will have finished* his work *by June.*

However, the future perfect form *must* be used when the verb describes activities or conditions continuing over a period of time, as in this example:

Dr. Evans *will have taught* for forty years when she retires. (*Will have taught* describes activity continuing over a period of time.)

NOTE: The **future perfect continuous form** (*will have been* + Verb-*ing*) is used to describe the same kind of activities or conditions as the future perfect. The following two sentences mean approximately the same thing:

Dr. Evans *will have taught* for forty years when she retires.

Dr. Evans *will have been teaching* for forty years when she retires.

The future perfect form, however, is generally acceptable, whereas the future perfect continuous form is often not acceptable. Thus it might be well, as a rule of thumb, to use future perfect in such instances.

▶ *Now do Exercise 6E at the end of the chapter.*

Past and Past Continuous Forms   6A

For this exercise, refer to Section 6.1, pages 109–111.

A. Fill in the blank in each of the following sentences with either the past form or
the past continuous form of the verb and any adverbial given.

Examples

My guests _____ while I was fixing dinner. (arrive)
Answer:
My guests _____ arrived _____ while I was fixing dinner.

We _____ when the storm broke. (hike)
Answer:
We _____ were hiking _____ when the storm broke.

1. The children were playing when their parents suddenly
    _____ . (arrive)

2. It _____ when I woke up this morning. (not, rain)

3. The students _____ interested when the bell rang. (just,
    become)

4. While Bill _____ in the den, I telephoned. (be)

5. When I arrived this morning, the students _____ a new
    song. (practice)

6. Paul _____ on his car when I visited him. (always, work)

7. John _____ his instructors when he was an
    undergraduate. (not, always, believe)

8. The water in the mineral springs that we visited last week
    _____ of sulphur. (smell)

9. The plane _____ along the runway when I got to the
    airport. (already, taxi)

10. The floats and bands were still lining up when the mayor
    _____ the signal for the parade to start. (give)

11. Robert _____ time while he was attending college. He
    graduated with close to an A average. (not, always, waste)

12. The marching band _____ beautiful to the proud
    parents at the game. (sound)

13. We _____ on a walk along the beach when a thunder
    storm blew up and kept us from going out. (plan)

14. While I _____ lunch ready for a friend, she called to say
    that her car would not start and that she could not come. (get)

15. What were you doing last summer? I _____ in the
    Middle East last summer. (travel)

16. Everything at the students' potluck dinner _____ delicious. (taste)

17. Something in the house was always going out of order just when it _____ most inconvenient. (be)

18. Your train _____ on time when I checked ten minutes ago. (not, run)

19. Jane _____ very happy when I saw her yesterday. (seem)

20. The students in our class usually _____ written examinations to oral examinations. (prefer)

B. Using the expression given, write a complete sentence for each item below. If the verb given is in the past form, use the past continuous form of the verb you choose; if it is in the past continuous form, use the past form of the verb you choose.

Example

When the orchestra began to play,
Possible answer:
When the orchestra began to play, the audience was still arriving.

While we were studying the road map,
Possible answer:
While we were studying the road map, a small airplane landed on the highway ahead of us.

1. When the orchestra began to play,

_____

2. While we were studying the road map,

_____

3. It was not raining when

_____

4. While I was listening to the election returns,

_____

5. When the guests arrived,

_____

6. The orchestra members were practicing for the concert when

_____

7. When the snow began to fall,

_____

8. While we were exploring the ruins,

_____

9. John was not paying attention when

_____

10. When the electricity went off,

_____

For this exercise, refer to Section 6.1, pages 109–111. Write a paragraph of 100–150 words that begins with:

1. "While I was vacationing in ———, . . ."

2. "When he was a child, my best friend [or my brother, my cousin, or other person] was always taking something apart and putting it together again."

3. "While I was studying for my last hour quiz [or final examination, driver's test, or other], . . ."

4. "When I was driving [or walking, flying, riding, or other] to ———, . . ."

5. "I was thinking of you when . . ."

Write a short composition of 200–250 words that begins with:

1. "The election returns were just coming in when . . ."

2. "The newscasters were predicting victory for [name a person, team, or other possibility] when . . ."

3. "In our city the traffic of the day was just beginning when . . ."

4. "Funds were running low in our town [or club, class, or other] treasury when . . ."

Past and Past Perfect Forms   6C

For this exercise, refer to Section 6.2, pages 111–13.

A. Fill in the blank in each of the following sentences with the past form or the past perfect form of the verb, plus *not* or any adverbial given in parentheses. If both forms are acceptable, give both.

Examples

After the audience _____ the
auditorium, several students took the speaker out for coffee. (leave)
Answer:
After the audience _____ had left (or left) _____ the
auditorium, several students took the speaker out for coffee. (leave)

The term _____ before the
students were on their way home. (scarcely, end)
Answer:
The term _____ had scarcely ended _____ before the
students were on their way home.

1. After the students _____ their
performance, they returned to the dressing rooms. (give)

2. Unfortunately, we _____ when the real excitement at the rodeo began. (already, leave)

3. Before Ellen _____ her hand at painting, she had studied the piano for years. (try)

4. Although the meeting had been announced well in advance, there

_____ enough members present for a quorum. (not, be)

5. When the students _____ their processional march, the audience sat down. (complete)

6. John _____ his car to the city because it had broken down. (not, drive)

7. Since Paul _____ off to college, his younger brother and sister had a few more chores to do. (go)

8. Before the family _____ down to dinner, there was a knock on the front door. (sit)

9. By the time the third encore was offered, most of the audience

_____ nearly enough. (hear)

10. Although the drama critic from the newspaper had not applauded at the end of the play, her review the next day

_____ the players very happy. (make)

11. Julia _____ out of her car when her first guest arrived. (just, get)

12. As soon as the speaker _____, many students eagerly began to ask questions. (finish)

13. By the time we _____ the tire, the plane had already come and gone. (fix)

14. After the children had opened their presents, there

_____ cake and ice cream for everyone. (be)

15. By the time the rain _____, it was too late to go to the beach. (stop)

B. Using the expression given, write a complete sentence for each item below. Use the past form if the past perfect form of a verb is given; use the past perfect form if the past form is given.

Examples

After the newscast had ended, _____

Possible answer:
    After the newscast had ended, our whole group burst into enthusiastic
    discussion of the latest events at the Olympics.

Because _____ ,
we did not have to take a taxi to the theater.
Possible answer:
   Because it had stopped raining, we did not have to take a taxi
   to the theater.

1. After the newscast had ended,

   _____

2. Because _____ ,
   we did not have to take a taxi to the theater.

3. When the children had finished playing,

   _____

4. After _____ ,
   we left the restaurant.

5. I had just mailed you a letter when _____ .

   _____

6. I did not go to the movies because _____ .

   _____

7. Because our team had never before won a game,

   _____

8. As soon as _____ ,
   the students all left on vacation.

   _____

9. I did not arrive on time for the flight although

   _____

10. By the time the newscast was over,

   _____

C. Rewrite each of the following sentences, using a prepositional phrase if a subordinate clause is used, or a subordinate clause if a prepositional phrase is used.

Examples

   After we had completed a survey of the ruins, we felt ready to begin our dig in earnest.
   Answer:
      After having completed (or *completing*) *a survey of the ruins,* we felt ready to begin our dig in earnest.

   After not having spoken Portuguese for many years, Dr. Prentice decided on a trip to Brazil for his next vacation.
   Answer:
      After he had not spoken Portuguese for many years, Dr. Prentice decided on a trip to Brazil for his next vacation.

1. *After we had arrived at our hotel,* we took out a map of the city.

_____

_____

2. *After having had lunch,* we set out to explore the area.

_____

_____

3. *After we had seen some of the sights of the city,* we sat down to rest in a beautiful park.

_____

_____

4. *After walking so much,* we felt like having some refreshments.

_____

_____

5. *After we had located a food vendor,* we chose some unfamiliar but delicious things to eat.

_____

_____

6. *After having finished our snack,* we consulted our map.

_____

_____

7. *After we had checked some points of interest,* we decided to go back to the hotel by a different route.

_____

_____

8. *Before going very far,* we came to an old mission that we wanted to see.

_____

_____

9. *After we had walked through the beautiful buildings and grounds,* we decided that we had explored enough for one day.

_____

_____

_____

10. *After having made sure of our directions,* we found our way back to the hotel.

_____

_____

Nonindependent Verb Forms

For this exercise, refer to Section 6.2, pages 111–13. Rewrite the sentences in each group below as a paragraph. Show the time relationships between activities by sometimes changing the past form of the verb to the past perfect form. You may combine two sentences into one sentence, using such expressions as *after* and *before*, or you may supply adverbials such as *then*.

A. Begin your paragraph with "Before Paul went to college, . . ." and use the following sentences:

1. He became an expert swimmer.

2. He swam at the age of three.

3. In high school he won a state championship for high diving.

4. He also became an expert surfer.

5. He went to college.

6. He tried out for the swimming team.

7. He made the team.

8. He swam with the team for two years.

9. He entered the Olympics.

10. He won a Gold Medal.

11. He returned home a hero.

12. His friends were not surprised.

B. Begin your paragraph with "Before Agnes de Mille choreographed the ballet *Rodeo* in 1942, . . ." Follow the same directions as for A, using the following sentences:

1. The major ballet companies presented only a few American ballets.

2. The Ballet Theater performed Eugene Loring's ballet *Billy the Kid* in 1938.

3. The company also performed his ballet *The Great American Goof* in 1940.

4. The Ballet Russe produced the American Marc Platoff's ballet *Ghost Town* in 1939.

5. Agnes de Mille created the ballet *Rodeo.*

6. *Rodeo* was an unqualified success.

7. *Billy the Kid* was the first important American ballet.

8. *Rodeo* was the second.

9. *Rodeo* conclusively proved the value of the American genre of ballet.

10. The Ballet Russe invited other American choreographers to contribute to its repertory.

6E   Future Continuous and Future Perfect Forms

For this exercise, refer to Section 6.3, pages 113–14. Complete each of the following items to form a sentence, using a clause or, when indicated, an adverbial expression.

Examples

I will be fixing dinner when _____
Possible answer:
I will be fixing dinner when _____ you arrive. _____

I will have finished my preparations (+ adverbial of time)

_____
Possible answer:
I will have finished my preparations
_____ by six o'clock. _____

1. I will be cleaning my house when _____

2. John will have finished his thesis (+ adverbial of time)

   _____

3. The cereus is going to be blooming (+ adverbial of time)

   _____

4. That car will have seen its last days by the time that

   _____

5. The senior citizens will be celebrating the opening of their new recreation

   hall when _____

6. The play will have ended by the time that _____

7. The newspaper will be printing its final edition when

   _____

8. The plane will have landed by the time that _____

9. The students will be having dinner when _____

10. The Andersons will have built their new house (+ adverbial of time)

   _____

SENTENCE PATTERNS THAT REQUIRE SPECIAL USAGE OF VERB FORMS

7

Some sentence patterns require the use of specific verb forms. These patterns all contain a main clause and a subordinate clause. Depending on the sentence pattern, specific verb forms occur in the main clause, and other specific verb forms occur in the subordinate clause. The sentence patterns that require such special usage of verb forms are:

(1) Conditional sentences (sentences containing *if*-clauses)

(2) Sentences with *wish*

(3) Some sentences expressing future time

(4) Sentences with verbs like *demand* and verb phrases like *be necessary*

(5) Indirect discourse (sentences with verbs like *say* and *ask*)

Verb forms that occur in these sentence patterns are said to occur in **sequence** with each other. The sentence patterns in which they occur are said to require **sequence of tenses** (verb forms). A characteristic of verb forms required in these sentence patterns is that often their tenses do not agree with the times they describe, as will be seen throughout this chapter.[1]

VERB FORMS USED IN CONDITIONAL SENTENCES 7.1

Conditional sentences include a main clause and a subordinate clause, usually introduced by *if.* The condition is expressed in the *if*-clause, which is also referred to as the "condition." Conditional sentences are of two types: *real*, in

---

[1]See also note in Section 24, page 25.

which the condition is *possible;* and *contrary* to *fact* (or *unreal*), in which the condition does not (or did not) exist. The verb forms used depend on whether the condition is real or contrary to fact, and on whether the condition relates to present or past time.

In all conditional sentences, either the main or the *if*-clause may precede. Note the punctuation in the following examples:

> *If the weather permits,* we will go for a walk this afternoon. (When the *if*-clause precedes, use a comma.)

> We will go for a walk this afternoon *if the weather permits.* (When the main clause precedes, do not use a comma.)

Throughout this discussion, *will* + Verb is used for future forms and *would* + Verb for conditional forms with all subjects. See the note on *will/shall* on page 90 and Note 2 on *would/should* on pages 128–29.

Present Real Conditions

A **present real condition** is one in which the condition expressed is *possible* at the present time (present from the speaker's point of view). The time expressed in the *if*-clause (the condition) may be present or future; the time expressed in the main clause is generally future. Several different verb forms may be used in both clauses, but a general rule that avoids predictable errors is: *Use the present form of the verb in the* if-*clause, and use the future form of the verb in the main clause.*

if-Clause: Verb Forms Used in Present Real Condition

Both present and future time may be expressed with the present form of the verb in the *if*-clause.

Examples

> If you *are* free now [possibly you are], I *will leave* for your office immediately. (*Are*, the present form of the verb, describes present time in the *if*-clause.)

> If Al *arrives* in time [possibly he will], he *will join* us for lunch. (*Arrives*, the present form of the verb, describes future time in the *if*-clause.)

It will be seen that other forms may be used to describe both present and future time in the *if*-clause. However, a major restriction is this: Even though the time expressed in the *if*-clause may be future, future verb forms (*will* or *am/is/are going to*) are not used in the *if*-clause.

NOTE: As a general rule, *will* should not be used in the *if*-clause of a real conditional sentence; also, *would* should not be used in the *if*-clause of a contrary-to-fact sentence (see pages 127–30). However, both *will* and *would* do occur with modal meanings in conditional and other kinds of sentences. These usages are discussed in Chapter 4, especially. Section 4.2, pages 56–57.

Some other forms that may occur in the *if*-clause are the following.

Present continuous form in *if*-clause   The usage is the same as that for independent usage. (See Chapter 5, Section 5.1.)

Example

> If Helen *is working* in the garden now, I will come by sometime in the afternoon. (The present continuous form *is working* describes continuing activity.)

Compare this sentence with:

> If Helen *works* in the garden every morning, I will come by sometime in the afternoon. (The present form *works* describes repeated or habitual activity.)

Present perfect (or present perfect continuous) form in *if*-clause   The usage is the same as that for independent usage. (See Chapter 5, Section 5.3.)

Example

> If Helen *has worked* (or *has been working*) in the garden all morning, she will want to rest before lunch.

Present forms of modals to express future meaning in *if*-clause   Modals other than *will* and *shall* may be used to express future meaning in the *if*-clause.

Examples

> If your paper *must be handed* in on Monday, I will type it for you over the weekend.

> If I *can* not *be* home by six, I will telephone you.

NOTE: Some additional usages in the present real condition are these:

(1) *Should* + Verb

> If I *should miss* my plane today, I will telephone you.

This usage is more common in British English than in American English, where "If I miss my plane" is the more frequent form.

(2) *be* (present subjunctive of *be*). Examples:

> If that statement *be* true, you will receive support for your proposal.

> If that statement *be not true*, the proposal will surely fail.

This usage is formal and has become uncommon in present-day usage.

Main Clause: Verb Forms Used in Present Real Condition

The main clause in the present real condition generally expresses future time. Future time may be expressed in any of the usual ways, including the following.

Tense forms and modals that express future time

Examples

If John finishes his work today [possibly he will],
he *will leave* tomorrow.
he *is going to* leave tomorrow.
he *is leaving* tomorrow.
he *leaves* tomorrow.
he *can (may, must) leave* tomorrow.

Imperative (with or without *please*)

Examples

(Please) Pay us a visit if you have time.

(Please) Do not *hesitate* to ask for my help if you need it.

Here, future activity is implied.

let's + Verb

Example

Let's go to the art exhibit if there is time.

Again, future activity is implied.

NOTE: Other verb forms that may occur in the main clause are: present form expressing present time and present perfect; *ought to* and *should* in expressing obligation; and *might* and *could* in asking permission and expressing possibility.

Examples

If you are happy, I *am* happy.

If you have already finished your project, you *have earned* a reward.

If all goes as planned, we *should be* able to leave at three o'clock.

If you have finished reading the paper, *could* I please *borrow* it?

▶ *Now do Exercise 7A at the end of the Chapter.*

Past Real Conditions

A past real condition is one in which the condition expressed was *possible* in past time (past from the speaker's point of view). A common pattern is that past indicative verb forms are used in both the *if*-clause (the condition) and the main clause.

Sentence Patterns That Require Special Usage of Verb Forms

Example

> If Dr. Allen *was* at the meeting yesterday [possibly he was], I *was* not aware of the fact. I did not see him. (The time of the condition is past; *past indicative* is used in both clauses.)

Here is the sentence changed so that it is contrary to fact (a condition that will be discussed shortly):

> If Dr. Allen *were* at the meeting now [but he is not], he *would* surely *express* his ideas. (The time of the condition is present; *past subjunctive* is used in the *if*-clause, conditional in the main clause.)

NOTE: Other verb forms can occur in both clauses, as in these examples:

> If your letter *arrived* in this morning's mail [possibly it did], it *will* probably *be* on my desk by two o'clock this afternoon. (Past form in the *if*-clause, and future form in the main clause.)

> If Paula *was* not *working* in her garden this afternoon [I thought it possible that she was], she *must have gone* shopping instead. (Past continuous indicative form in the *if*-clause, and present perfect form in the main clause.)

The important point is that the condition expressed be *possible* in *past time*.

Now do Exercise 7B at the end of the chapter. ◀

Present Contrary-to-Fact Conditions

A **present contrary-to-fact condition** (also called a **present unreal condition**) is one in which the condition expressed does not exist at the present time (present from the speaker's point of view). Generally the past form of the verb is used in the *if*-clause (the condition), and the conditional form (*would* + Verb) is used in the main clause.

Examples

> If I *had* time [but I do not], I *would go* for a walk.

> If I *did* not *have* letters to write [but I do], I *would go* for a walk.

> If you *had* chores to do, you *would* not *go* for a walk.

The condition expressed may be one that does not exist at the present time but will possibly exist at some time in the future.

Example

> If you *came* with us [maybe you will, maybe you will not], my uncle *would let* us take out the sailboat.

NOTE: The present real condition expresses almost the same meaning as the present contrary-to-fact condition expressing future possibility. The following present real condition expresses approximately the same idea as the sample sentence just given:

> If you *come* with us [maybe you will, maybe you will not], my uncle will let us take out the sailboat.

The difference that some native speakers might feel is that the contrary-to-fact condition expresses a stronger doubt of the condition's being realized.

Past form of *be* in *if*-contrary-to-fact condition

The past form of *be* in an *if*-contrary-to-fact condition is *were* for all subjects.

Examples

> If I *were* in your place [but I am not], I would go on a vacation.
>
> If Anne *were* here [but she is not], she would help us.

NOTE 1: The past form used in the *if*-clause is actually a past subjunctive form. The past subjunctive form of all verbs except *be* is the same as the past indicative form. The past subjunctive of *be* is *were* for all subjects. Some grammarians now accept *was* as well as *were* for first- and third-person-singular subjects in informal usage. Compare these sets of sentences:

> If I *were* in your place [but I am not], I would go on a vacation. (Standard)
> If I *was* in your place [but I am not], I would go on a vacation. (Informal)
>
> If Anne *were* here [but she is not], she would help us. (Standard)
> If Anne *was* here [but she is not], she would help us. (Informal)

The same is true of usage after *wish,* as in these examples:

> I *wish* that I *were* (or *was*) with you.
> We all *wish* that Anne *were* (or *was*) here.

NOTE 2: *Would* + Verb is used for all subjects in the conditional form. For example: example:

> I, you, he, she, it, we, they *would* go

For conditional forms, traditional usage prescribed *should* for first-person subjects (as in "If I were asked, I *should go*") and *would* for second- and third-person subjects. *Would* is now accepted usage for all subjects and is used in all examples in this text. (Compare the note on the usage of *will* and *shall* on page 90.)

Generally, forms with *would* do not occur in an *if*-clause. *Would* occurs, however, with the modal meaning of *be willing to,* as discussed in Chapter 4 (especially Section 4.2), and in this usage does occur in *if*-clauses.

Could + Verb and *might* + Verb can occur with their special modal meanings in any pattern where *would* + Verb can occur, and these forms are also classified as conditional forms.

If you let me borrow your car today, I *could go* to the library for you.

If Margaret budgeted her money more carefully, she *might be able* to afford a trip to Alaska next summer.

Two other verb forms used in present contrary-to-fact conditions are the past continuous subjunctive form and the conditional continuous form. The **past continuous subjunctive form** (*were* + Verb-*ing* for all subjects) may be used in the condition (the *if*-clause) if emphasis on the continuing nature of the activity is intended.

Examples

If I *were looking* for a new car [but I am not], I would surely check on gas mileage.

If I *were* not *writing* a term paper this weekend [but I am], I would plan to go to the beach with you.

The **conditional continuous form** (*would be* + Verb-*ing* for all subjects) may be used in the main clause if emphasis on the continuing nature of the activity is intended.

If my research for my term paper were complete [but it is not], I *would* probably *be dining* with my family at home this minute.

If my car were in good working condition [but it is not], I *would* not *be traveling* on this plane right now.

Now do Exercise 7C at the end of the chapter. ◄

Past Contrary-to-Fact Conditions

A **past contrary-to-fact condition** (also called a **past unreal condition**) is one in which the condition expressed is contrary to fact at a time in the past (past from the speaker's point of view). Generally the past perfect form is used in the *if*-clause (the condition), and the past conditional form — *would have, could have,* or *might have* + past participle — is used in the main clause.

Examples

If I *had been* in your place [but I was not], I *would have been* very proud of the award.

If Jane *had* not *promised* to baby-sit this evening [but she did], she *would have helped* with your party.

NOTE 1: The past perfect continuous form (briefly presented in the note on page 113) may be used in the *if*-clause if a continuing activity interrupted by another activity is being described.

Examples

> If I *had been planning* on a walk [but I was not], I would have changed my mind after one look at the sky.

> If I *had* not *been saying* good-bye to guests at the time of your telephone call [but I was], I would have told you about our new house right then.

The **past conditional continuous form** may be used in the main clause if emphasis on the continuing nature of the activity is intended.

Examples

> If your telephone call *had come* through ten minutes later [but it did not], I *would have been sitting* in the airport waiting for you right now.

> If my car had not broken down [but it did], I *would* undoubtedly *have been arriving* at your house this minute.

NOTE 2: In this section, the *standard* rules for the usage of verb forms, or sequence, in conditional sentences have been given. It is possible to have "mixed conditions," as in these examples:

> If I *knew* the answer to your question, I *could have been* a millionaire years ago. (The *if*-clause expresses a condition contrary to fact in present time, and the main clause expresses past time.)

> If I *had received* your letter yesterday, I *would be* with you now. (The *if*-clause expresses a condition contrary to fact in past time, and the main clause expresses present time.)

Many mixed conditions can be unacceptable, however, and as a general rule, it is best to follow the standard rules for usage of verb forms in conditional sentences.

▶ *Now do Exercise 7D at the end of the chapter.*

Further Points About Conditions

A special use of the *if*-condition is in the form of an exclamatory sentence, in which a main clause need not be stated. The meaning of such an exclamatory sentence is equivalent to that of a statement with *wish*. The word *only* is usually included and intensifies the meaning expressed.

Examples

> If only that were true! (Meaning: I wish that that were true.)

> If only you had been there! (Meaning: I wish that you had been there.)

If-clauses, like other subordinate clauses, may be stated as elliptical clauses. An elliptical clause of this kind is one with the subject and verb or auxiliary omitted. (See Volume II, Section 15.5 for further discussion. Also see note on page 8 for comment on conditions expressed without *if*.)

Examples

Full-form: *If I am delayed,* I will telephone.
Elliptical: *If delayed,* I will telephone.

Full-form: *If I had been delayed,* I would have telephoned.
Elliptical: *If delayed,* I would have telephoned.

Now do Exercises 7E and 7F at the end of the chapter. ◀

VERB FORMS IN CLAUSES   7.2
FOLLOWING *WISH* [2]

The basic pattern of verb forms with the verb *wish* is this:

Subject 1 + *wish* (that) Subject 2 + Verb 2

An example is:

$\underset{\text{S1}}{\underline{George\ wishes}}$ (that) $\underset{\text{S2}}{\underline{the\ weather}}$ $\underset{\text{V2}}{\underline{were}}$ better.

In this sentence, *George* is Subject 1, the subject of *wish;* *the weather* is Subject 2, the subject of *were,* and *were* is Verb 2.

The form of Verb 2 depends on the time relationship between *wish* (in any form) and Verb 2. The use of *that* is optional. Rules for the form of Verb 2 may be summed up as follows.

Rule 1 If the time of *wish* and the time of Verb 2 are the same, use the past subjunctive of Verb 2.

Examples

John *wishes* that he $\overset{\text{V2}}{knew}$ an answer to your question. (Meaning: "John wishes *now* that he knew an answer to your question *now*." The time of *wishes* and of V2 is the same: present time.)

John *wished* that he $\overset{\text{V2}}{knew}$ an answer to your question. (Possible meaning: "John wished *yesterday* that he knew an answer to your question *yesterday*." The time of *wished* and of V2 is the same: past time.)

Be, as explained earlier, is the only verb whose past subjunctive form is different from its indicative form. The past subjunctive form is *were* for all subjects. Some grammarians feel that *was* is now acceptable for first- and third-person-singular subjects in informal usage. Compare these sets of sentences:

I wish that I *were* with you. (Standard)
I wish that I *was* with you. (Informal)

---

[2] *Wish* may also be followed by *to* + Verb, as in "John *wishes to sing*," and "John *wishes me to sing*."

I wish that it *were* a nice day. (Standard)

I wish that it *was* a nice day. (Informal)

Compare this with the comment on usage Note 1 on page 128.

NOTE: A refinement of Rule 1 is that only status verbs may be used *unmodified* (without adverbials) in the past to express the same time as *wish*. Other verbs (process verbs) may be used *if modified by an adverbial* to show repeated or habitual activity. For example:

I wish that John *had* a new car. (*Had* is the past subjunctive form, *unmodified*, of the status verb *have*. The form *bought*, for example, which is the past subjunctive form of the process verb *buy*, would not be acceptable in this sentence.)

I wish that John *bought* a new car *every year*. (*Bought* is acceptable in this sentence; it is *modified* by the adverbial *every year* indicating a repeated or habitual activity.)

See the note in Section 5.1, page 89, for a discussion of *status* and *process verbs*.

Rule 2   If the time of Verb 2 is past in relation to the time of *wish*, use the past perfect form of Verb 2.

Examples

George *wishes* that *he had known* an answer to your question. (Possible meaning: "George wishes *now* that he had known an answer to your question *yesterday*." Verb 2 describes past time in relation to *wishes*.)

George *wished* that he *had known* an answer to your question. (Possible meaning: "George wished *yesterday* that he had known an answer to your question *the day before yesterday*." Verb 2 describes past time in relation to *wished*.)

Rule 3   If the time of Verb 2 is future in relation to the time of *wish*, use the conditional form (*would/could/might* + Verb) of Verb 2.

Examples

Ellen *wishes* that you *would come* to the party. (Possible meaning: "Ellen wishes *now* that you would come to the party *tomorrow*." Verb 2 describes future time in relation to *wishes*.)

Ellen *wished* that you *would come* to the party. (Possible meaning: "Ellen wished *yesterday* that you would come to the party *tomorrow*." Verb 2 describes future time in relation to *wished*.)

An important exception to Rule 3, however, is this: If the subject of *wish* and the subject of Verb 2 are the same, generally do not use the conditional form with *would*; use *could* or *might* instead. (*Might* is more common in British English than in American English.)

Examples

Ellen wishes that she *could* (or *might*) *attend* the party. (Not *would attend*)

Ellen wished that she *could* (or *might*) *attend* the party. (Not *would attend*)

NOTE: An exception to the above guideline occurs when two conditions are present:

(1) The subject of *wish* and the subject of V2 are the same.

(2) The logical agent of V2 is different from the subject of V2. The logical agent is the person or thing that initiates or initiated an activity or condition.

Here is a sentence in which *would* is correct:

I *wish* I *would receive* a letter.

The subjects of *wish* and *would receive* are the same (I), but the logical agent — the person who would send the letter — is not the same as the subject of *would receive* (I). The sentence "I wish I would write a letter" is not acceptable because the subject and the logical agent are the same.

Now do Exercises 7G and 7H at the end of the chapter. ◀

PRESENT FORM TO EXPRESS FUTURE TIME 7.3
IN SUBORDINATE CLAUSES
WITH ADVERBIAL FUNCTION

This kind of sentence contains a main clause that expresses future time and a subordinate clause with adverbial function that expresses future time and is introduced by a time-expression (*after, before, until, when, while,* or such an expression as *by the time that* or *as soon as*). A subordinate clause with adverbial function[3] may follow or precede the main clause and is commonly said to "modify" the verb — in this case, to describe the time of the action of the verb. Any way of expressing future time may be used in the main clause, but future forms (*will* + Verb and *am/is/are going to* + Verb) cannot be used in the subordinate clause; the present form is generally used.

Examples

I *will wait* here until Louise *arrives*. OR:
Until Louise *arrives*, I *will wait* here.

I *will get* the car while you *close* up the house. OR:
While you *close* up the house, I *will get* the car.

---

[3]Subordinate clauses with adverbial function are discussed in Volume II, Section 15.5.

Some other ways of expressing future time in the main clause are:

I will be studying when you get here.

I will have finished my chores before you get here.

Close (Please close) the door before you leave.

Let's have some coffee before we leave.

I plan to study in the library until it closes.

I may travel before I settle down to a job.

Optional Forms in the Subordinate Clause

Although the present form is always acceptable in the subordinate clause, the present perfect form and the present continuous form may sometimes be optionally used. The two sentences in each of the following pairs are acceptable and have approximately the same meaning:

I will wait here until Louise *arrives*.

I will wait here until Louise *has arrived*.

     (Completed action: present form *or* present perfect form.)

I will get the car while you *close* up the house.

I will get the car while you *are closing* up the house.

     (Continuing action: present form *or* present continuous form.)

It is important to note that the present form is acceptable in both sentences. However, present continuous would not be acceptable in the first pair of sentences, and present perfect would not be acceptable in the second pair.

This rule of thumb may generally be followed: To express future time in a subordinate clause with adverbial function introduced by a time-expression, use the simple present form.

NOTE: These rules for usage of verb forms pertain only to subordinate clauses that are used adverbially. The rule would not apply to this sentence:

The time *when we will leave* is not certain.

When we will leave is a subordinate clause that expresses future time, but it modifies the noun *time*. Thus it is being used adjectivally, not adverbially.[4]

Also, the rule pertains only to subordinate clauses with adverbial function that are introduced by time-expressions. It does not apply to clauses that begin with subordinate conjunctions such as *although* and *because*. The future form may be used after such words, as in these examples:

We will have to walk home *although the ground will be muddy*.

We will have dinner without Charles *because he will get home late this evening*.

▶ *Now do Exercises 7I and 7J at the end of the chapter.*

---

[4]Clauses with adjectival function are discussed in Volume II, Chapter 12, Section 12.6, and Chapter 14, Section 14.9.

***Demand/be necessary* expressions** include the following:

ask that	propose that	be essential that
demand that	recommend that	be important that
insist that	request that	be necessary that
move that	suggest that	

With all of these expressions, *that* may sometimes be omitted but is commonly included.

With *demand/be necessary* expressions, the basic pattern is:

Subject 1 + *demand/be necessary* expression *that* Subject 2 + Verb 2 (present subjunctive).

An example is:

S1   S2   V2
Helen <u>*proposed*</u> that <u>*our club*</u> <u>*have*</u> a picnic next weekend.

In this sentence, *Helen* is Subject 1, the subject of *proposed* (a *demand/be necessary* expression). *Our club* is Subject 2, the subject of *have*; *have* is Verb 2.

After any form of the *demand/be necessary* expression (present, past, future, present perfect, and so on), Verb 2 generally occurs in the present subjunctive form. This form is the same as the base form of the verb for all subjects.

Examples

The students *request*
The students *are requesting*
The students *requested*   that they *have* more time
The students *will request*   to complete their papers.
The students *have requested*

I *move*
I *moved*
I *will move*   that the meeting *be adjourned*.
I *have moved*

The negative form is *not* + present subjunctive.

Examples

It *is* important
It *was* important   that the committee *not reach*
It *will be* important   a decision without hearing all
It *has* often *been* important   of the facts.

In the above examples, any other form of the *demand/be necessary* expression that fit the context could also have occurred.

NOTE 1: Two other forms of Verb 2 besides the present subjunctive occur, but much more commonly in British English than in American English, where they are quite rare:

(1) The form *should* + Verb occurs, as in this example:

The students *requested* that they *should have* more time to complete their papers.

(2) An indicative form that agrees in time with the time of the *demand/be necessary* verb expression occurs, as in this example:

The doctor *recommended* that John *took* more exercise.
(*Took* is past indicative agreeing in time with the past form of *recommended*.)

NOTE 2: Some *demand/be necessary* expressions (including *ask, insist, suggest,* and *be essential*) also occur as **reporting** *(say/ask)* expressions introducing indirect discourse (see Section 7.5). They then occur with different rules of sequence. Compare the following sentences:

John *insisted* that he *pay* for our theater tickets. (*Insisted* is here a *demand/be necessary* verb; *pay* is a present subjunctive form with future meaning in relation to *insisted*.)

John *insisted* (= *said*) that he *would enjoy* being our host at the theater. (*Insisted* is a reporting [*say/ask*] verb; *would enjoy* is a conditional form with future meaning in relation to *insisted*, as required in indirect discourse.)

Other *demand/be necessary* verb expressions (among them *ask, demand, move, propose, request, be essential,* and *be necessary*) may also be followed by *to* + Verb, as in "Emily *asked to sing*," and "Emily *asked me to sing*"; "It *was necessary to leave*," and "It *was necessary for us to leave*."

▶ *Now do Exercises 7K and 7L at the end of the chapter.*

7.5 INDIRECT DISCOURSE

The term **indirect discourse** is generally defined as "someone else's words or thoughts" or "the speaker's words or thoughts at another time." Indirect discourse follows reporting words such as *say* and *ask*. There are two kinds of indirect discourse: **indirect statements** and **indirect questions**. Indirect questions are also called *dependent interrogative clauses*.[5] Indirect statements follow **say-words,** which include: *agree, announce, believe, decide, feel, know, observe, read, reply, report, respond, say, state, think, write,* and such expressions as *be sure* and *be of the opinion*. For example:

---

[5]Indirect statements and indirect questions function as the direct objects of *say* and *ask* words, as nouns might do. Thus they are sometimes referred to as *noun clauses*.

DIRECT STATEMENT	INDIRECT STATEMENT
Philip walks to class every day.	Lillian *says (that) Philip walks to class every day.*

Indirect questions follow **ask-words** and some *say*-words. *Ask*-words include: *ask, inquire, wonder,* and such expressions as *be a question of*. Some examples:

DIRECT QUESTION	INDIRECT QUESTIONS
Does Philip walk to class every day?	Helen *wonders whether* (or *if*) *Philip walks to class every day.*
	Helen *does* not *know whether* (or *if*) *Philip walks to class every day.*

Indirect discourse involves two special kinds of rules: rules of word order (patterns), and rules for special usage of verb forms.

Word Order (Patterns) in Indirect Discourse

Word order in indirect discourse depends on the form of the direct statement or question. In the examples below, the following symbols are used:

S	= Subject	V	= Verb
DO	= Direct object	Aux	= Auxiliary
Prep	= Preposition	Remainder	= Complements and adverbials following the verb
OP	= Object of preposition		

Indirect Statements, yes/no Questions, and Information Questions with *wh*-Adv

These all take the same forms and follow the same rules of word order as direct statements.

DIRECT STATEMENT	INDIRECT STATEMENT
The party [S] ended [V] early.	John says *(that) the party [S] ended [V] early.*
The party [S] did [Aux] not last [V] long.	John says *(that) the party [S] did [Aux] not last [V] long.*

Note that the use of *that* in indirect statements is optional.

DIRECT *yes/no* QUESTION	INDIRECT *yes/no* QUESTION
Was [V] it [S] a large party?	I wonder *whether* (or *if*) *it [S] was [V] a large party.*
Did [Aux] Paula [S] go [V] to the party?	I do not know *whether* (or *if*) *Paula [S] went [V] to the party.*

Indirect questions must always have an introductory word. Indirect *yes/no* questions are introduced by *whether* or *if*, which are used interchangeably.

DIRECT *wh*-ADV QUESTION	INDIRECT *wh*-ADV QUESTION
Where was the party? (V S)	I wonder *where the party was*. (S V)
Why *did Anne leave* the party early? (Aux S V)	I do not know *why Anne left the party early*. (S V)
Why *didn't Anne speak* with her friends? (Aux S V)	Everyone is asking *why Anne did not speak with her friends*. (S Aux V)

Note that the indirect *wh*-Adv question uses the same question word as the direct question.

Indirect Questions with *wh*-N Forms (Interrogative Pronouns and Interrogative Adjective + Noun Phrases)[6]

The *wh*-N form in an indirect question always fills a nominal function. The word order depends on the function of the *wh*-N form, whether it is a pronoun, such as *who* or *whom*, or an Interrogative Adjective + Noun phrase, such as *what artist*, *what pianist*, or *whose children*, (see the following examples). An indirect question with the *wh*-N form as *subject* follows the order Subject + Verb.

DIRECT *wh*-N FORM QUESTION	INDIRECT *wh*-N FORM QUESTION
Who went to *the concert?* (S V)	I wonder *who went to the concert*. (S V)
What artist was on the program? (S V)	I will ask *what artist was* on the program. (S V)

In an indirect question with the *wh*-N form as *direct object*, the direct object has initial position and the rest of the clause follows direct statement word order.[7]

DIRECT *wh*-N FORM QUESTION	INDIRECT *wh*-N FORM QUESTION
Who (m) will we have as a guest conductor next week? (DO Aux S V)	I wonder *who (m) we will have* as a guest conductor next week. (DO S Aux V)
What pianist will we hear next week? (DO Aux S V)	I do not know *what pianist we will hear* next week. (DO S Aux V)

In an indirect question with a *wh*-N form as the *object of a preposition*, two orders are possible. The object of the preposition may be in initial position with the preposition at the end of the clause, or the prepositional phrase consisting of the Preposition + Object may be in initial position. The latter order is now considered to be formal; both orders are now accepted on all levels of usage. In both cases, the remainder of the clause follows direct statement word order.

---

[6]See Chapter 2, Section 2.8, and Volume II, Section 14.10, for further discussion of interrogative forms and patterns.

[7]The forms *whom* and *who* both occur in initial position in object functions, as do *whomever* and *whoever*. *Who* and *whoever* are both accepted in informal usage (generally, spoken English), but *whom* and *whomever* are generally required in written English. Interrogative pronouns and their case forms are discussed in detail in Volume II, Section 14.10.

DIRECT *wh*-N FORM QUESTION	INDIRECT *wh*-N FORM QUESTION
Who (m) did you speak with? with OP, did Aux, you S, speak V, with Prep	*My friends asked who (m) I had spoken with.* who OP, I S, had spoken Aux V, with Prep
With whom did you speak? (Formal) With Prep, whom OP, did Aux, you S, speak V	*My friends asked with whom I had spoken.* (Formal) with Prep, whom OP, I S, had spoken Aux V
Whose children did you speak with? Whose children OP, did Aux, you S, speak V, with Prep	*My friends asked whose children I had spoken with.* whose children OP, I S, had Aux, spoken V, with Prep
With whose children did you speak? (Formal) With Prep, whose children OP, did Aux, you S, speak V	*My friends asked with whose children I had spoken.* (Formal) with Prep, whose OP, children, I S, had Aux, spoken V

NOTE: The other kinds of clauses containing *wh*-N forms, relative and indefinite relative clauses, follow the same rules of word order as indirect questions (dependent interrogative clauses). Relative and indefinite relative pronouns and the clauses they occur in are discussed in Section 1.3, pages 8–9, and also in Volume II, Sections 14.8, 14.9, and 14.11.

Rules for Usage of Verb Forms in Indirect Discourse

The rules for the usage of verb forms are the same for indirect statements and indirect questions. There are two categories of rules, depending on the form of the *say/ask* verb.

Rules for Usage of Verb Forms Following a *say/ask* Verb in the Present System

The present system of verb forms includes the present form and all other verb forms containing a present auxiliary (present continuous, future, future continuous, present perfect, present perfect continuous, future perfect, future perfect continuous, and all forms with modals in the present form). The present system also includes imperatives, *let's* + Verb, and *please* + Verb.

After a *say/ask* verb in the present system, use the same form of the verb as would have been used in direct discourse.

Examples

Direct statement: Dorothy *rides* her bicycle every day.

Indirect statement: Bill *says* (that) Dorothy *rides* her bicycle every day.

Direct statement: Dorothy *rode* her bicycle to school yesterday.

Indirect statement: Bill *says* (that) Dorothy *rode* her bicycle to school yesterday.

Direct question: *Does* Dorothy *ride* her bicycle to school every day?

Indirect question: Bill *has wondered* whether Dorothy *rides* her bicycle to school every day.

Rules for Usage of Verb Forms Following a *say/ask* Verb in the Past System

The **past system** of verb forms includes the past form and all other verb forms containing a past auxiliary (past continuous, past perfect, past perfect continuous, conditional, past conditional, and all forms with modals in the past form).

Rules for usage of verb forms after a *say/ask* verb in the past system depend on the time relationship between the *say/ask* verb and the following verb.

(1) When the *say/ask* verb is in the past system, activities or conditions occurring at the same time (present time from the point of view of the *say/ask* verb) must be described with a past form.

Examples

Direct statement: Carl *is* in the library.

Indirect statement: Laura *said* [at three o'clock] (that) Carl *was* in the library [at three o'clock]. (*Said* and *was* describe the same time in the past.)

Direct question: *Is* Carl in the library?

Indirect question: Laura *asked* [at three o'clock] whether Carl *was* in the library [at three o'clock]. (*Asked* and *was* describe the same time in the past.)

(2) When the *say/ask* verb is in the past system, activities or conditions that occurred before that time (past time from the point of view of the *say/ask* verb) must be described with past perfect.

Examples

Direct statement: Carl *was* in the library.

Indirect statement: Laura *said* [at three o'clock] (that) Carl *had been* in the library [at two o'clock]. (*Had been* describes past time in relation to *said*.)

Direct question: *Was* Carl in the library?

Indirect question: Laura *asked* [at three o'clock] whether Carl *had been* in the library [at two o'clock]. (*Had been* describes past time in relation to *asked*.)

(3) When the *say/ask* verb is in the past system, activities or conditions to take place after that time (future time from the point of view of the *say/ask* verb) must be described with the conditional.

Examples

Direct statement: Carl *will be* in the library.

Indirect statement: Laura *said* [at three o'clock] that Carl *would be* in the library [at four o'clock]. (*Would be* describes future time in relation to *said*.)

Direct question: *Will* Carl *be* in the library?

Indirect question: Laura *asked* [at three o'clock] whether Carl *would be* in the library [at four o'clock]. (*Would be* describes future time in relation to *asked*.)

Two errors in tense usage in indirect discourse are frequently made by both native and nonnative speakers of English: the use of present form and the use of future form after reporting words like *say* and *ask* that are being used to describe past time. These are examples of correct forms in such instances:

Direct statement: Lillian *is* a student at the university now.

Indirect statement: John *said* that Lillian *was* a student at the university now.

Direct statement: George *will telephone* us tomorrow.

Indirect statement: Ellen *said* that George *would* telephone us tomorrow.

Although *was* describes present time and *would telephone* describes future time, neither present form nor future form is acceptable after a verb form describing past time such as *said*. It must be noted, however, that the use of present and future forms after *say/ask* verbs in the past system seems to be increasingly more common, especially on the informal level.

An optional exception to the rule occurs when indirect discourse describes general truths (laws of nature and the like). In such cases, the present form may be used, as in this example:

Direct statement: The normal human temperature *is* 98.6° Fahrenheit or 37° centigrade.

Indirect statement: The doctor said that the normal human temperature *was* (or *is*) 98.6° Fahrenheit or 37° centigrade.

Punctuation in Indirect Questions

Note that indirect questions introduced by *say/ask* verbs in statement patterns, such as "Laura asked" and "I do not know," are punctuated as statements, normally with periods at the ends, as in the preceding examples. If indirect questions are introduced by *say/ask* verbs in question patterns, such as "Did Laura ask" and "Don't you know," they are punctuated as questions, with question marks at the ends of the complete sentences.

Examples

Laura asked where Carl was.

Did Laura ask where Carl was?

I do not know why Anne left the party early.

Don't you know why Anne left the party early?

Reporting Printed Material

It is a convention that either past or present forms of *say/ask* verbs may be used in reporting printed and written material — books, articles, letters, and so on.

Examples

I have just read an excellent book on gardening.

The author said that it was a good idea to prune roses twice a year. OR: *The author says* that it is a good idea to prune roses twice a year.

I have just received a letter from a friend.

He said that he was planning to go skiing next month. OR: *He says* that he is planning to go skiing next month.

Nonindependent Verb Forms and Complex Sentences in Indirect Discourse

The examples in this section have included only verb forms used independently, as described in Chapter 5. Similar rules apply to indirect discourse, both statements and questions, containing verb forms that cannot occur independently (as described in Chapter 6) or containing verb forms required by some sentence patterns (as described in this chapter).

After a *say/ask* verb in the *present system*, the same forms of the verb occur as in direct discourse.

Examples

Direct statement: Paul *was studying* when the bell *rang*.

Indirect statement: Helen *thinks* that Paul *was studying* when the bell *rang*.

Direct question: *Will* the bus driver *wait* for us until we *arrive?*

Indirect question: I *will ask* whether the bus driver *will wait* for us until we *arrive*.

After a *say/ask* verb in the *past system*, similar rules to those for verb forms used independently apply. Generally present and future forms do not occur. Also, a basic rule is that activities or conditions occurring before those described by a *say/ask* verb in the past system are described by a past perfect or a past conditional form.

Example

Direct statement: Harry *would help* us if he *were* here.

Indirect statement: Laura *said* that Harry *would have helped* us if he *had been* here.

An exception is that in indirect discourse with sentences containing *demand/be necessary* expressions, the present subjunctive does not change.

Example

Direct statement: John *requested* that his cousin *be asked* to play the piano.

Indirect statement: Paula *said* that John *had requested* that his cousin *be asked* to play the piano.

Now do Exercises 7M, 7N, and 7O at the end of the chapter. ◀

Present Real Conditions   7A

For this exercise, refer to Section 7.1, pages 123–26. Fill in the blank in each sentence below with an appropriate form of the modal, if any; and the verb in parentheses; and the word *not*, is given.

With some items in this exercise, more than one form of the verb may be acceptable in general usage. For purposes of this practice, however, fill in the blanks in *if*-clauses with the present form and the blanks in main clauses with the future form.

Examples

If everyone _____ ready, we will leave for the mountains at seven o'clock. (be)
Answer:
If everyone _____is_____ ready, we will leave for the mountains at seven o'clock.

If the weather permits, our class _____ on a hike tomorrow morning. (go)
Answer:
If the weather permits, our class _____will go_____ on a hike tomorrow morning.

1. If I _____ time to pack today, I will leave by car tomorrow. (have)

2. If my car _____ ready now, I will call for it tomorrow. (not, be)

3. If the mayor can attend our meeting, he _____. (speak)

4. If your package is delivered by tomorrow, we _____ you. (not, call)

5. Please leave a message in the mailbox if there _____ no one at home this afternoon. (be)

6. If an announcement of the new library hours _____ in the newspaper today, please let me know. (not, appear)

7. I _____ you until tomorrow if I should arrive home after ten this evening. (not, telephone)

8. If our club meeting is held in a classroom, we _____ our lunches with us. (may, not, bring)

9. I am going to make a soufflé if there _____ enough eggs in the refrigerator. (be)

10. If it is true that the concert has been canceled, we _____ tickets for another performance. (receive)

11. Please do not worry if you _____ late. (must, arrive)

12. If I _____ my assignments before three o'clock, I will not be able to go for a walk with you. (not, finish)

13. We _____ in the lounge if your plane should be delayed. (can, meet)

14. If there should not be time to mail a postcard from London, I _____ you one from Madrid. (send)

15. Your instructor _____ a report before Tuesday if a field trip is being planned for Saturday. (not, expect)

16. If you _____ for a moment, Mr. Adams will give you a visitor's permit to use the library. (can, wait)

17. I _____ back later if the baby is sleeping. (come)

18. If visitors to the campus _____ other arrangements, they are met at the airport by a student committee. (not, have)

19. It _____ in the mountains before evening if it is not already snowing there. (snow)

20. If you are working on your paper now, I _____ you again later. (call)

7B Past Real Conditions

For this exercise, refer to Section 7.1, page 127. Fill in the blank in each sentence below with the appropriate form of the verb in parentheses and *not*, if given.

Example

If Harry _____ at home, he did not answer the doorbell. *(be)*
Answer:
If Harry ____was____ at home, he did not answer the doorbell.

1. If it was not your brother who answered the telephone, it _____ someone who sounded just like him. (be)

2. If Dr. Wilson was at the meeting last evening, I _____ aware of her presence. (not, be)

3. If our term paper was due yesterday, no one _____ me the information. (give)

4. If Paul _____ off your book, he surely did so by mistake. (carry)

5. If the telephone rang, I _____ it. (not, hear)

6. If Mr. Calhoun _____ at home, I did not see any signs of his presence. (be)

7. If our instructor was not ill, why _____ he _____ to class? (not, come)

8. If there _____ a meeting last night, I did not receive a notice of it. (be)

9. If it _____ last night, I was not aware of the fact. (rain)

10. If there was a thunderstorm last night, I _____ awakened by it. (not, be)

For this exercise, refer to Section 7.1, pages 127–29. Fill in the blank in each sentence below with an appropriate form of the modal given, if any, and the verb in parentheses and *not*, if given.

Example

If the post office _____ open, I would mail your letter today. (be)
Answer:
If the post office _____ were _____ open, I would mail your letter today.

1. If it _____ possible for Mr. Andrews to be at our meeting this evening, he would probably support your proposal. (be)

2. If it _____ so close to the end of the semester, another field trip might be planned. (not, be)

3. If Dr. Gray were teaching this semester, he _____ the person to ask about historical sites in the area. (be.)

4. If there were fewer students on the campus, we _____ a new dormitory. (not, need)

5. We could probably go to the game if we _____ on our assignments all afternoon. (work)

6. Fred would have more time to spend with his friends if he _____ the piano. (not, play)

7. One of the students _____ you sightseeing if there were not a meeting scheduled this afternoon. (can, take)

8. Some students _____ Dr. McKay's lecture if it were scheduled for Thursday instead of Friday evening. (can, not, attend)

9. If you _____ time to take a longer vacation, you could visit Disneyland. (have)

10. If John _____ with you, he would tell you so. (not, agree)

11. If the library were open on Sunday, I _____ the research on my term paper today. (can, start)

12. If the weather were nicer today, I _____ here at home. (not, be)

13. You might enjoy a visit to our new art gallery if you _____ for contemporary painting. (care)

14. I would surely like to go to the movies with you if I _____ so much homework to do. (not, have)

15. Our adviser would charter a plane if there _____ more students interested in a trip to Washington. (be)

16. The air would be a lot clearer than it is if there _____ so many cars on the freeways. (not, be)

Exercises

17. If I _____ time to go to the library this afternoon, I would pick up your books for you. (have)

18. If it _____ raining so hard, we could go for a walk. (not, be)

19. If I knew your friends, I _____ surely _____ them. (like)

20. Even if you left for the store immediately, you _____ there before closing time. (can, not, get)

7D Past Contrary-to-Fact Conditions

For this exercise, refer to Section 7.1, pages 129–30. Fill in the blank in each sentence below with the appropriate form of the modal given, if any; the verb in parentheses; and *not,* if given.

Example

If you had called me, I _____ your plane.
(meet)
Answer:
If you had called me, ___I would have met___ your plane.

1. If your plane had arrived ten minutes sooner, you _____ the governor at the airport. (see)

2. If the traffic had been lighter, John _____ so late. (not, arrive)

3. If the horse show _____ on time, the horses would have been less restless. (start)

4. If the student play _____ such a success, the Drama Society would not have been able to continue. (not, be)

5. If news of our horse show had been more widespread, there _____ _____ a larger audience attending it.
   (be)

6. There _____ so many students taking the comprehensive examination if it had been scheduled a week earlier. (not, be)

7. If there had been more cars on the freeway during the storm, probably more accidents _____. (occur)

8. Wheat _____ so much this year if there had not been a drought last summer. (not, cost)

9. If the date of our meeting had been changed, all members of the group _____ notification. (receive)

10. All concert tickets _____ good for a later date if the performance had not been given as planned. (be)

11. If I had heard of your visit in time, I _____ plans for you to speak to our class. (can, make)

12. Jerry _____ to graduate school if he had not received a scholarship. (not, may, go)

13. If it _____ harder last night, there might have been skiing in the mountains this weekend. (snow)

14. I would have telephoned you tomorrow if I _____ you today. (not, see)

15. If you had not told me about the ballet company's special performance, I

    _____ it. (may, miss)

16. I _____ the announcement of your award if the newspaper had been late this morning. (not, may, see)

17. If my typewriter had been working yesterday, I _____ my term paper. (can, type)

18. I _____ you at the door if I had not been watching television. (hear)

19. If it _____ longer last night, we would not have had to water the plants today. (rain)

20. I would have telephoned you earlier if your letter _____ so late. (not, arrive)

Conditional Sentences of All Types   7E

For this exercise, refer to Section 7.1, pages 123–31. Complete each of the following items to form a conditional sentence. Write out each sentence in both of these orders: (a) subordinate clause + main clause (a comma is used in this order); (b) main clause + subordinate clause (no comma is generally used in this order).

Example

   If you are free now,
   Possible answers:
   a. _____ If you are free now, I will come over right away. _____

   b. _____ I will come over right away if you are free now. _____

1. If you are free now,

   a. _____

   b. _____

2. If it does not rain today,

   a. _____

   b. _____

3. If I were in your place,

   a. _____

   b. _____

4. Our dog would have barked if

   a. _____

   b. _____

5. If I did not have so much to do today,

   a. _____

   b. _____

6. Phyllis will not be able to go to Alaska this summer if

   a. _____

   b. _____

7. If our meeting had started on time,

   a. _____

   b. _____

8. I will telephone you this evening if

   a. _____

   b. _____

9. If the newspaper was delivered this morning,

   a. _____

   b. _____

10. Our team would not have had a chance at the silver cup if

   a. _____

   b. _____

11. If you mailed your invitations today,

   a. _____

   b. _____

12. The city council is going to renovate the library if

   a. _____

   b. _____

13. If it were not raining,

   a. _____

   b. _____

14. There would not be so many automobile accidents if

   a. _____

   b. _____

15. If there is no one at home this afternoon,

    a. _____

    b. _____

16. Please come to our party if

    a. _____

    b. _____

17. If there had not been a notice about the game in the newspaper,

    a. _____

    b. _____

18. More handcrafted articles would be produced if

    a. _____

    b. _____

19. If my car cannot be repaired by five o'clock,

    a. _____

    b. _____

20. Your dog would not have run away if

    a. _____

    b. _____

21. If Dr. Bullard was at last night's meeting,

    a. _____

    b. _____

22. Let's go on a picnic if

    a. _____

    b. _____

23. If there were not so much traffic at this time of day,

    a. _____

    b. _____

24. I did not see Paul at the airport if

    a. _____

    b. _____

25. If Emily's plane arrives late,

    a. _____

    b. _____

7F   Directed Writing

For this exercise, refer to Section 7.1, pages 123–31.
A. Write a paragraph of 100–150 words according to the following instructions:

1. Begin with: "If I ever write a book, it will be about . . ." Tell what will be in your book.

2. Think of a make of car, such as a Ford or a Cadillac. Begin your paragraph with: "If I bought a new car, I would choose (or not choose) a . . ."

3. Suppose that a friend tells you of a problem or a decision he must make. Give him your advice. Begin your paragraph with "If I were you, . . ."

4. Begin with: "If I had known a year ago what I know now, . . ."

5. Begin with: "If only I had not . . ."

B. Write a short composition of 200–250 words according to the following instructions:

1. Begin with: "If telephones with video screens come into use in private homes . . ." (Or discuss what will happen if another device is invented or comes into common use.)

2. Discuss what might happen if an invented language, such as Esperanto, were adopted for communication throughout the world.

3. Discuss an event that might have happened but did not.

7G   Verb Forms in Clauses Following *wish*

For this exercise, refer to Section 7.2, pages 131–33.
A. Fill in the blank with the appropriate form of the verb given in parentheses.

Example

Anne wishes that she _____ here now. (be)
Answer:
Anne wishes that she _____were_____ here now.

1. We all wish that Tom _____ here now. (be)

2. Some students wish that they _____ more time just now to participate in sports. (have)

3. When I lived next door to the Browns, they often wished that they

   _____ such a large house. (not, own)

4. During the holidays I often wished that you _____ here to enjoy them with us. (be)

5. The whole class wished that your visit _____ longer than it did. (last)

6. We all wish that it _____ so much during your visit last week. (not, rain)

7. Carl wishes that you _____ his recital last week. (not, miss)

8. Janet's doctor wishes that she _____ more exercise in the future. (get)

9. Janet wishes that she herself _____ more walks in the future. (take)

10. I wish that Bill _____ more letters next year. (write)

11. I wish that I _____ you next year. (visit)

12. I wish that I _____ more letters next year. (receive)

B. Complete each of the following items so as to form a sentence, including the words in parentheses. In giving your answer, write a complete sentence. Keep in mind that the conjunction *that* is optional.

Example

I wish that (now)

_____

Possible answer:
_____ I wish that I had time for a walk now. _____

1. I wish that (now)

_____

2. The president expressed the wish that (at this time)

_____

_____

3. Some people wish that (not, now)

_____

4. Our instructor wishes that (last week)

_____

5. My friends have often wished that (last summer)

_____

_____

6. The children in the neighborhood wished that (not, last night)

_____

_____

7. John wishes that he (in the future)

_____

8. I wished that our class (next summer)

_____

Exercises

9. We all wish that (not, tomorrow)

_____

10. I have sometimes wished that I (next year)

_____

_____

7H Directed Writing

For this exercise, refer to Section 7.2, pages 131–33.
A. Write a paragraph of 100–150 words according to the following instructions:

1. Begin with: "I wish that I had enough time to . . ."

2. Write a paragraph about something you wish were so, but is not.

3. Begin with: "I wish that I had gone to ——— on my last vacation."

4. Begin with: "I wish that I had not bought ———."

5. Begin with: "I wish that I could meet ———."

6. Begin with: "I wish that my best friend [or brother, sister, or other person] would not waste so much time on ———."

B. Write a short composition of 200–250 words according to the following instructions:

1. Begin with: "I wish that the school I go to were not so large [or were larger]."

2. Begin with: "I wish that I had lived in [choose a year]."

3. Begin with: "I wish that I could be a [name of profession]."

7I Present Form for Future Time

For this exercise, refer to Section 7.3, pages 133–34.
A. Fill in the blank in each of the following sentences with an appropriate form of the verb given in parentheses. Keep in mind that although present perfect or present continuous may be used in a specific sentence, present form is always acceptable and should be practiced in this exercise.

Example

I will finish my homework before the library _____ .
(close)
I will finish my homework before the library _____ closes _____ .

1. I will be through with my chores by the time that the guests _____

_____ . (arrive)

2. The car will not be repaired before the garage _____
today. (close)

3. When the slide projector and screen _____ ready, the lecture will begin. (be)

4. Before vacation _____, the students are going to have comprehensive examinations. (begin)

5. The proctor is not going to start the examination until everyone _____ seated. (be)

6. As soon as the sun _____, we are leaving. (rise)

7. We are not planning a visit home until the school term _____. (end)

8. We may wait here until the rain _____. (stop)

9. The bus cannot leave before the tour of the gardens _____ over. (be)

10. When you _____, turn off the lights. (leave)

11. Don't forget to write to me while you _____ on vacation. (be)

12. After the mail _____, please call me. (arrive)

13. Please don't open the presents until the guests _____ here. (be)

14. As soon as the restaurant _____, let's have lunch. (open)

15. Let's not tell the good news until everyone _____ here. (get)

16. Eleanor expects to be here by the time that the concert _____. (begin)

17. The students do not want to leave on vacation before their grades _____ announced. (be)

18. I hope to be ready to go out before you _____. (call)

19. As soon as the school term _____, some of my friends plan to leave for Mexico. (end)

20. While you _____ dinner, I will finish this letter. (prepare)

B. Complete the following items by writing a subordinate clause so as to form a sentence. Give both orders for each sentence: (a) main clause + subordinate clause (no comma); (b) subordinate clause + main clause (comma). Write out the complete sentence in your answer. Be sure to punctuate your sentences correctly.

Example

1. Elizabeth will finish her thesis before
Possible answers:
a. _____ Elizabeth will finish her thesis before the term ends. _____
b. _____ Before the term ends, Elizabeth will finish her thesis. _____

1. Carl will finish his errands before

a. _____

b. _____

2. The recital will not begin until

a. _____

b. _____

3. The boy next door is going to wash the car while

   a. _____

   b. _____

4. I am not going to watch television until

   a. _____

   b. _____

5. Jane can telephone after

   a. _____

   b. _____

6. You may not be happy to see me when

   a. _____

   b. _____

7. Please write to me as soon as

   a. _____

   b. _____

8. Please don't begin the chores until

   a. _____

   b. _____

9. Let's play a game of chess while

   a. _____

   b. _____

10. I expect to have my homework assignments finished by the time that

    a. _____

    _____

    b. _____

    _____

11. I hope to get a driver's license as soon as

    a. _____

    _____

    b. _____

    _____

12. I will be cleaning my house when

    a. _____

    b. _____

Sentence Patterns That Require Special Usage of Verb Forms

13. I will not be practicing the piano when

   a. _____

   b. _____

14. The plane will have landed by the time that

   a. _____

   b. _____

15. We will not have finished dinner when

   a. _____

   b. _____

Directed Writing   7J

For this exercise, refer to Section 7.3, pages 133–34. Write a paragraph of 100–150 words on the topic(s) below. In each paragraph that you write, use sentences containing a main clause and a subordinate clause, like the sentences given as examples in this section. Include subordinate conjunctions such as *after, before, until, when,* and *while,* and expressions such as *by the time that* and *as soon as.*

1. Describe what will happen when you go on a picnic. You may begin, for example, with "My friends and I will meet a half hour before the school bus arrives. After we get on the bus, . . ."

2. Describe what you will do while you wait for a friend to pick you up at the airport. You may begin, for example, with "I will get my luggage before I do anything else. Then I will . . ."

3. Describe what you will do on a shopping trip in the city. You may begin, for example, with "I will get to the city early before the stores are crowded. Then I will . . ."

4. Describe how you will spend a day at a park, a zoo, a museum, an art gallery, or another place of interest. You may begin, for example, with "We will plan to arrive at ——— when it opens for the day. Then we will . . ."

demand/be necessary Expressions   7K

For this exercise, refer to Section 7.4, pages 135–36.
A. Fill in the blank in each sentence below with an appropriate form of the verb in parentheses to complete the *demand/be necessary* sequence, and use the word *not* when given.

Examples

   It will be necessary that each voter _____ . (register)
   Answer:
   It will be necessary that each voter _____ register _____

   Mr. Wilson insisted that George _____ for his own lunch. (not, pay)

   Mr. Wilson insisted that George _____ not pay _____ for his own lunch.

1. The registrar requests that each student _____ up his registration materials on the date assigned. (pick)

2. At our next committee meeting I will demand that a vote on our proposal _____ postponed. (not, be)

3. It was necessary that we _____ up camp before leaving on our hike. (set)

4. Our instructor asked that students _____ transistor radios with them on the hike. (not, bring)

5. Carl's doctor recommended that he _____ an exercise program immediately. (start)

6. Our tour conductor suggested that the bus _____ for another fifteen minutes. (not, leave)

7. It is essential that no one _____ a word about the winners of our awards before the annual banquet. (say)

8. Many students have requested that they _____ charged late fines for books due in the library during the mid-semester break. (not, be)

9. It will be important that everyone _____ on time for the examination. (arrive)

10. I move that the meeting _____ adjourned. (be)

B. Complete each of the items in the following exercise with a clause so as to form a complete sentence following the *demand/be necessary* sequence.

Suppose that you have injured your ankle while hiking on a rough path. Describe your experience, following these instructions.

1. My doctor will put a cast on my foot. Then he will insist that _____
_____
_____

2. He will probably recommend that _____
_____
_____

3. It will be necessary that _____
_____
_____

4. I will ask that my friends _____
_____
_____

Sentence Patterns That Require Special Usage of Verb Forms

5. After the doctor takes the cast off my foot, he will probably suggest that _____

_____

_____

C. Again, for each item below, supply a clause to complete the sentence.

When completed, the items below describe in order the happenings at a meeting of a club to which you belong. The occasion is that you make a proposal of some sort (for example, a proposal that your club have a project to clean up litter on the public streets, start a nursery school for children of mothers who work, or carry out another such project). The proposal will be discussed and voted on.

1. At our next club meeting I will propose that _____

_____

_____

2. Another member will probably recommend that _____

_____

_____

3. Another member may request that _____

_____

_____

4. The president will probably suggest that _____

_____

_____

5. I will ask that _____

_____

_____

6. Members may insist that _____

_____

_____

7. It will be important that _____

_____

_____

8. After discussion, someone may move that _____

_____

_____

9. It will then be necessary that _____

_____

_____

10. Finally someone will move that _____

_____

_____

7L   Directed Writing

For this exercise, refer to Section 7.4, pages 135–36.
A. Write a paragraph of 100–150 words according to the following instructions:

1. Suppose that a friend has asked you your suggestions for studying for an examination. Write a paragraph telling your suggestions. Use such expressions as *suggest that, recommend that, be important that,* and *be necessary that.*

2. Suppose that a friend is going to visit your school (or another place with which you are familiar). Write a paragraph giving him your suggestions of what he should do and see on his visit. Use such expressions as *insist that, recommend that, suggest that,* and *be essential that.*

B. Write a short composition of 200–250 words according to the following instructions:

1. Consider a problem that exists on your school campus, in the city where you are living, or elsewhere. Write a letter to the editor of your school or local paper giving your suggestions for improving the situation. Use such expressions as *ask that, propose that, recommend that, request that, suggest that, be essential that,* and *be necessary that.*

2. Suppose that a friend of yours asks you how to apply for something: admission to a college or university, a charge account at a department store, a driver's license, or other. Write a paragraph giving him information on procedures. Use such expressions as *ask that* ("The person you see or write to will ask that you . . ."), *request that* ("It will be requested that you . . .") and *be necessary that.*

7M   Indirect Discourse

For this exercise, refer to Section 7.5, pages 136–45.
A. Fill in the blank with an appropriate form of the verb in parentheses and *not*, if given.

Example

I think that it _____ last night. (rain)
Answer:
I think that it _____ rained _____ last night.

1. Most of the students say that they usually _____ breakfast at 6:30. (have)

Sentence Patterns That Require Special Usage of Verb Forms

2. Our instructor says that he _____ last summer in Canada. (spend)

3. Howard says that he _____ here tomorrow. (not, be)

4. My neighbor tells me that he _____ to Hawaii twice since last January. (fly)

5. It is often said that the world _____ a small place. (be)

6. You may be sure that your project _____ my full support during the coming year. (have)

7. Everyone is saying that the city _____ a new airport at this time. (not, need)

8. I will tell you what the newspaper _____ on this subject yesterday evening. (say)

9. It has been rumored that one of the presidential candidates _____ _____ on our campus next week. (speak)

10. Francis writes that if he _____ time (have), he _____ _____ us next summer. (visit)

11. I am sure that you _____ going to England next year. (not, regret)

12. I often wonder how my friends in other parts of the world _____ _____ their time every day. (spend)

13. I have often thought that your instructor would recommend that you ____ _____ Italian in Italy before graduation. (study)

14. John's friends have often asked him why he _____ to study medicine but decided to study law instead. (not, want)

15. Your adviser will ask you where you _____ since the beginning of the term. (live)

B. Follow the same instructions as for A.

1. Peter said that Dr. Reeves _____ on sabbatical leave at this time. (be)

2. The newspaper reported this morning that the meeting last night _____ a large audience. (attract)

3. Before the meeting began, several members of our group stated that they _____ their services for the benefit concert next week. (volunteer)

4. Lillian wrote that she _____ here before tomorrow morning. (not, arrive)

5. After I had read your report, I decided that I _____ copies to all of the members of our committee. (give)

6. It was announced in the newspaper this morning that an international dance festival _____ place here next spring. (take)

7. Our instructor asked us whether we still _____ any questions about the assignment he had just given us. (have)

8. During a panel discussion on television, one member inquired whether any organizations _____ assistance on the project in question in previous years. (offer)

9. The instructor asked the students where they _____ to go on their field trip next spring. (like)

10. I wondered why Bill _____ before the party was over. (leave)

7N   Indirect Discourse

For this exercise, refer to Section 7.5, pages 136–43.
A. Form one sentence from the two clauses given in each item using *whether* or *if* or the *wh*-word in the direct question. Be sure to follow the rules for word order and special usage of verb forms in indirect discourse. Rewrite the whole sentence.

Examples

I wonder. Will it rain today?
Answer:

_____ I wonder whether (or *if*) it will rain today. _____

I asked. When are Bill's cousins leaving?
Answer:

_____ I asked when Bill's cousins were leaving. _____

1. We wonder. Will class end early tomorrow?

    _____

2. I will ask. When is the library open?

    _____

3. Our friends wonder. Why did we stay at the library so late last night?

    _____

    _____

4. The students are all asking. Where will the examination be held?

    _____

    _____

5. Will you please ask? Is our instructor in his office now?

    _____

    _____

6. We wondered. Will class end early tomorrow?

    _____

7. I asked. When is the library open?

_____

8. Our friends wondered. Why did we stay at the library so late last night?

_____

_____

9. The students all asked. Where will the examination be held?

_____

_____

10. Did you ask? Is our instructor in his office now?

_____

_____

B. Form one sentence from the two clauses given in each item below. Be sure to follow rules of sequence and rules of word order. Rewrite the whole sentence.

Examples

I wonder. Who is on duty today?
Answer:

_____ I wonder who is on duty today. _____

Carl asked. Whom did the students speak with?
Answer:

_____ Carl asked whom the students had spoken with. _____

1. I wonder. Who is playing the lead role in the new play?

_____

_____

2. My friends are asking. Whom did you see at the play?

_____

3. We want to know. Whose friends did you speak with at the play?

_____

_____

4. Let's ask. Who wants to see the play?

_____

5. Will you ask? Whom will Paul invite to the play?

_____

6. I wondered. Whose student is playing the lead role in the new play?

_____

_____

Exercises

7. My friends asked. Whom did you see at the play?

8. We wanted to know. Whom did you speak with at the play?

9. We wondered. Whose roommate will Art invite to the play?

10. Did you ask? Whom will Art invite to the play?

C. Add a clause to each of the following items to form a sentence containing an indirect statement or question. Write out the whole sentence in giving your answer. Keep in mind that in indirect statements the use of *that* following verbs and some verbal expressions is optional.

Example

The latest weather report states (that)
Answer:
     The latest weather report states that it may rain before evening.

1. The latest weather report states (that)

2. Our instructor always says (that)

3. I have often thought (that)

4. Most students know (that)

5. The students in our class will surely all agree (that)

6. I will ask whether

7. John wonders whether

8. A question often asked on drivers' tests is whether

9. The custodian has wondered where

10. I have often been asked why

D. Follow the same instructions as those given for A, but include the adverbial given in parentheses.

Example

Our instructor said yesterday (that)   (last week)_____
_____Our instructor said yesterday that he had gone_____
_____to a professional meeting last week._____

1. One of my friends said yesterday (that)   (last week) _____
   _____

2. John told us (that)   (now) _____
   _____

3. It was stated in the newspaper this morning (that)   (tomorrow) _____
   _____

4. All club members at the meeting agreed (that)   (as soon as possible next
   month) _____
   _____

5. After hearing your news, I decided (that)   (next week) _____
   _____

6. Rosemary asked me whether   (last winter) _____
   _____

7. Everyone in our class wondered where   (tomorrow) _____
   _____

8. We asked George why   (now) _____
   _____

9. Everyone at the party asked me how   (last summer) _____
   _____

10. The question raised at our class meeting was whether   (tomorrow) _____
    _____

E. Add a clause to each of the following items to form an indirect question. Use *who* as subject and *whom* as object. Use the time adverbial given.

Example

I wonder who _____ tomorrow.
Possible answer:
I wonder who _____will be at the party_____ tomorrow.

1. I wonder who _____ now.

2. We all know whom _____ yesterday.

3. The students wonder whom _____ with tomorrow.

4. Let's ask who _____ now.

5. Will you ask whom _____ tomorrow?

6. I wondered who _____ now.

7. We all knew whom _____ yesterday.

8. The students wondered whom _____ with tomorrow.

9. We did not ask who _____ now.

10. Did you want to know whom _____ tomorrow?

70   Directed Writing

For this exercise, refer to Section 7.5, pages 136–43.

A. Select a short news story from a newspaper. Then rewrite it according to the following instructions:

1. Begin your paragraph with "This article in today's newspaper reports that . . ." Use such expressions as "it says that," "the reporter's opinion is that," and so on.

2. Begin your paragraph with "This article in today's newspaper reported that . . ." Use such expressions as "it said that," "the reporter's opinion was that," and so on.

B. Write a paragraph of 100–150 words according to the following instructions:

1. Suppose that you have just received a letter from a friend. Tell another friend what is in the letter. Use such expressions as "My friend says that," "he [or she] tells me that," "he [or she] asks," and "he [or she] wonders."

2. Suppose that yesterday you saw a friend whom you had not seen for some time. Tell another friend about your conversation. Use such expressions as "My friend said that," "asked," "replied," and "inquired."

C. Write a short composition of 200–250 words according to the following instructions: Suppose that you have just attended a lecture on a topic in your major field of study. Write a summary of the lecture. Use such expressions as "the lecturer first stated that," "he [or she] said that," "I agreed that," and "After the lecture I asked him [or her]."

VERBALS **8**

TYPES AND FORMS OF VERBALS[1] 8.1

A **verbal** is a verb form that does not have *tense*. There are three kinds of verbals in English: the **infinitive**, the **gerund**, and the **participle.** Verbals may occur independently as words or in phrases with modifiers and/or complements of various kinds.

Examples

Infinitive: Let's plan *to meet.*

Infinitive phrase: Let's plan *to meet each other again soon.*

Gerund: *Singing* is fun.

Gerund phrase: *Loudly singing to oneself in the shower* is fun.

Participle: *Barking,* the dog next door woke the neighborhood.

Participial phrase: *Barking loudly,* the dog next door woke the neighborhood.

Verbals are often described as verb forms that function as other parts of speech. They may function as nouns, adjectives, or adverbs do. When they function like nouns, they are said to have a **nominal** function; when they function like adjectives, they are said to have an **adjectival** function; when they function like adverbs, they are said to have an **adverbial** function.

---

[1]This section includes Verb-*ing* forms (gerunds and participles) and past participle forms. The spelling rules for adding -*ing* to base verb forms are given in Chapter 2, Section 2.3. The rules for adding -*ed* to base forms to form the past participles of regular verbs are also given in that section. The past participles of irregular verbs are given in Appendix B.

Infinitives

Infinitive Forms

The infinitive may occur with or without *to,* as in these examples:

> The Andersons allow their son *to drive* their car.
> The Andersons let their son *drive* their car.

The infinitive without *to* is sometimes referred to as the *base form* of the verb or the bare infinitive, as noted in Chapter 2. The terms Verb and *to* + Verb will be used for infinitives in this chapter.

The forms of the infinitive are:

	ACTIVE VOICE	PASSIVE VOICE
PRESENT	(to) see	(to) be seen
PRESENT CONTINUOUS	(to) be seeing	(to) be being seen
PERFECT	(to) have seen	(to) have been seen
PERFECT CONTINUOUS	(to) have been seeing	(to) have been being seen

Infinitive Functions

The infinitive may have a nominal, an adjectival, or an adverbial function.

Examples

> Nominal function: *To see* is *to believe.* (*To see* is a subject; *to believe* is a subject complement.)

> Adjectival function: The person *to see* is Anne Gardner. (*To see* modifies the noun *person.*)

> Adverbial function: We must hurry *to get* home before dinner. (*To get* describes purpose; infinitives that describe purpose are said to be adverbial in function. An alternate form is *in order to get.*)

Gerunds

Gerund Forms

	ACTIVE VOICE	PASSIVE VOICE
PRESENT	seeing	being seen
PERFECT	having seen	having been seen

Gerund Functions

The gerund always has a *nominal* function.

Examples

> *Seeing* is *believing.* (*Seeing* is a subject; *believing* is a subject complement, a nominal function.)
>
> Do you enjoy *shopping?* (*Shopping* is a direct object, a nominal function.)
>
> Does Jim know anything about *sailing?* (*Sailing* is the object of a preposition, a nominal function.)

The term Verb-*ing* will be used for gerunds in this chapter.

Participles

Participle Forms

The forms of the participle are the same as those of the gerund but also include a *past participle.*

	ACTIVE VOICE	PASSIVE VOICE
PRESENT	seeing	being seen
PERFECT	having seen	having been seen
PAST PARTICIPLE	(no active form)	seen

Participle Functions

Participles function as parts of verb forms such as *am seeing* and *have seen*, and also as verbals. Participles functioning as verbals always have an *adjectival* function.

Examples

> We had a picnic by a *running* stream. (The present participle, *running*, modifies the noun *stream*. It therefore functions as an adjectival.)
>
> Your car has a *broken* axle. (The past participle, *broken*, modifies the noun *axle*.)
>
> *Walking down the street*, Barry met a friend. (The participial phrase *walking down the street* "modifies" the subject of the clause, *Barry*. In other words, Barry is the logical subject of *walking*.)

The term Verb-*ing* will be used for present participles and the term "past participle" for past participles in this chapter.)

NOTE: A participle or participial phrase that modifies the subject of a clause may occur in the following positions:

Initial:	*Walking down the street*, Barry met a friend.
Medial:	Barry, *walking down the street*, met a friend.
Final:	Barry met a friend, *walking down the street*.

If the participle or participial phrase modifies the subject, *Barry*, as in the above examples, the participle or participial phrase is set off by commas as in the examples. However, if the writer wishes to indicate that the participial phrase modifies *friend* (rather than *Barry*), only the final position may occur, and without a comma, as in this example:

> Barry met a friend *walking down the street*. (*Friend* is the logical subject of *walking down the street*.)

8.2 TENSE AND TIME OF VERBALS: PRESENT VS. PERFECT FORMS

Verbals all have present and perfect *forms*, as listed in Section 8.1. They have no *tense*; however, they describe *time relative* to that of the main verb. If the time of the activity described by the verbal is the same as that described by the main verb, a present form of the verbal is used. If the time of the activity described by the verbal is before that described by the main verb, a perfect form of the verbal is used.

Examples — infinitive use

> It *is* nice *to see* you. (Both forms describe present time. This statement might be made at the beginning of a meeting.)

> It *is* nice *to have seen* you. (*To have seen* describes activity before present time described by *is*. This statement might be made at the close of a meeting.)

Examples — gerund use

> We *appreciated* your *helping* us last week. (Both forms describe the same time in the past.)

> We *appreciate* your *having helped* us last week. (*Having helped* describes activity before *appreciate*.)

Examples — participle use

> *Studying* hard, George lost track of time. (Both forms describe the same time in the past.)

> *Having studied* hard, George felt prepared for his examination. (*Having studied* describes activity before *prepared*.)

NOTE: If a word like *before* or *after* makes the time relationship clear, the simple form of Verb-*ing* is commonly used, as in this example:

> *After having studied hard*, George went to bed. OR:
> *After studying hard*, George went to bed.

▶ *Now do Exercise 8A at the end of the chapter.*

Both Verb-*ing* (in this case, the present participle) and the past participle may occur before nouns or as subjective complements following linking verbs, according to these rules:

(1) If the word modified is the *subject* or *performer* of the activity described by the participle, the Verb-*ing* form is used.

(2) If the word modified is the *object* of the activity described by the participle, the past participle is used.

Here are examples of the usage. The situation to be described is this:

Last night's speaker interested the audience. (The subject or performer of the verb *interested* is *speaker;* the object of *interested* is *audience.*)

The Verb-*ing* form, *interesting,* is used in these instances:

Last night's speaker was *interesting.* He was an *interesting* speaker. (The word modified, *speaker,* is the performer of the activity described by *interesting* in both examples.)

The past participle, *interested,* is used in these instances:

The audience was *interested.* The speaker had an *interested* audience. (The word modified, *audience,* is the object or recipient of the activity described by *interested* in both examples.)

Many verbs that occur in these situations describe emotional reactions. Such verbs include the following: *annoy, appall, bore, charm, enchant, excite, exhaust, fascinate, interest, please, shock, thrill, tire.*

Now do Exercise 8B at the end of the chapter. ◄

VERB + VERBAL COMBINATIONS   8.4

Some verbs may be followed by verbals. Depending on the verbs that they follow, the verbals occur in different forms and different patterns, as presented in the following sections. Throughout the discussion, the term "Possessive," as in Section 8.5, is used to refer to the possessive form of a noun, as in "I appreciated *Paul's* helping with the program"; or to a possessive adjective, as in "I appreciated *his* helping with the program." The term "Nominal," as in Section 8.8, is used to refer to nouns and noun phrases in the base form as in "We persuaded *Bill* to enter the contest"; and to pronouns in the objective form, as in "We persuaded *him* to enter the contest."

NOTE: The subject of a gerund is generally a possessive form, such as *Paul's* in *Paul's helping* and *his* in *his helping,* is the example sentences just given. Occasionally the base form of a noun or the objective form of a pronoun occurs in this position, as in "I appreciated Paul [*or* him] helping with the program." This usage is generally informal and not accepted as standard. Occasionally there may be a slight difference in meaning when one form is used rather than the other. For example, in a sentence like "I cannot imagine *Dr. Allen riding* a bicycle," there may be more emphasis on *Dr. Allen* than on *riding*, as different from "I cannot imagine *Dr. Allen's riding* a bicycle." However, the general rule of using the possessive forms normally holds. See also Volume II, Chapter 14, Section 14.2, for a comment on this usage.

8.5   VERB (± POSSESSIVE) + VERB-*ing*

Some verbs are followed by Verb-*ing* (a gerund), or by the possessive form of a noun or a possessive adjective (*my, your, his, her, its, our, their*) + Verb-*ing*.

Examples

Do you enjoy *singing*? (*Singing* is a Verb-*ing* form.)

Do you enjoy *Lillian's singing*? (*Lillian's* is the possessive form of a noun + *singing*.)

Do you enjoy *her singing*? (*Her* is a possessive adjective + *singing*.)

Some common verbs that are followed by (Possessive) Verb-*ing* are the following:

admit	enjoy	mind	resent
appreciate	escape	miss	resist
avoid	finish	postpone	stop
consider	imagine	practice	suggest
deny	keep (or, keep on)	quit	

A special usage is *go* +Verb-*ing*, in which Verb-*ing* describes an activity, as in these examples:

I *went shopping* yesterday afternoon.

Some of the students *have gone hiking* this weekend.

Other common expressions with *go* are these; *(to go) bicycling, fishing, hunting, riding, sailing, sightseeing, skating, skiing, swimming, walking.*

8.6   VERB + *to* + VERB

Some verbs are followed by *to* + Verb (the infinitive with *to*), as in this example:

I *hope to see* you again soon.

Some common verbs followed by *to* + Verb are the following:

afford[2]	deserve	hope	prepare
agree	endeavor	know how (what,	pretend
appear	fail	when, where)[3]	promise
care	guarantee	learn	refuse
choose	happen	manage	seem
decide	have (= must)	mean (= intend)	threaten
demand	hesitate	offer	

Now do Exercise 8C at the end of the chapter. ◄

VERBS THAT ARE FOLLOWED BY *to* + VERB   8.7
OR BY VERB-*ing*

Some verbs may be followed by *to* + Verb or by Verb-*ing* (a gerund), as in this example:

When did you *begin to study* English? OR:

When did you *begin studying* English?

Some common verbs followed by both forms are the following:

allow	dread	regret
bear	forget	remember
begin	intend	stand
continue	like	start
deserve	neglect	try
dislike	prefer	

Two verbs in this category — *bear* and *stand,* both in the sense of *endure* — generally occur with *can* or *could* in the negative and question forms:

I *cannot bear (stand) to stay* indoors on spring days. OR:

I *cannot bear (stand) staying* indoors on spring days.

Allow occurs in the following patterns:

The library *allows patrons to borrow* books for three weeks. (*allow* + Nominal + *to* + Verb)

Do the owners of this property *allow swimming* here? (*allow* + Verb-*ing*)

Will the owners of this property *allow our swimming* here? (*allow* + Possessive + Verb-*ing*)

Four verbs in this category — *forget, remember, regret,* and *try* — express different meanings when followed by *to* + Verb than when followed by Verb-*ing*, as in these examples:

---

[2]*Afford* generally occurs with the modal forms *can* or *could:* Can Carole *afford to buy* a new car? Carole *can* not *afford to buy* a new car. Carole *can afford to buy* a bicycle.

[3]Examples: Do you *know how to play* the piano? I *do* not *know what to do.* I *know where to buy* ice cream. Do you *know when to meet* the plane?

Some club members *may have forgotten to send* their annual dues. They did not send their annual dues.)

Some club members *may have forgotten sending* their annual dues. (They sent their annual dues but have forgotten that they did.)

Jane *remembered to send* her aunt a birthday card. (Jane sent her aunt a birthday card.)

Jane *remembered sending* her aunt a birthday card. (Jane remembered that she had sent her aunt a birthday card.)

I *regret to tell* you that Randy is in the hospital. (I am sorry that I must tell you that Randy is in the hospital.)

I *regret telling* you that Randy is in the hospital. (I am sorry that I told you that Randy was in the hospital.)

Try to get to bed early tonight because tomorrow will be a long day. (Attempt to get to bed early.)

Try getting to bed early for a few nights. It may make you feel better. (Experiment with getting to bed early.)

▶ *Now do Exercise 8D at the end of the chapter.*

8.8   VERB + NOMINAL + *to* + VERB

Some verbs are followed by a Nominal (such as a noun or pronoun) + *to* + Verb, as in this example:

We *advised the hikers to start* down the mountain soon.

Some common verbs in this category are the following:

advise	condemn	forbid	persuade
allow	convince	force	provoke
cause	dare	implore	remind
caution	defy	instruct	teach
challenge	direct	invite	tell
coerce	enable	oblige	tempt
command	encourage	order	urge
compel	entitle	permit	warn

Allow also occurs in the patterns given in Section 8.7. *Encourage* also occurs in the patterns given in Section 8.5

8.9   VERBS THAT ARE FOLLOWED EITHER BY *to* + VERB, OR BY *(for)* NOMINAL + *to* +VERB

Some verbs are followed by *to* + Verb or by Nominal + *to* + Verb, as in these examples:

We *asked to see* the new book exhibit. (Verb + *to* + Verb)

We *asked Dorothy to see* the new book exhibit. (Verb + Nominal + *to* + Verb)

Some common verbs in this category are the following. The verbs marked with an asterisk (*) also occur with Verb-*ing*.

ask	expect	need	want
beg	*hate	prepare	wish
desire	*like	promise	
*dislike	*love	train	

Other verbs are followed by *to* + Verb or by *for* + Nominal + *to* + Verb, as in these examples:

We *have arranged to stay* with friends in New York. (Verb + *to* + Verb)

We *have arranged for John to stay* with friends in New York. (Verb + *for* + Nominal + *to* + Verb)

Some common verbs in this category are the following. Again, the verbs marked with an asterisk (*) also occur with Verb-*ing* but only without a nominal.

arrange	hope	mean	*stand
*bear	*intend	plan[4]	wait
care	long	prepare	

In some dialects of English, the word *for* is added to create the pattern Verb + *for* + Nominal + *to* + Verb. This pattern occurs following verbs other than those given in the preceding list. With verbs other than those listed, the usage is generally considered nonstandard and characteristic of the speech of certain regions.

NOTE: Verbs that occur in the pattern Verb + Nominal + *to* + Verb (or another verbal, as discussed in Section 8.11) are called **causative verbs.** The general meaning is that the subject of the verb "causes" the subject of the verbal to perform the action described by the verbal. Some examples:

Our instructor *asked us to hand* in our papers promptly.

We *have planned for you to have* dinner with us.

Anne *let someone borrow* her notes.

Now do Exercise 8E at the end of the chapter. ◀

ELLIPTICAL FORMS OF VERB + *to* + VERB   8.10

Verb + *to* + Verb may appear in elliptical constructions ending with *to* rather than with *to* + Verb. ("Elliptical constructions" are constructions in which words are omitted but understood.)

---

[4] *Plan* may also be followed by *on* + Verb-*ing*, as in "We *are planning on* taking a trip."

Mr. Cooper could not drive us to the picnic, but our neighbors offered *to*. (Meaning: Our neighbors offered *to drive us to the picnic*.)

Helen does not know how to play chess, but Paul knows *how to*. (Meaning: Paul knows *how to play chess*.)

▶ *Now do Exercise 8F at the end of the chapter.*

8.11 *Have, let, make, help,* AND VERBS OF PERCEPTION

have, let, make

When an infinitive following *have, let,* or *make* is in the active voice, the pattern Nominal + Verb (the bare infinitive) occurs. In these cases the nominal is the subject of the bare infinitive and the performer of the activity described by the bare infinitive.

Examples

We *had a gas station attendant take* the car to the garage. (*A gas station attendant* is the subject of the bare infinitive *take* and also the performer of the activity described by *take*.)

We *let another attendant wash* the car. (*Another attendant* is the subject and the performer of the activity described by *wash*.)

We *made him vacuum* the interior of the car. (*Him* is the subject and the performer of the activity described by *vacuum*.)

Only *have* and *let* can be followed by passive verbal forms. These passive verbal forms are actually passive infinitive forms, but they are "reduced," or incomplete, forms and do not always look like infinitives. They will be referred to simply as "verbals." In the case of passive forms of verbals, the subject of the verbal is not the performer but the object of the activity described by the verbal. The passive forms following *have* and *let* are not the same.

Have is followed by the past participle.

Example

We *had the car taken* to the garage by a gas station attendant. (The subject of the verbal, *taken*, is *the car. The car*, however, is the object of the activity described; the actual performer, or agent, is *a gas station attendant*.)

Let is followed by Nominal + *be* + Past Participle.

Example

We *let the car be washed* by another attendant. (The subject of the verbal, *be washed*, is *the car*. It is the object of the activity described; the performer, or agent, is *another attendant*.)

help

Help may be followed by Nominal + Verb (the bare infinitive) or by Nominal + *to* + Verb.

Example

Susan *helped her mother clean* the house. OR:
Susan *helped her mother to clean* the house.

Help is not usually followed by a passive form.

Verbs of Perception: *feel, hear, notice, observe, see, smell, watch*

These verbs of perception are followed by the same construction. In the *active* voice of the following verbal, either Verb (the bare infinitive) or Verb-*ing* is used.

Examples — active voice of verbals

We *heard* the children *sing* the song. OR:
We *heard* the children *singing* the song.

We *saw* the children *light* the candles. OR:
We *saw* the children *lighting* the candles.

In the *passive* voice of the following verbal, either the past participle or *be-ing* + the past participle is used.

Examples — passive voice of verbals

We *heard* the song *sung* (by the children).[5] OR:
We *heard* the song *being sung* (by the children).

We *saw* the candles *lighted* by the children. OR:
We *saw* the candles *being lighted* by the children.

NOTE: After *smell*, only the forms Verb-*ing* and *be-ing* + the past participle generally occur, as in these examples:

We *smelled* something *burning*, probably rubber.
We *smelled* something *being burned*, probably rubber.

---

[5]As in the case of most passive forms, the agent (*by* + Nominal) may or may not be expressed.

Form Following Main Verb in Passive Voice

If *make, help,* or the verbs of perception occur in the passive voice, *to* + Verb rather than the bare infinitive is used, as in these examples:

> An attendant *was made to wash* the car.
>
> John *was seen to leave* the room. (OR: John *was seen leaving* the room.)

Have does not have a passive form in this kind of construction. *Let* occurs with a passive only in such expressions as "They *were let* go."

▶ *Now do Exercise 8G at the end of the chapter.*

8.12   VERB + *to* + VERB-*ing*

A few expressions are followed by *to* + Verb-*ing*. Common expressions are these:

(be) accustomed to   look forward to
(be) opposed to   object to
(be) used to

Examples

> John is *accustomed to getting* up early.
>
> We are *opposed to letting* dogs roam unleashed.
>
> Are you *used to driving* in heavy traffic?
>
> We will *look forward to seeing* you again soon.
>
> Ellen's roommate *does* not *object to* her *practicing* the flute.

Other linking verbs may occur with *accustomed to, opposed to,* and *used to,* as in this example:

> We soon *became accustomed to living* in the high altitude of Mexico City.

▶ *Now do Exercises 8H and 8I at the end of the chapter.*

For this exercise, refer to Sections 8.1–8.2, pages 167–70.

A. Present vs. Perfect Verbal Forms

Fill in the blank in each of the following sentences with the *present* or the *perfect form* of the verbal indicated.

Examples

_____ up the mountain, we became hungry.
(Verb-*ing*: *hike*, same time as *became*)
Answer:

_____ Hiking _____ up the mountain, we became hungry.

_____ the top of the mountain,
we had lunch. (Verb-*ing*: *reach*, time before *had*)
Answer:

_____ Having reached _____ the top of the mountain,
we had lunch.

1. _____ cheerfully, Al left the party.(Verb-*ing*: *smile*, same time as *left*)

2. _____ his hostess, Al left the party. (Verb-*ing*: *thank*, time before *left*)

3. Most of the voters consider Edwin Johnson to _____ an excellent mayor. (*be*, same time as *consider*)

4. Some of the voters consider him to _____ the best qualified candidate for mayor in many years. (*be*, time before *consider*)

5. Susan enjoys _____ people. (Verb-*ing*: *meet*, same time as *enjoys*)

6. Elaine Harrison enjoys _____ so many interesting people during her last stay in Washington. (Verb-*ing*: *meet*, time before *enjoys*)

7. Your _____ letters so promptly is always appreciated by your friends. (Verb-*ing*: *answer*, same time as *is*)

8. I appreciate your _____ my last letter so promptly. (Verb-*ing*: *answer*, time before *appreciate*)

9. To _____ a concert by every famous pianist in the world is Teresa's only ambition. (*attend*, same time as *is*)

10. To _____ Vladimir Horowitz play is one of Teresa's happiest childhood memories. (*hear*, time before *is*)

B. Active vs. Passive Verbal Forms

Fill in the blank in each of the following sentences with the *active* or the *passive form* of the verbal indicated.

Examples

Wayne likes to _____ to parties. (go)
Answer:
Wayne likes to _____go_____ to parties.

Wayne likes to _____ to parties by his friends.
(invite)
Answer:
Wayne likes to _____be invited_____ to parties by his friends.

1. _____ friends is one of Anne's favorite pastimes. (Verb-*ing: telephone*)

2. _____ by her friends is one of the things she enjoys most. (Verb-*ing : telephone*)

3. Andrew happened to _____ some friends at the game yesterday. (*see*)

4. Andrew happened to _____ by some friends at the game yesterday. (*see*)

5. _____ rapidly, George hoped to finish going through the newspaper before dinner. (Verb-*ing: read*)

6. _____ by a telephone call, George reluctantly put down his newspaper. (Verb-*ing : interrupt*, time before *put down*)

7. _____ her work, Emily decided to go for a walk. (Verb-*ing : finish*, time before *decided*)

8. _____ early by a barking dog, Emily had already finished her work by noon. (Verb-*ing: awaken*, time before *had finished*)

9. To _____ as a main speaker at a conference has been Dr. Knight's ambition for years. (*invite*, same time as *has been*)

10. To _____ as a main speaker at this year's conference is, in Dr. Knight's opinion, a great honor. (*invite*, time before *is)*

C. Simple vs. Continuous Verbal Forms
Fill in the blank in each of the following sentences with the *simple* or the *continuous* form of the verbal indicated.

Examples

Grace sometimes likes to _____ her house. (clean)
Answer:
Grace sometimes likes to _____clean_____ her house.

Grace does not like to _____ her house when company arrives. (continuous: clean)
Answer:
Grace does not like to _____be cleaning_____ her house when company arrives.

Verbals

1. Barry likes to _____ . (study)

2. Barry likes to _____ at his desk by nine o'clock every morning. (continuous: study)

3. You seem to _____ almost everything written on the subject of gardening. (*read*: time before *seem*)

4. You seem to _____ a lot of gardening lately. (*do*, time before *seem*; both forms acceptable)

5. I must _____ soon.   (*leave*; both forms acceptable)

Present Participle vs. Past Participle   8B

For this section, refer to Section 8.3, page 171. Fill in the blank in each of the following sentences with either Verb-*ing* or the past participle. Use a form of the verb given in the first sentence.

Example

Last Saturday's game *excited* the fans.

The game was _____ . The

_____ fans cheered wildly. It was an

_____ game. The fans were _____ .

Answers:

The game was _____ exciting _____ . The

_____ excited _____ fans cheered wildly. It was an

_____ exciting _____ game. The fans were

_____ excited _____ .

1. The students' performance in their play *pleased* their teacher. The students'

performance was _____ to their teacher. The

_____ teacher congratulated them. It was a

_____ performance. Their teacher was

_____ .

2. Anne's singing *charms* her friends. Anne's singing is

_____ . Her _____ friends often ask

her to sing. Her voice is _____ to her friends.

Her friends are _____ .

3. The mayor's announcement about a lack of money in the treasury *shocked*

his committee. His announcement was _____ . The

_____ committee wondered how to improve the

condition. It was a _____ announcement. The

committee was _____ .

4. Some nursery school children *annoyed* parents and teachers attending the parent-teacher meeting. The children were _____. The _____ parents and teachers tried to quiet them. They created an _____ disturbance. The parents and teachers were _____.

5 One of the piano students *thrilled* everyone who attended the graduation performance. His performance was _____. He played to a _____ audience. It was a _____ performance. Everyone was _____.

6. Last week's hockey game *excited* the spectators thoroughly. The game was _____. The team played to thoroughly _____ spectators. It was an _____ game. The spectators were thoroughly _____.

7. News of an approaching hurricane *appalled* all seashore residents in the vicinity yesterday. The news was _____. The _____ residents did not know whether to leave or to stay. It was _____ news. The residents were _____.

8. A plan to clean up litter has *pleased* our whole neighborhood. Many _____ neighbors have offered their cooperation. The plan is _____. It is a very _____ plan. The whole neighborhood is _____.

9. Publicity about his heroism in saving a friend from drowning has not *pleased* Paul. The publicity has not been _____ to Paul. Paul's _____ parents, however, have bought copies of every newspaper that reported the incident. He has not found the publicity _____. He has not been _____.

10. The news on television today *has* not *interested* us very much. The news has not been _____. The news has not found us an _____ audience. It has not been very _____ news. We have not been _____ by the news.

11. The grown-up conversation at the children's party yesterday *bored* the children. The conversation was _____. The _____ children became noisy. It was _____ conversation. The children were _____.

12. Exercise *tires* some people. Some people find exercise

    _____ . Some _____ people have

    lain down on the grass to rest. If exercise is too _____ , it

    is not beneficial, I am sure. Are you _____ from today's
    exercise?

13. Ellen's work *fascinates* her. She finds her work _____ .

    Her _____ friends like to hear about her work.

    It is _____ work. Ellen's friends are also

    _____ .

14. Your new house *enchants* everyone in the neighborhood. Your house is

    _____ . I have been told so by your

    _____ neighbors. It is an _____

    house. The neighbors are _____ .

15. Hot weather *exhausts* some people. They find hot weather

    _____ . They become _____ by hot

    weather. This _____ weather is fortunately made more

    bearable by air conditioning. These _____ people stay
    indoors as much as possible during hot weather.

Verb (± Possessive) + Verb-*ing*,   8C
and Verb + *to* + Verb

For this exercise, refer to Sections 8.4–8.6, pages 171–73. Fill in the blank in each of
the following sentences with either *to* + Verb or Verb-*ing*, using the verb given in
parentheses.

Examples

Emily managed _____ from college in three years.
(graduate)
Answer:
Emily managed _____ to graduate _____ from college in three years.

Let's practice _____ Spanish. (speak)
Answer:
Let's practice _____ speaking _____ Spanish.

1. Our new neighbors appear _____ pleasant people. (be)

2. We all appreciate your _____ our meeting. (attend)

3. Can you be prepared _____ in half an hour? (leave)

4. More and more people stop _____ every day. (smoke)

5. Janet Wilson has offered _____ us to the airport. (drive)

6. Our guest speaker admitted _____ the author of a best-selling mystery story. (be)

7. Anne learned _____ Spanish in Mexico. (speak)

8. Can you afford _____ to Hawaii next summer? (travel)

9. John resisted _____ out for a walk until he finished studying. (go)

10. I am sorry that I failed _____ your letter promptly. (answer)

11. Many people endeavor _____ another language. (learn)

12. Our instructor avoided _____ yes or no to our questions about the quiz. (say)

13. I hope that you do not resent my _____ at this early hour. (telephone)

14. Would you care _____ shopping with us? (come)

15. George is considering _____ a house. (buy)

16. The man who changed my flat tire refused _____ any payment for doing so. (accept)

17. I keep (on) _____ about your idea for a book. (think)

18. Everyone at the party seemed _____ himself. (enjoy)

19. Ellen suggested our not _____ out this evening. (go)

20. It is threatening _____. (rain)

21. Most of my friends have quit _____ if they ever did smoke. (smoke)

22. What time do you have _____ for home? (leave)

23. We have missed _____ you lately. (see)

24. I hope _____ you again soon. (see)

25. Will you promise not _____ my news until tomorrow? (tell)

26. Do you often practice _____ Italian? (speak)

27. Mr. Keith denied _____ the anonymous donor of a large gift of money to the library. (be)

28. The manufacturer of this cassette guarantees _____ you your money back if you are not satisfied. (give)

29. Patricia barely escaped _____ over a cliff on a hike last week. (fall)

30. I happened _____ an old friend yesterday. (run across)

31. We have chosen not _____ a trip next summer. (take)

32. Philip always postpones _____ decisions. (make)

33. A student demanded _____ to the head librarian about an overdue book fine. (speak)

Verbals

34. Have you finished _____ for the test tomorrow? (study)

35. Please do not hesitate _____ for anything you need. (ask)

36. Can you imagine _____ all of your assignments by Friday evening? (finish)

37. The children's father only pretended not _____ their joke. (understand)

38. Do you mean _____ to San Francisco next week? (fly)

39. We have surely enjoyed your _____ this evening. (sing)

40. Let's agree _____ next week. (meet)

41. Michael always manages not _____ late. (be)

42. Do you mind my _____ in this chair? (sit)

43. Would you mind our not _____ to the movies today? (go)

44. Does your nephew know how _____ the violin? (play)

45. I do not know what _____. (wear)

46. Do you know when _____ for the bus station? (leave)

47. I do not know where _____ lunch today. (have)

48. Let's go _____ this morning. (shop)

49. George went _____ this afternoon. (swim)

50. Have you ever gone _____ in the mountains? (camp)

Verbs That Are Followed by *to* + Verb   8D
or by Verb-*ing*

For this exercise, refer to Section 8.7, pages 173–74. Complete each of the following sentences with the appropriate verbal or, in cases where two forms are possible, with both appropriate verbals.

Example

When did you begin _____
English? (study)
Answer:
When did you begin _____ to study/studying _____
English?

1. Have you begun _____ your vacation? (plan)

2. We had better start _____ ready to go to the airport. (get)

3. What time do you prefer _____ dinner? (eat)

4. Peter continued _____ long after his friends had gone to bed. (read)

5. Do you plan _____ away this summer? (go)

6. Do you like _____ letters? (write)

7. Do you dislike _____? (type)

8. Our team deserved _____ the game. (win)

9. Some people dread _____ letters. (write)

10. Many people neglect _____ their cars when they park. (lock)

11. What do you intend _____ this evening? (do)

12. Sarah cannot bear _____ mystery stories. (read)

13. Do you think that you can stand _____ the children practice their songs this afternoon? (hear)

14. Do the regulations allow _____ on this lake? (boat)

15. Do the regulations allow our _____ on this lake? (boat)

16. Do the regulations allow visitors _____ on this lake? (boat)

17. Mr. Pearson may have forgotten _____ his water bill. (pay) (Meaning: He did not pay his water bill.)

    Mr. Pearson may have forgotten _____ his telephone bill. (pay) (Meaning: He paid his telephone bill but has forgotten that he did.)

18. Anne remembered _____ postage stamps. (buy) (Meaning: She thought to buy postage stamps and did so.)

    Anne remembered _____ postage stamps, but she could not find them in her desk. (buy) (Meaning: She remembered that she had bought postage stamps.)

19. I regret _____ you that we are out of the item that you ordered. (inform) (Meaning: I am sorry that I must give you this disappointing information.)

    I regret _____ you that we are out of the item that you ordered because I was mistaken. (inform) (Meaning: I regret that I gave you this information because I was mistaken.)

20. Try _____ more economical. (be) (Meaning: Attempt to be.)

    Try _____ more economical. You will be better off. (be) (Meaning: Experiment with being more economical.)

For this exercise, refer to Sections 8.8–8.9, pages 174-75. Fill in the blanks in the sentences below with either Nominal + *to* + Verb or *for* + Nominal + *to* + Verb. Note that you may need to change the forms of pronouns.

Example

    I want to go to Alaska next summer.

    I want _____ to Alaska next summer, too. (you, go)
    Answer:
    I want   you to go   to Alaska next summer, too.

    We will arrange to see Helen before long.

    We will arrange _____ us before
    long. (Helen, visit)
    Answer:
    We will arrange _____ for Helen to visit _____ us before
    long.

1. Do you want to go to the movies with us?

    Do you want _____ to the movies with you? (I, go)

2. We hope to have dinner with you soon.

    We hope _____ dinner with us soon.
    (you, have)

3. We asked to see Anne's new painting.

    We asked _____ Anne's new painting.
    (our friends, see)

4. Our club has arranged to have a picnic next Sunday.

    Our club has arranged _____ the
    picnic. (guests, attend)

5. Would you care to go to the library with me?

    Would you care _____ to the library with you? (I, go)

6. Do you wish to attend the concert tonight?

    Do you wish _____ the concert
    tonight? (he, attend)

7. The house painter is waiting to call us until his schedule is definite.

    We are waiting _____ us when his
    schedule is definite. (the house painter, call)

8. Elizabeth begged to try the new piano.

    Elizabeth begged _____ the new
    piano. (her sister, try)

9. How can you stand to wait until June to see your parents?

How can you stand _____ until June? (they, wait)

10. We all long to see you.

We all long _____ us. (you, visit)

11. Is your brother preparing to be a lawyer?

Are his studies preparing _____ a lawyer? (he, be)

12. I will prepare to have you come to dinner with us.

I will prepare _____ dinner with us. (you, have)

13. What do you expect to do next summer?

What do you expect _____ next summer? (your friends, do)

14. You do not need to help with cleaning up.

We do not need _____ with cleaning up. (anyone, help)

15. How long do the Bensons plan to stay in New York?

When do you plan _____? (we, meet)

16. Ellen is training to be a dancer.

Ellen is training _____ newspapers. (her dog, fetch)

17. Alan promised to weed the garden this Saturday.

Alan promised _____ the garden this Saturday. (his father, weed)

18. What do you intend to help with at the bazaar?

What do you intend _____ with? (I, help)

19. I did not mean to be so late getting to the airport.

I did not mean _____. (you, wait)

20. What do you like to do during the summer?

What do you like _____ _____ during the summer? (your family, do)

Verbals

For this exercise, refer to Section 8.10, page 176. Complete each sentence below with the elliptical *to* construction of the sentence given in parentheses.

Example

George wants to buy a new car, but _____ .
(he cannot afford to buy a new car)
Answer:
George wants to buy a new car, but _____ he cannot afford to _____ .

1. We can have lunch in town if _____ .
(you care to have lunch in town)

2. Carole has never visited Alaska, but _____ .
(she would love to visit Alaska)

3. Our instructor has never shown us slides of his trip to China, but _____ .
(he has promised to show us slides of his trip to China)

4. Eileen swims beautifully because _____when she was a child.
(she learned how to swim)

5. Jim's parents do not want him to play football, so _____

_____ .
(he has promised them not to play football)

6. If I forget to return your pen, _____ ?
(will you remind me to return your pen)

7. Barry wanted to come with us, so _____ .
(we invited him to come with us)

8. Margaret knows how to speak Basque because _____when she was in Spain.
(she learned how to speak Basque)

9. We can go to the zoo this afternoon if _____ .
(you would care to go to the zoo)

10. I am going to take an umbrella with me this morning if _____ .
(you are going to take an umbrella with you)

11. You may park in this space if _____ .
(you wish to park in this space)

12. If you wish to borrow some books from the library, you may, because _____

_____ . (you are entitled to borrow books from the library)

13. I always park my car in this lot, and _____ .
(no one has ever told me not to park in this lot)

14. Arthur is thinking of entering an essay contest, and _____

_____ .
(we are urging him to enter the contest)

15. Bob knows how to bake cookies because _____

_____ .
(one of his friends taught him how to bake cookies)

8G *have/let/make/help* and Verbs of Perception

For this exercise, refer to Section 8.11, pages 176–78. Fill in the blanks in the sentences below with the appropriate form(s) of the verb given in parentheses. Where indicated, two forms are acceptable; give both.

Examples

    A friend let Walter ———————— his tennis racket. (use)
    Answer:
    A friend let Walter ———— use ———— his tennis racket.

    We had our house ———————————— last year. (paint: passive)
    Answer:
    We had our house ———— painted ———— last year.

1. Bad weather forced us ——————— in the mountains another day. (stay)

2. Jeff's haste caused him ———————— his car. (wreck)

3. We had a student ———————— up the yard. (clean)

4. Helen's parents do not permit her ———————— to school. (drive)

5. A neighbor allows us ———————— on his tennis court. (play)

6. Some parents make their children ——————— their homework before watching television. (do)

7. Drivers are cautioned not ——————— through underpasses after heavy rains. (go)

8. This pass entitles you ———————— all games. (attend)

9. George had his hair ——————— yesterday. (cut: passive)

10. The theater critic for our newspaper urged everyone not

    ———————————— the new play. (miss)

11. The park guards permit no one ———————— a dog without a leash. (walk)

12. We had to let our car ———————— to the garage by a tow truck. (take: passive)

13. A friend challenged Christine ———————— a game of chess. (play)

14. Heavy traffic caused us ———————— . (delay: passive)

15. Gordon does not let anyone else ———————— his car. (drive)

16. Heavy snows compel drivers ———————— special tires. (use)

17. Do you advise me ———————— a new car or wait? (buy)

18. We felt a tremor ———————————— the house. (shake: two forms)

                                                             Verbals

19. A policeman at the site of the accident directed all traffic

_____ a detour. (make)

20. We allowed our car _____ to another parking space. (move: passive)

21. We heard someone _____ our doorbell. (ring: two forms)

22. Joyce's friends persuaded her _____ tennis. (play)

23. The students in our class have all implored the instructor

_____ the deadline for the term paper. (extend)

24. We felt our house _____ by a powerful wind. (shake: passive, two forms)

25. We heard someone _____ on the door. (knock: two forms)

26. Someone was heard _____ on the door. (knock: two forms)

27. The English Club invited us _____ a reception in honor of their retiring president. (attend)

28. We noticed a car _____ into the driveway. (turn: two forms)

29. We convinced George not _____ before dinner. (leave)

30. Margaret's bonus enabled her _____ presents for all of her friends. (buy)

31. We observed a dog _____ a swim in the campus pool. (take: two forms)

32. The beautiful weather yesterday tempted us _____ farther than we had planned. (walk)

33. Regulations forbid anyone _____ papers on the library tables. (leave)

34. I smell something _____ . (burn)

35. Elaine Saunders always urges her children _____ new things. (try)

36. Robert's friends dared him _____ a rodeo. (enter)

37. I saw you _____ the letter. (mail: two forms)

38. The students were all obliged _____ for the bell to ring. (wait)

39. Dr. Raymond's secretary must often remind her _____ lunch. (eat)

40. Peter's friends teased him and provoked him _____ . (retaliate)

41. A bus driver watched the children

_____ the street. (cross: two forms)

42. Rosemary's father taught her (how) _____. (drive)

43. Signs warn picnickers not _____ private roads to the lake. (enter)

44. The children next door are not often allowed _____ up late. (stay)

45. Harry helped the proctor _____ the examination papers. (distribute: two forms)

46. A nurse told us _____. (seat: passive)

47. She told us not _____. (worry)

48. All squadron leaders commanded their troups _____ at attention during inspection. (stand)

49. Albert's parents made him _____ for the window he had broken. (pay)

50. Albert was made _____ for the window he had broken. (pay)

8H   Verb + *to* + Verb / Verb + *to* + Verb-*ing*

For this exercise, refer to Section 8.12, page 178. Fill in the blanks in the following sentences with either Verb (the bare infinitive) or Verb-*ing*.

Examples

When do you expect to _____ on your vacation? (leave)
Answer:
When do you expect to _____leave_____ on your vacation?

We are looking forward to _____ Rome. (visit)
Answer:
We are looking forward to _____visiting_____ Rome.

1. Do you like to _____? (sing)

2. We are accustomed to _____ to school. (walk)

3. Many people in the city are opposed to _____ for parking spaces downtown. (pay)

4. You must promise to _____ us again soon. (visit)

5. Are you getting used to _____ in the country? (live)

6. It is expected to _____ today. (rain)

7. You must plan to _____ dinner with us tomorrow. (have)

8. Let's look forward to _____ again soon. (meet)

9. Would you object to my _____ this window? (open)

10. Janet longs to _____ all over the world. (travel)

For this exercise, refer to Sections 8.1–8.12, pages 167–78.

A. Write a paragraph of 100–150 words according to the following instructions:

1. Tell about your plans for next weekend. Use such expressions as *decide, hope, intend, plan, want,* and *wish.*

2. Describe how you cooked something, made something, repaired something, or accomplished some other task. Use such expressions as *begin, continue, decide, postpone, start,* and *wait.*

3. Tell what you did on your last weekend. Use *go* + Verb-*ing* to describe your activities. For example, "First I went shopping. Then . . ."

B. Write a paragraph of 100–150 words according to the following instructions:

1. Describe how you are going to help a friend do something, such as study for a test, clean his or her apartment, or shop for something. Use such expressions as *allow, ask, have, make,* and *let.*

2. Describe your experience in taking care of a friend's children or acting as a teacher's substitute in a class. Use such expressions as *allow, ask, dare, encourage, forbid, let, make, pretend, tell,* and *watch.*

3. Pretend that you visited a friend in the hospital. Describe the nurse's visit to his room, telling what she made her patient do or let her patient do. Use such expressions as *allow, encourage, forbid, have, let, make, promise,* and *talk.*

PHRASAL VERBS **9**

Phrasal verbs are combinations of verbs and words like *down, in, off, on, out, over,* and *up* that together express a unit of meaning. Examples are *call on,* which may express the meaning *visit,* and *call up,* which may express the meaning *telephone.* Most words like *down, in,* and so on are classified as both prepositions and adverbs in dictionaries and grammars. How they are classified depends on how they function where they occur. This chapter explains how they are classified and how they function in phrasal verbs. Phrasal verbs may be combinations of Verb + Adverb, Verb + Preposition, or Verb + Adverb + Preposition. Verb + Adverb and Verb + Preposition are the two largest categories and are often called **two-word verbs.**

Adverbs in phrasal verbs are called by various names, often **particles.** The important point is that phrasal verbs including prepositions and those including adverbs, or particles, pattern differently from each other in such a way that they form two separate categories.

A summary of the rules follows.

Verb + Preposition Combinations

A Verb + Preposition combination, such as *call on,* must always have an object, which is normally the *object of the preposition.* With these combinations, the preposition is generally not separated from the verb. The preposition precedes its object in sentences like the following:

> George *called on some friends* yesterday.
> George *called on them* yesterday.

Verb + Preposition combinations are often referred to as **inseparable.**

Verb + Adverb Combinations

A Verb + Adverb combination, such as *call up*, may occur with or without an object. If there is an object, it functions as the *direct object of the verb.* When a Verb + Adverb combination occurs with a direct object that is not a personal pronoun, the adverb may precede or follow it, as in these examples:

> George *called up some friends* yesterday. OR:
> George *called some friends up* yesterday.

In both of these sentences, *some friends* is a direct object that is not a personal pronoun. In the second sentence, the adverb *up* is separated from the verb form *called.*

If, however, the direct object is a personal pronoun, the adverb must follow it and be separated from the verb form, as in this sentence:

> George *called them up* yesterday.

The direct object, *them*, is a personal pronoun. Verb + Adverb combinations that pattern in this way with direct objects are often referred to as **separable.**

Note that *call up* is one of the Verb + Adverb combinations that may also occur without a direct object, as in this sentence:

> George *called up* yesterday.

Usage of Phrasal Verbs

There are at least 3,000 phrasal verbs in use in present-day English, both American and British. Most of them have multiple meanings. Some have essentially the same meanings as their base verbs, that is, the verbs when they occur by themselves. Examples are most of the Verb + Preposition combinations, such as *look at* and *listen to*, in which the preposition adds only direction or specificity. Other meanings seem quite unrelated to either the verb or to the adverb or preposition in the combination. Examples are the Verb + Adverb combination *turn out* in such a sentence as "A large crowd *turned out*," which means "A large crowd gathered"; and the Verb + Adverb + Preposition combination *put up with* in such a sentence as "The patient *put up with* much suffering during his illness," which means "The patient endured much suffering during his illness."

The level of usage of phrasal verbs is generally considered to be informal, and there is often a more formal one-word equivalent of a phrasal verb. In present-day usage, however, phrasal verbs are so well established that they frequently defy the substitution of equivalents. Only some of the most common phrasal verbs and meanings are included in this text. Slang and other nonstandard usages have not been given. More extensive listings may be found in standard dictionaries and in specialized dictionaries that give two-word and other phrasal verbs.

NOTE: Many phrasal verbs have developed noun derivatives in present-day English. Common examples are these: *backup, blowout, breakdown, cleanup, countdown, dropout, feedback, giveaway, handout, letdown, mixup, playback, throwaway,* and *washout.* Some occur in the Verb-*ing* form, such as *cheering up, cooling off,* and *going over.* Some occur adjectivally as well as nominally; one hears of a *backup procedure, a letdown feeling,* and *a cooling-off period.* However, since there are many phrasal verbs that have not developed noun and adjective forms and there are no general rules about forming nouns and adjectives from phrasal verbs, it seems best to learn such terms as individual vocabulary items in context.

VERB + PREPOSITION COMBINATIONS 9.2

Phrasal verbs in this category are often called inseparable two-word verbs because the verb and the preposition are either inseparable or only optionally separable. Keep in mind that a Verb + Preposition combination always has a stated object, which is the object of the preposition.

Inseparable Patterns

The verb and the preposition in the phrasal verb combination are inseparable in all kinds of constructions, with the exception of a few in which they are optionally separable. (These will be listed under "Optionally Separable Patterns.") Here are some examples of Verb + Preposition in inseparable patterns.

TYPE OF CONSTRUCTION	EXAMPLES
Statement	The committee *called on* a lawyer.
	The committee *did* not *call on* a lawyer.
yes/no question	*Did* the committee *call on* a lawyer?
wh-Adv question	Why *did* the committee *call on* a lawyer?
Passive statement	A lawyer *was called on* by the committee.
Passive question	Was a lawyer *called on* by the committee?
Infinitive phrase modifying noun headword *(lawyer)*	The committee knew *the lawyer to call on*.

Optionally Separable Patterns

The verb and the preposition in the phrasal-verb combination are optionally separable in all constructions that contain a *wh*-N form, such as *whom, whose, what,* or *which*, as the object of the preposition. These constructions include relative clauses, indefinite relative clauses, and some direct and indirect questions. Following are some examples.

TYPE OF CONSTRUCTION	EXAMPLES
Direct question	*Who(m) did* the committee call on? OR:
	On whom did the committee *call*? (Formal.)
Relative clause	A lawyer *who(m) the committee called on* advised them. OR:
	A lawyer *on whom the committee called* advised them. (Formal.)

NOTE 1: An adverb or another short adverbial expression may optionally separate the verb and the preposition, as in this example:

The committee *called promptly on* a lawyer.

The order Verb + Adverbial + Preposition, however, is often awkward, and it is usually better to place the adverbial in one of its usual positions in the sentence, as in "*Promptly* the committee *called on* a lawyer," or "The committee *called on* a lawyer *promptly*."

NOTE 2: The phrasal-verb combination of Verb + Preposition + Object of Preposition should not be confused with a Verb + a Prepositional Phrase that functions as an adverbial modifier.[1]

Examples

The committee *called on* a lawyer. (*Called on* is the two-word verb meaning *visited*.)

The committee called *on Monday*. (*On Monday* is a prepositional phrase functioning as an adverbial modifier of time modifying the verb *called*, meaning *visited* or *telephoned*.)

The committee *called on* a lawyer *on Monday*. OR: *On Monday* the committee *called on* a lawyer. (*Called on* is a two-word verb, and *on Monday* is a prepositional phrase modifying *called on*.)

Common Verb + Preposition Combinations

Some common Verb + Preposition + Object of Preposition combinations are included in the following lists. Note that in Verb + Preposition combinations, the verb is usually intransitive, and the combination has essentially the same meaning as the verb used by itself. Generally the preposition only adds a meaning of direction or specificity.

Verb + *at*	glance at, laugh at, look at (=regard; inspect with a view to buying; watch); point at, smile at, stare at, wonder at (*or* wonder about)
Verb + *for*	call for (=come to a person to escort him to another place; demand); care for (= like; tend), hope for, look for (=search for), shop for, vote for (*or* against), wait for, wish for
Verb + *from*	differ from, escape from, recover from, retire from
Verb + *in*	believe in, confide in, engage in, participate in, result in, succeed in
Verb + *of*	beware of (usually occurs only in the infinitive and imperative forms), consist of (also *consist in*, in British usage)
Verb + *of* or *about*	dream of (*or* about), speak of (*or* about),[2] talk of (*or* about), think of (*or* about)

---

[1]See Volume II, Chapter 17, for a discussion of prepositions and prepositional phrases.

[2]Generally use *speak of* or *speak about* for persons and things, and use *speak about* or *speak on* when referring to subject matter. "Al often *speaks of* (or *about*) you," but "Al will *speak on* (or *about*) American ballet next Thursday evening."

Verb + *on*	agree on (*agree on* a subject, but *agree with* a person), call on (=ask for the assistance of; visit), decide on, depend on, insist on, knock on, lecture on
Verb + *to*	listen to, object to, subscribe to
Verb + *with*	associate with, cooperate with

Now do Exercise 9A at the end of the chapter. ◀

SEPARABLE AND INSEPARABLE PATTERNS 9.3 OF VERB + ADVERB COMBINATIONS

Some Verb + Adverb combinations occur as transitive (having objects), some as intransitive (not having objects), and some as both transitive and intransitive. If there is an object, it functions as the direct object of the verb. Generally if the base verb is transitive, the Verb + Adverb combination is transitive; if the base verb is intransitive, the Verb + Adverb combination is intransitive; and if the base verb has both a transitive and an intransitive sense, the Verb + Adverb combination occurs as both transitive and intransitive. Phrasal verbs consisting of Verb + Adverb are often called separable two-word verbs because the verb and the adverb may be separated by a direct object.

Exceptions to this rule include the intransitive verbs *go, look,* and *run* in the transitive combinations *go over, look over, look up,* and *run over.*

Rules of Word Order for Verb + Adverb + Direct Object (Transitive Two-Word Verbs)

With the specific exceptions that will be given shortly (under the heading "Other Constructions in Which Verb + Adverb Must Follow Inseparable Order"), the rules of word order for Verb + Adverb + Direct Object are these.

Rule 1   When the direct object is not a personal pronoun, the order of Verb and Adverb may be optionally separable or inseparable. Here are some examples.

TYPE OF CONSTRUCTION	EXAMPLES
Statement	Clifford *checked over his work.* OR: Clifford *checked his work over.*
	Clifford did not *check over his work.* OR: Clifford *did* not *check his work over.*
yes/no question	*Did* Clifford *check over* his work? OR: *Did* Clifford *check his work over?*

Rule 2   When the direct object is a personal pronoun, the order of the Verb and Adverb *must* be separable, as in these examples.

TYPE OF CONSTRUCTION	EXAMPLES
Statement	Clifford *checked it over.*
yes/no question	*Did* Clifford *check it over?*

Other Constructions in Which Verb + Adverb Must Follow Inseparable Order

Verb + Adverb combinations *must be inseparable* in passive constructions; in constructions that contain a *wh*-N form such as *whom, whose, what,* or *which* as the direct object (that is, relative clauses, indefinite relative clauses, and some direct and indirect questions); and in infinitive phrases that modify noun and pronoun headwords. Here are some examples.

TYPE OF CONSTRUCTION	EXAMPLES
Passive statement	The work *was checked over* by every member of the committee.
	It *was checked over.*
Passive *yes/no* question	*Was* the work *checked over?*
	Was it *checked over?*
Relative clause	The work *that the committee checked over* was well done.
Indefinite relative clause	*What work the committee checked over* was well done.
Direct *wh*-N form question	*Who(m) did* the committee *call up?*
	Whose work did the committee *check over?*
Indirect *wh*-N form question	John wondered *who(m) the committee had called up.*
Infinitive phrase modifying noun headword	Clifford gave me *his report to check over.*
Infinitive phrase modifying pronoun headword	He brought *it to check over.*

When a noun is the direct object of an infinitive, Rule 1 is followed, as in these examples:

John asked me *to check over his report* (or, *to check his report over*). (The direct object, *his report,* is not a personal pronoun. *Check over* is optionally separated.)

John asked me *to check it over.* (The direct object is a personal pronoun, and *check over* must be separated.)

NOTE: An adverb or another short adverbial may generally occur between a verb and an adverb, as in these examples:

Clifford *checked carefully over* his work.
Clifford *checked* it *carefully over.*
The work *was checked carefully over.*

This order, however, often seems awkward, and it is probably best avoided.

VERB + ADVERB COMBINATIONS + DIRECT   9.4
OBJECT (TRANSITIVE TWO-WORD VERBS)

Some Verb + Adverb combinations always occur as transitive — that is, with direct objects — in standard usage. They pattern like *check over* in the examples in Section 9.3.

Some common Verb + Adverb combinations that always occur with direct objects are the following:

bring about: cause to happen

bring back: return; recall

bring up: raise (as of children); mention (a subject)

call off: call away; cancel

check over: examine for accuracy

do over: do again

drink up: drink completely

eat up:[3] eat completely

figure out: understand; work out (a solution)

fill in (or *fill out*): complete (as a form or application)

fill up: fill completely

give away: give (intensive meaning); reveal (a secret)

hand back: return

hand out: distribute

have on: wear

jot down: write quickly

keep back:[4] withhold; fail to tell

let down: disappoint

look over: read over; examine

look up:[5] seek and find information (especially relating to an entry in a dictionary or other reference work); go and visit

mark down: note in writing; reduce the price of

pick out: choose

point out: mention

put aside: stop doing something with the intention of continuing the activity later

put away: place things where they belong when not in use

put off: postpone

put on: don (clothes); informal usage: mislead someone

take back: return; retract (what one has said)

take down: write down

take in: understand; deceive

take up: discuss; study a subject; adopt (a cause)

talk over: discuss

think over: consider carefully

throw away: discard (often with a sense of waste)

use up: use completely

wash off: wash

wrap up: wrap

write down: take down on paper

Now do Exercise 9B at the end of the chapter. ◀

---

[3]Both *drink up* and *eat up* occur intransitively in informal but not in standard usage. Examples: "Drink up!" and "Eat up!"

[4]*Keep back* also occurs in the list in Section 9.7 but with different meanings.

[5]*Look up* also occurs without a direct object, but in a different meaning: *look up* in the sense of "gaze upward."

9.5 VERB + ADVERB COMBINATIONS (INTRANSITIVE TWO-WORD VERBS)

The Verb + Adverb combinations listed in this section are intransitive, that is, they do not take direct objects. They generally are not separated.[6]

Examples

> Dr. Benson *grew up* in New York. (*Grew up* means grew from childhood to adulthood.)
>
> Where *did* Carl *grow up*?

Some common Verb + Adverb combinations that occur only as intransitive, except for *break down* and *fall over*, are included in the following list.

> *break down:* cease to function (the transitive meaning of this combination is fairly unrelated: to break something into parts)
> *come about:* happen; change course (as of a ship)
> *fall over:* topple toward the ground (transitive meaning with reflexive pronouns is figurative: *fall over oneself* means *make unseemly effort*[7])
> *fall through:* not develop; not be successful
> *go off:* go (somewhere indefinite); explode
> *grow up:* grow from childhood to adulthood
> *lie down:* settle in a reclining position
> *rest up:* rest until refreshed
> *sit down:* move from a standing to a sitting position
> *sit up:* sit erectly
> *speak up:* speak loudly enough to be heard; speak or write so as to make one's opinions known

Some intransitive Verb + Adverb combinations are associated with Verb + Preposition or Prepositional Phrase.

Examples

> Two men *got out of the taxi*. (Verb + Adverb + Preposition + Object of Preposition)
>
> Two men *got out*. (Verb + Adverb)
>
> John and Helen *got into the taxi*. (Verb + Preposition + Object of Preposition)
>
> John and Helen *got in*. (Verb + Adverb)
>
> Common combinations of this type include the following:

---

[6]One or more adverbs may occur with Intransitive Verb + Particle, as in these examples:

> Dr. Benson grew up *happily* in New York.
> *Unfortunately*, Carl's plans for his vacation have fallen through.
> Carl's plans for his vacation have *unfortunately* fallen through.

It is usually best not to place an adverb between a verb and particle. For example, in the above sentences, the orders *grew happily up* and *fallen unfortunately through* would be awkward.

[7]The reflexive pronouns are *myself, yourself, himself, herself, itself, ourselves, yourselves,* and *themselves.*

get in: associated with *get into* an automobile, a canoe, a car, a motor boat, a small airplane, a taxi, or some other small, usually privately owned conveyance

get out: associated with *get out of* the small conveyances listed above with *get into*

get on: associated with *get on* an airplane, a bus, a ship, a train, or some other large, usually public conveyance; also, get on a bicycle or a motorcycle

get off: associated with *get off* the conveyances listed above with *get on*

move in: associated with *move into* an apartment, a hotel, a house, or other residence

move out: associated with *move out of* a residence

sign on: associated with *sign on the air* (as of radio or television): begin broadcasting

sign off: associated with *sign off the air* (as of radio or television): stop broadcasting

Now do Exercise 9C at the end of the chapter. ◀

VERB + ADVERB COMBINATIONS ± DIRECT 9.6 OBJECT (DIRECT OBJECT STATED OR IMPLIED)

Many Verb + Adverb combinations occur both with and without direct objects. They behave in several different ways. One group occurs with a direct object that is either stated or implied. Note the different word orders of *call up* (meaning "telephone") with direct objects that are not personal pronouns and direct objects that are personal pronouns.

Examples

Carl *called up Helen* yesterday.

Carl *called Helen up* yesterday.

Carl *called her up* yesterday.

(In the above examples the direct objects, *Helen* and *her*, are stated.)

Carl *called up*.

(In this example, a direct object is not stated but implied.)

Some common Verb + Adverb combinations in this category are the following:

call back: return a telephone call

call up: telephone; summon

clean up: clean completely

finish up: finish completely

give up: surrender

keep up: continue; remain in position

lock up: lock; lock all the doors and windows

pass by: pass

save up: save (usually money)

▶ *Now do Exercise 9D at the end of the chapter.*

9.7 VERB + ADVERB COMBINATIONS (TRANSITIVE AND INTRANSITIVE)

A Verb + Adverb combination in this category may occur in a transitive form with a stated direct object. The direct object is usually animate. It may also occur in an intransitive form. The direct object in a transitive use becomes the subject in the corresponding intransitive use. Note the different word orders of *cheer up* with direct objects that are not personal pronouns and direct objects that are personal pronouns.

Examples

Paul *cheered up his friends.*
Paul *cheered his friends up.* } Transitive use with the direct objects *his friends* and *them*.
Paul *cheered them up.*

His friends cheered up. } The direct objects *his friends* and *them* in the transitive use become the subjects in the intransitive use.
They cheered up.

(*Paul,* of course, may also have been the subject with the intransitive meaning of the verb in such a sentence as "Paul cheered up.")

Some common Verb + Adverb combinations in this category are the following. If two meanings are given, the first is transitive, and the second is intransitive. An asterisk (*) means that the combination occurs as both transitive and intransitive, but with different meanings.

cheer up: make or become cheerful

cool off: make or become less angry or upset[8]

get up: cause to stand up or to stand up oneself; cause to leave a bed or to leave a bed oneself after sleeping

hurry up: hurry

keep back: hold back or stay back

pick up: learn informally (transitive meaning only); come or go to take someone or something somewhere (transitive meaning only); improve (intransitive meaning only). Also many other informal meanings

---

[8]Also given in list for Section 9.8.

pull through: help someone recover, or recover oneself, from sickness or difficulties

quiet down: make or become quiet

*run off: produce printed materials as with a ditto machine; run away

*run over: hit, usually with a car or other moving vehicle (transitive meaning only). *Also:* review, usually printed materials (transitive meaning only). *Also:* run toward or from (intransitive meaning only).

show off: display something or someone for attention; display oneself for attention

sign up: put someone's name on a list; put one's own name on a list

stand up: place someone or something in a standing position; rise to or be in a standing position

*take off: remove clothing (transitive meaning only). *Also:* depart, as of an airplane (intransitive meaning only)

*turn out: produce work or results (transitive meaning only). *Also:* gather, as of an audience or other crowd attending an event such as a rally (intransitive meaning only)

wake up: cause to stop sleeping; stop sleeping

*wash up: wash, as of dishes (transitive meaning only). *Also:* wash one's face and hands (intransitive meaning only).

Now do Exercise 9E at the end of the chapter. ◀

VERB + ADVERB COMBINATIONS 9.8 (TRANSITIVE AND INTRANSITIVE): DIRECT OBJECT BECOMES SUBJECT

In this category only the direct object in the transitive usage can act as subject of the intransitive Verb + Adverb combination and is generally inanimate.

Examples

I *am heating up the soup.*
I *am heating the soup up.*
I *am heating it up.*

Transitive use with inanimate direct objects *the soup* and *it*

The soup *is heating up.*
It *is heating up.*

Only the direct objects in the transitive use can be the subject of the intransitive verb

Some common Verb + Adverb combinations in this category are the following. If two meanings are given, the first meaning is transitive, the second intransitive.

blow away: blow (with direction)

burn down: burn completely (buildings, forests, and other large, upright things) *burn up:* burn completely (papers, leaves, and other small, low things)

cool off:[9] make or become cool

heat up: heat completely

shut down: close (a business, factory, and so on)

turn up: discover; appear

wear out: make or become unusable through use (as of clothing and machinery)

work out: develop; succeed

▶ *Now do Exercise 9F at the end of the chapter.*

9.9   VERB + ADVERB COMBINATIONS: ALL PATTERNS IN SECTIONS 9.6, 9.7, AND 9.8

These Verb + Adverb combinations can have stated or implied direct objects, as in the list in Section 9.6, and be transitive or intransitive, as in the lists in Sections 9.7 and 9.8. These combinations often have to do with means of transportation (airplanes, automobiles, motorcycles, and so on).

Examples

Anne *backed up the car.*	Transitive use with direct objects
Anne *backed the car up.*	*the car* and *it*
Anne *backed it up.*	

Anne *backed up.*   Direct object implied but not stated

The car *backed up.* Direct object of transitive verb is
It *backed up.*   subject

Some common Verb + Adverb combinations in this category are the following. If two meanings are given, the first is transitive, the second intransitive.

back up: move backward

close up: close (a house, an office, a store, and so on)

drive off: drive away

open up: open (a building, a library, an office, a store; make open for business or become open for business)

pull up: stop (a bus, a car, a motorcycle, a taxi; also a horse)

---

[9]Also given in list for Section 9.7.

slow down (or *up*): make go more slowly; go more slowly

speed up: make go faster; go faster

Now do Exercise 9G at the end of the chapter. ◀

VERB + ADVERB (± PREPOSITION 9.10 + OBJECT OF PREPOSITION)

Some Verb + Adverb combinations may be followed by prepositional phrases. Phrasal verbs in this category are intransitive. They are generally inseparable.

Examples

Paul *gets along with most people.* (*Gets* = verb; *along* = adverb; *with* = preposition; *most people* = object of preposition. Meaning: Paul maintains good relationships with most people.)

Does Paul *get along with* most people?

How *does* Paul *get along with* most people?

Paul is easy *to get along with.*

In questions and relative clauses in which the object of the preposition is an interrogative pronoun or a relative pronoun, the following order — inseparable — is usual:

Who(m) *does*n't Paul *get along with?*

George, who(m) Paul *gets along with,* has just been assigned to work with Paul.

NOTE: In questions and relative clauses like those above, the order Preposition + Object may occur, as in *With whom does Paul not get along? George, with whom Paul gets along,...* This order is, however, considered very formal in present-day English.

Most phrasal verbs in this category also occur without Preposition + Object of Preposition, as in these examples:

How *are* you *getting along?* (Meaning: How is your life progressing? How is everything with you?)

Some friends *dropped in on us* yesterday evening. OR: Some friends *dropped in* yesterday evening. (Meaning: Some friends came to visit us informally, without an invitation or advance notice.)

Some common Verb + Adverb (± Preposition + Object of Preposition) combinations are the following. Those that may occur as Verb + Adverb without a following preposition are marked with an asterisk (*).

*catch up (with someone/something): overtake; get up to date on (in British English, *catch someone up* also occurs)

drop in (*on* someone): visit informally without an invitation or advance notice

drop out (*of* an activity): cease to participate in

fall in love (*with* someone/something): begin to love (*in love* = adverbial particle; Verb + Adverb without Preposition and Object = *fall in love*)

get along (*with* someone): maintain relationship with. *Get along* (*with* something = job, occupation, chore): manage

get through (*with* something): finish

get together (*with* someone): meet with

give in (*to* someone/something): yield to

go back (*on* someone/something = a promise, one's word): betray; rescind. (The expression *go back* occurs also as *go* + *back* in the sense of *go* + adverb of direction).

go on (*with* an activity): continue

go through (*with* an activity): continue to completion, often with a sense of difficulty or unpleasantness

keep up (*with* someone/something): stay abreast of other persons or things

look down (*on* someone/something): regard with contempt (*Look down* occurs also as *look* +*down* in the literal sense of *look* + adverb of direction.)

look up (*to* someone/something): regard with respect. (*Look up* occurs also as *look* + adverb of direction.)

put up (*with* someone/something): endure

▶ *Now do Exercise 9H at the end of the chapter.*

For this exercise, refer to Section 9.2, pages 197–99.

A. Fill in the blank in each sentence with the appropriate preposition. Choose from the lists of verbs combining with *at, for, from,* and *in* that were given in Section 9.2.

Example

    Eileen looked ——————————— her cousin with interest. (regard)

    Answer:

    Eileen looked ———— at ———— her cousin with interest.

1. Eileen looked ——————————— her friends in a dreamy manner. (=regard)

2. She asked them what time they were going to call ——————————— her that evening. (= come to escort her to another place)

3. Her good news called ——————————— a celebration. (= demanded)

4. John's car differs ——————————— yours only in its color scheme.

5. Do you believe ——————————— the accuracy of these statistics?

6. George thought that his story was funny, but nobody laughed

    ——————————— it.

7. Would you care ——————————— some tea? (= like)

8. Let us hope ——————————— good weather for the party tomorrow.

9. The dog next door escaped ——————————— his kennel.

10. I was looking ——————————— an old movie on television when you called. (= regard; watch)

11. Catherine has been looking ——————————— new cars for a month. (= regard; inspect with a view to buying)

12. He has been looking ——————————— a new car to replace his old one. (= search for)

13. Mr. Dillard has just retired ——————————— his position as vice-president of his firm.

14. Did your brother engage ——————————— competitive sports when he was a student?

15. It is not polite to point ——————————— people.

16. How many people must vote ——————————— the proposal in question in order for it to be adopted?

17. What is the greatest number of people who may vote ——————————— the proposal in order for it not to be adopted?

18. I hope that Patricia will recover ——————————— her cold in time to come to our party.

19. Everyone in our club will have to participate _____ preparations for the fall reception if it is to be a success.

20. I must study for tomorrow's quiz. I have only glanced _____ my notes.

21. We will wait _____ you until you get back from class.

22. I hope that George will persevere _____ his efforts to get an A in physics.

23. Margaret and her cousin smiled _____ each other.

24. I wondered _____ Harold's decision to apply to medical school instead of law school.

25. Francis had wished _____ a horse of his own for years, and finally he was able to buy one.

26. Jimmie had never seen an elephant before, and he just stared

    _____ it.

27. The severity of the rains last week resulted _____ the closing of several main streets.

28. Fortunately a group of citizens succeeded _____ their efforts to mark out several bicycle routes through the city.

29. Helen is always busy because she has her father to care _____.

30. Fred is glad that he has his sister to confide _____.

31. I do not know what to get my brother for his birthday. He is a difficult person to

    shop _____.

32. Margaret smiled encouragingly _____ her cousin.

33. Dr. Edwards does not care greatly _____ modern art.

34. The passengers all waited patiently _____ the plane to take off.

35. Everyone does not believe firmly _____ exercise as a way to health and happiness.

B. As in Part A of this exercise, fill in the blank in each sentence with the appropriate preposition. Choose from the list of verbs combining with *of, of/about, on, to,* and *with* that was given in Section 9.2. In some cases both *of* and *about* may be acceptable.

1. Beware _____ the dog.

2. Helen and Arthur have agreed _____ a date for their wedding.

3. Expert gardeners do not always agree _____ each other on the best ways to grow their favorite plants.

4. Be sure to listen _____ the evening news on television.

5. Howard Williams has been associated _____ a leading law firm since he graduated from law school.

6. The students have been talking _____ their plans after graduation for months.

7. Students are cooperating _____ local highway personnel in cleaning up litter along the roads.

8. Bill can always be depended _____ to keep his promises.

9. What do you think _____ the new art show?

10. What do you think _____ going on a picnic this Saturday?

11. My aunt will insist _____ our staying for lunch.

12. Phyllis has often spoken _____ you.

13. What part of the plan for a new auditorium do you object _____?

14. What do Jane's duties in her new job consist _____?

15. What is Dr. Ellis going to speak _____ tomorrow evening?

16. I believe that Dr. Ellis will lecture _____ jade carvings tomorrow evening.

17. Someone is knocking _____ the door.

18. Margaret's new job is something to dream _____.

19. A site for the new civic auditorium has yet to be decided _____.

20. Tell me which of these magazines to subscribe _____.

21. Fred speaks enthusiastically _____ his instructors.

22. The committee has not agreed unanimously _____ a chairman.

23. Alice has decided firmly _____ law as a profession.

24. Please cooperate fully _____ your new club president.

25. Sometimes students do not listen carefully enough _____ the instructions for taking an examination.

Verb + Adverb Combination + Direct Object   9B

For this exercise, refer to Sections 9.3–9.4, pages 199–201.
A. Phrasal verbs for this exercise are from *bring about* through *eat up* on the list in Section 9.4. Follow these instructions: (a) rewrite the sentence using a different order of Verb and Adverb; (b) rewrite the sentence changing the direct object to a pronoun, following the rule of word order for pronoun direct objects.

Example

Your story *has brought back* many memories.

Answer:

a. _____ Your story *has brought* many memories *back*. _____

_____ Your story *has brought* them *back*. _____

1. Lucy's aunt *brought up* those children.

a. _____

b. _____

2. Have you *checked over* your test papers?

    a. _____

    b. _____

3. The city council *called off* the band concert because of rain.

    a. _____

    b. _____

4. The new administration *has* not *brought about* many changes.

    a. _____

    b. _____

5. The mayor *will bring up* the matter of a new budget today.

    a. _____

    b. _____

6. My secretary *will do over* this letter.

    a. _____

    b. _____

7. Please *drink up* all of your milk.

    a. _____

    b. _____

8. If you *do* not *eat up* all your vegetables, you may not have any dessert.

    a. _____

      _____

    b. _____

      _____

9. Alan *must check over* some papers.

    a. _____

    b. _____

10. The garage attendant *has* not *brought back* my car.

    a. _____

    b. _____

B. Phrasal verbs for this exercise are from *figure out* through *point out* on the list in Section 9.4. Follow these instructions: (a) fill in the blank with a two-word verb corresponding to the expression given in parentheses; (b) rewrite the sentence using a different order of verb and adverb; (c) rewrite the sentence changing the direct object to a pronoun, following the rule of word order for pronoun direct objects.

Example

Mr. Wilson _____ a great deal of money to charity.
(give: intensive meaning)

Answer:

a. Mr. Wilson _____gives away_____ a great deal of money to charity.

b. _____Mr. Wilson gives a great deal of money away to charity._____

c. _____Mr. Wilson gives it away to charity._____

1. a. Last night's speaker _____ some interesting facts. (mention)

    b. _____

    c. _____

2. a. I have to go to the library and _____ some words in the unabridged dictionary. (seek and find information)

    b. _____

    _____

    c. _____

    _____

3. a. Please _____ this job application form. (complete)

    b. _____

    c. _____

4. a. The campus bookstore has _____ the price on nearly all of its books. (reduce)

    b. _____

    _____

    c. _____

    _____

5. a. "How much gas do you need today?" "Just _____ the tank, please." (fill completely)

    b. _____

    c. _____

6. a. Tell me all of the facts in the matter. Do not _____ the facts. (withhold; fail to tell)

    b. _____

    _____

    c. _____

    _____

7. a. Our instructor always _____ test papers promptly. (return)

b. _____

c. _____

8. a. Our instructor _____ course syllabuses at the beginning of the semester. (distribute)

b. _____

_____

c. _____

_____

9. a. I cannot quite _____ these instructions. (understand)

b. _____

c. _____

10. a. Have you _____ this report? (read over; examine)

b. _____

_____

c. _____

_____

11. a. The day of the parade was cold and gray, and everyone

_____ heavy winter clothes. (wear)

b. _____

_____

c. _____

_____

12. a. Lillian will never _____ her friends. (disappoint)

b. _____

c. _____

13. a. I _____ some notes while you were speaking. (write)

b. _____

c. _____

14. a. I must go shopping because I must _____ several presents. (choose)

b. _____

c. _____

15. a. Lewis never _____ secrets. (reveal)

b. _____

c. _____

C. Phrasal verbs for this exercise are from *put aside* through *write down* on the list in Section 9.4. Fill in each blank with a two-word verb corresponding to the expression given in parentheses.

1. The students all _____ their warmest clothes for their trip to the mountains. (don)

2. I have just been given some extra chores and must _____ my promise to go shopping with you. (retract)

3. Our instructor has _____ our test until next week. (postpone)

4. Please bring the notes that you have _____ to our next class meeting. (write)

5. Let's _____ our work for a while and relax. (stop doing something with the intention of continuing the activity later)

6. It is time for dinner, children. Please _____ your toys. (place them where they belong when not in use)

7. At tomorrow's class meeting, the matter of the comprehensive examination will be _____. (discuss; two possible answers)

8. Paul _____ several job offers before he decided which one to accept. (consider carefully)

9. Let me _____ my hands before I look at your letter. (wash)

10. Somebody has _____ all of the hot water. (use completely)

11. I have decided to buy this book. Will you please _____ it _____ for me? (wrap)

12. Let's _____ plans for our trip with a travel agent. (discuss)

13. You may borrow the notes that I _____ in class while you were absent. (write down)

14. The reading assignment for today's class contained too much information to be _____ on one reading. (understand)

15. These old newspapers are not to be _____. They can be recycled. (discard with sense of waste)

Verb + Adverb Combinations (Intransitive)   9C

For this exercise, refer to Section 9.5, pages 202–203. Complete each sentence below with a two-word verb equivalent to the term in parentheses. Choose from the list in Section 9.5.

Example

A truck _____ on the highway and delayed traffic for hours. (cease to function)
Answer:
A truck _____ broke down _____ on the highway and delayed traffic for hours.

1. Everyone will have to _____ to be heard in this large auditorium. (speak loudly enough to be heard)

2. You have some excellent ideas about our club project. I hope that you will _____ at the meeting today. (speak so as to make one's opinions known)

3. Our plans for the weekend have _____ because Stephen broke a leg yesterday. (not develop; not be successful)

4. You must be tired after your trip. Would you like to _____ before dinner? (rest until refreshed)

5. What a loud noise! It sounds as though a bomb _____. (explode)

6. I do not know where Paula is. She has just _____ somewhere. (go somewhere indefinite)

7. Please _____. (move from standing to sitting position)

8. Whenever we light the fire, our dog _____ in front of the fireplace. (settle in a reclining position)

9. We cannot watch television. Our television set has _____. (cease to function)

10. During the storm last night, a huge tree _____ and damaged our front porch. (topple toward the ground)

11. It is fun to watch children _____. (grow from childhood to adulthood)

12. A new tenant has been found for your apartment. When are you planning to _____? (vacate a residence)

13. When does the new tenant want to _____? (take up residence)

14. There is room for one more in this taxi. Please _____. (enter)

15. When the taxi arrived, three people _____. (exit from)

16. The plane is due to depart in fifteen minutes. Passengers with tickets may now _____. (board)

17. The train will stop in this station for ten minutes. Passengers with through tickets should not _____. (leave)

18. What time do your local television stations _____? (start broadcasting)

19. What time do your local television stations _____? (stop broadcasting)

20. It is time to _____ for your afternoon nap. (settle in a reclining position)

Phrasal Verbs

For this exercise, refer to Section 9.6, pages 203–204. For each item below, (a) fill in the blank with a two-word verb equivalent of the expression given in parentheses; (b) complete the sentence with a different word order of Verb + Adverb; (c) complete the sentence using a pronoun direct object and using correct word order; (d) complete the sentence using the two-word verb without a direct object. Choose from the list in Section 9.6.

Example

    a. I must _____clean up_____ the house before my guests arrive.

       (clean completely)

    b. I must _____clean the house up_____

    c. I must _____clean it up_____

    d. I must _____clean up_____

1. a. You can _____ the house while I get the car. (lock; lock all the doors and windows)

    b. You _____

    c. You _____

    d. You _____

2. a. George just _____ my sister. (telephone)

    b. George just _____

    c. George just _____

    d. George just _____

3. a. My sister is going to _____ George. (return a telephone call)

    b. My sister _____

    c. My sister _____

    d. My sister _____

4. a. Alice's brother just _____ the house. (pass)

    b. He _____

    c. He _____

    d. He _____

5. a. Do you plan to _____ your work before June? (finish completely)

    b. Do you plan to _____

    c. Do you plan to _____

    d. Do you plan to _____

6. a. Once Harry has an idea, he never _____ that idea. (surrender)

   b. He _____

   c. He _____

   d. He _____

7. a. I must _____ the yard before our party. (clean completely)

   b. I _____

   c. I _____

   d. I _____

8. a. You must _____ the good work. (continue)

   b. You _____

   c. You _____

   d. You _____

9. a. Pat has _____ money all year for a trip. (save)

   b. Pat _____

   c. Pat _____

   d. Pat _____

10. a. Do you think that you will _____ your chores before dinner? (finish)

   b. Will you _____

   c. Will you _____

   d. Will you _____

9E   Verb + Adverb Combinations (Transitive and Intransitive)

For this exercise, refer to Section 9.7, pages 204–205. For each item below, (a) fill in the blank with a two-word verb equivalent of the expression given in parentheses; (b) complete the sentence with a different word order of Verb + Adverb; (c) complete the sentence using a pronoun direct object; (d) complete the sentence using the two-word verb without a direct object. Choose from the list in Section 9.7.

Example

   a. The guide _____ hurried up _____ the hikers because it was getting dark. (hurry)

   b. The guide _____ hurried the hikers up because it was getting dark. _____

   c. The guide _____ hurried them up because it was getting dark. _____

   d. The guide _____ hurried up because it was getting dark. _____

Phrasal Verbs

1. a. Evelyn's good advice _____ the committee members. (make or become less angry or upset)

   b. Her good advice _____

   c. Her good advice _____

   d. The committee members _____

2. a. What time do you _____ the children in the morning? (cause to stop sleeping; stop sleeping)

   b. What time do you _____

   c. What time do you _____

   d. What time do the children _____

3. a. Please don't _____ the children before seven. (cause to leave a bed after sleeping)

   b. Please don't _____

   c. Please don't _____

   d. The children should not _____

4. a. Mrs. Penney is always _____ her children. (display others or oneself for attention)

   b. Mrs. Penney _____

   c. Mrs. Penney _____

   d. The children _____

5. a. An excellent doctor _____ our star athlete after a football accident. (help someone recover, or recover oneself, from sickness or difficulties)

   b. A doctor _____

   c. A doctor _____

   d. Our star athlete _____

6. a. Mr. Johnson _____ Bob so that he would not be late for school. (hurry)

   b. Mr. Johnson _____

   c. Mr. Johnson _____

   d. Bob _____

7. a. The registrar's office is _____ students to work during registration. (put a name on list)

   b. The registrar's office _____

   c. The registrar's office _____

   d. Students _____

Exercises

8. a. Please _____ the dishes. (wash)

b. Please _____

c. Please _____

d. Please _____

9. a. George _____ his new rubber tree in a large pot after bringing it home from the nursery. (place someone or something in a standing position; rise to or be in a standing position)

b. George _____

_____

c. George _____

_____

d. The rubber tree would not _____ in the pot but kept falling over.

(Different meaning: Gentlemen _____ when a lady enters a room.)

10. a. The ushers _____ the audience before curtain time. (make or become quiet)

b. The ushers _____

c. The ushers _____

d. The audience _____

The Verb + Adverb combinations in the following sentences have different transitive and intransitive meanings.

11. a. Our local newspaper _____ a morning edition every day at the present time. (produce work or results)

b. Our newspaper _____

_____

c. Our newspaper _____

_____

d. A capacity audience _____ for the performance last night. (gather)

12. a. John _____ his jacket. (remove)

b. John _____

c. John _____

d. The plane _____ on time just after we boarded. (depart)

13. a. Anne has never studied French formally. She just

_____ French. (learn informally)

    b. She just _____

    c. She just _____

    d. I hope that your spirits will soon _____. (improve)

14. a. A car nearly _____ our neighbor's dog yesterday. (hit)

    b. A car _____

    c. A car _____

    d. We all _____ to see whether he had been hurt. (run toward with direction)

15. a. Please have the printer _____ fifty copies of our announcement. (produce printed materials)

    b. Please have the printer _____

_____

    c. Please have the printer _____

_____

    d. Someone _____ with all my other copies. (run away)

Verb + Adverb Combinations (Transitive and Intransitive): Direct Object Becomes Subject   9F

For this exercise, refer to Section 9.8, pages 205–206. For each of the following items, (a) fill in the blank with a two-word verb equivalent of the expression given in parentheses; (b) complete the sentence with a pronoun direct object; (c) complete the sentence using the two-word verb. Choose from the list in Section 9.8.

Example

I have ___worn out___ this coat. (make unusable through use)

I have ___worn it out_____.

This coat ___has worn out_____.

1. a. Anne has _____ this frying pan. (make unusable through use)

    b. She has _____.

    c. This frying pan _____.

2. a. Be sure to _____ the leaves after you have finished raking. (burn completely)

    b. Be sure to _____.

    c. The leaves have not yet all _____.

3. a. Someone _____ the old barn on our property last fall. (burn completely)

   b. Someone _____.

   c. The old barn on our property _____.

4. a. The wind has _____ the clouds. (blow with direction)

   b. The wind has _____.

   c. The clouds _____.

5. a. Last night's rain has _____ the area considerably. (make or become cool)

   b. Last night's rain has _____ considerably.

   c. The area _____ considerably.

6. a. The furnace will quickly _____ the house. (heat completely)

   b. The furnace will quickly _____.

   c. The house _____.

7. a. The owners of a local mine have _____ the mine for repairs. (close)

   b. They have _____ for repairs.

   c. The mine _____ for repairs.

8. a. Bob will _____ the necessary plans for us. (develop; succeed)

   b. Bob will _____.

   c. The plans _____.

9. a. Researchers are always _____ new facts about history. (discover; appear)

   b. Researchers are always _____.

   c. New facts about history are always _____.

10. a. Jane is always _____ interesting people. (discover; appear)

    b. Jane is always _____.

    c. Interesting people _____.

9G   Verb + Adverb Combinations: All Patterns of Verb + Adverb in Sections 9.6, 9.7, and 9.8

For this exercise, refer to Section 9.9, pages 206–207. For each of the following items, (a) fill in the blank with a two-word verb equivalent of the expression given in parentheses; (b) complete the sentence with a pronoun direct object; (c) and (d) complete the sentences using the two-word verb without a direct object. Choose from the list in Section 9.9.

Phrasal Verbs

Example

    a. Bob <u>   pulled up   </u> his car a few minutes ago. (stop)

    b. Bob <u> </u> pulled it up <u>   </u>.

    c. Bob <u>   </u> pulled up <u>   </u>.

    d. The car <u>   </u> pulled up <u>   </u>.

1. a. Someone _____ his car and caused an accident. (move backwards)

    b. Someone _____

    c. Someone _____

    d. A car _____

2. a. A policeman _____ his motorcycle when he saw the accident. (make go faster; go faster)

    b. The policeman _____

    c. The policeman _____

    d. The motorcycle _____

3. a. A taxi driver _____ his cab when he saw the accident. (stop)

    b. The cab driver _____

    c. The cab driver _____

    d. The cab _____

4. a. A bus driver just _____ his bus when he saw the accident. (drive away)

    b. The bus driver just _____

    c. The bus driver just _____

    d. The bus just _____

5. a. Ruth _____ her car but did not stop. (make go more slowly; go more slowly)

    b. Ruth _____

    c. Ruth _____

    d. Ruth's car _____

6. a. What time does the librarian _____ the library in the morning? (open)

    b. What time does the librarian _____?

    c. What time does the librarian _____?

    d. What time does the library _____?

7. a. Does the librarian _____ the library at seven? (close)

   b. Does the librarian _____ at seven?

   c. Does the librarian _____ at seven?

   d. Does the library _____ at seven?

8. a. Helen _____ her horse when the guide signaled to stop. (stop)

   b. Helen _____ her horse.

   c. Helen _____

   d. The horse _____

9. a. The guards _____ the bank at ten o'clock. (open for business)

   b. The guards _____

   c. The guards _____

   d. The bank _____

10. a. The engineer _____ the train as it approached the city. (make go more slowly; go more slowly)

    b. The engineer _____

    c. The engineer _____

    d. The train _____

9H   Verb + Adverb (± Preposition + Object of Preposition)

For this exercise, refer to Section 9.10, pages 207–208.
A. Fill in the blank in each sentence below with the appropriate preposition. Choose from the list in Section 9.10.

Example

I am sure that Tom will not *give in* _____ discouragement because of one low grade. (yield to)

Answer:

I am sure that Tom will not *give in* ____ to ____ discouragement because of one low grade.

1. Edward *looks up* _____ his father. (regard with respect)

2. Alan is earning his way through school as a housecleaner. He does not *look down* _____ any kind of honest work. (regard with contempt)

3. Are you *going on* _____ your studies after you have finished your undergraduate work? (continue)

4. Anne started walking to school about ten minutes ago. I do not think that we can *catch up* _____ her. (overtake)

Phrasal Verbs

5. I am so far behind in my work that I think I will never *catch up*

    _____ it. (get up to date on)

6. When do you expect to *get through* _____ your work? (finish)

7. In my opinion Edward does not really need a new car. He just wants to *keep up* _____ his friends. (stay abreast of)

8. I have so much work to do at this time of year that I can hardly *keep up* _____ it. (stay abreast of)

9. How *are you getting along* _____ your teachers this year? (maintain relationship with)

10. How are you *getting along* _____ your work? (manage)

11. *Marilyn* did not want to sing, but she *gave in* _____ her friends' requests and did. (yield)

12. Arthur *fell in love* _____ Helen at first sight. (begin to love)

13. Joan *fell in love* _____ her new home the moment that she saw it. (begin to love)

14. Alan is sometimes hard *to put up* _____ because he is often late for appointments. (endure)

15. One often has *to put up* _____ a great deal of noise and traffic in a large city. (endure)

16. On major holidays we always try *to get together* _____ our families. (meet with)

17. George had *to drop out* _____ school last semester because he had been injured in an automobile accident. (cease to participate in)

18. Since we made all our arrangements for our trip, I think that we had better *go through* _____ them. (continue to completion)

19. Henry felt that he could not *go through* _____ his examination, and he told his adviser so. (continue to completion with a sense of difficulty or unpleasantness)

20. We see you too seldom. Please *drop in* _____ us some time soon. (visit informally without invitation or advance notice)

B. Complete each sentence below with a Verb + Adverb expression *without Preposition + Object*, equivalent to the expression in parentheses.

Example

I am so far behind in my work that I think I will never
_____ . (get up to date)

Answer:

I am so far behind in my work that I think I will never
        catch up   .

1. Anne left ten minutes ago. I do not think that we can

   _____. (overtake [her])

2. You do so many things all the time that I do not see how you

   _____. (stay abreast)

3. We have not seen you in a long time. Let's _____ soon.
   (meet)

4. George's accident has kept him out of school for nearly a year. I hope that he

   will not just _____. (cease to participate)

5. Mrs. Rogers was in the middle of vacuuming her living room when a neighbor

   just _____. (visit informally without an invitation or advance notice)

6. When Arthur met Helen, he _____ at first sight. (begin to
   love)

7. I am interested to hear that you have a new job. How are you

   _____? (manage)

8. No matter who disagrees with your views, if you think you are right, do not

   _____. (yield)

9. Pat has to finish a few chores before she leaves her office. She does not know

   when she will _____. (finish)

10. Mr. James suffered a great many setbacks before he succeeded in business. At

    times he thought that he could not _____. (continue his
    efforts)

Phrasal Verbs

APPENDIX A
PRONUNCIATION KEY FOR
AMERICAN ENGLISH

The following symbols are used to indicate pronunciation throughout the text. They are based on the Trager-Smith phonemic alphabet of American English. The underlined letter or letters in the key word that follows each symbol indicate the part of the word that is represented by the symbol.

VOWEL SOUNDS

SIMPLE

- /i/ still
- /e/ pen
- /æ/ (digraph a) pan
- /a/ father
- /ɔ/ (broken o) law
- /u/ put
- /ə/ (schwa) but, -er (sister)

COMPLEX

- /iy/ steel
- /ey/ pain
- /ay/ white
- /ɔy/ boy
- /aw/ out
- /uw/ boot
- /ow/ no

CONSONANT SOUNDS

- /p/ pat
- /b/ bat
- /t/ to
- /d/ do
- /k/ back
- /g/ bag
- /f/ fan
- /v/ van
- /s/ wince, say

- /z/ wins, zoo
- /l/ led
- /r/ red
- /m/ my, room
- /n/ no, run
- /h/ he
- /w/ wash
- /y/ year
- /č/ search

- /ǰ/ urge
- /š/ (esh) she, wash
- /ž/ (ezh) pleasure
- /θ/ (theta) thin
- /đ/ (eth) then
- /ŋ/ (ing) sing

SEMIVOWELS

/y/ and /w/ are called "semivowels." When they occur after vowels, as in *boy* (/bɔy/) and *no* (/now/), they are considered to be vowels. When they occur before vowels, as in *yes* (/yes/) and *wish* (/wiš/), they are considered to be consonants.

All vowel sounds are voiced. The following consonant sounds are voiceless: /p, t, k, f, s, č, š, θ, h/. All the other consonant sounds are voiced.

PRONUNCIATION OF *s* AND *d* ENDINGS

Pronunciation of *s* Third-Person-Singular Present Verb Form, Regular Noun Plural *s* Ending, and *'s* Possessive Ending

(1) The *s* ending is pronounced /s/, as in *say*, after voiceless sounds except /s, č, š/.

Examples

THIRD-PERSON-SINGULAR PRESENT: *taps*, /tæps/; *sits*, /sits/; *kicks*, /kiks/; *laughs*, /læfs/.

REGULAR NOUN PLURAL: *caps*, /kæps/; *mats*, /mæts/; *baths*, /bæθs/; *socks*, /saks/; *cuffs*, /kəfs/.

's POSSESSIVE: ape's, /eyps/; cat's /kæts/; Keith's, /kiyθs/; cook's /kuks/.

(2) The *s* ending is pronounced /z/, as in *zoo*, after voiced sounds except /z, ǰ, ž/.

Examples

THIRD-PERSON-SINGULAR PRESENT: *says*, /sez/; *sews*, /sowz/; *bids*, /bidz/; *digs*, /digz/; *shoves*, /šəvz/; *stirs*, /stərz/; *tells*, /telz/; *seems*, /siymz/; *means*, /miynz/.

REGULAR NOUN PLURAL: *plays*, /pleyz/; *rows*, /rowz/; *bananas*, /bənænəz/; *lids*, /lidz/; *gloves*, /gləvz/; *razors*, /reyzərz/; *wells*, /welz/; *brooms*, /bruwmz/; *plans*, /plænz/.

's POSSESSIVE: boy's /bɔyz/; dog's, /dɔgz/; man's /mænz/; women's, /wimənz/; dove's, /dəvz/; brother's, /brəðərz/; Bill's, /bilz/; ram's /ræmz/; Anne's, /ænz/.

(3) The *s* ending is pronounced as an unstressed syllable, /əz/, after /s, z, č, ǰ, š, ž/.

Examples

THIRD-PERSON-SINGULAR PRESENT: *misses*, /misəz/; *amazes*, /əmeyzəz/; *catches*, /kæčəz/; *judges*, /ǰəǰəz/; *washes*, /wašəz/.

REGULAR NOUN PLURAL: *classes*, /klæsəz/; *quizzes*, /kwizəz/; *watches*, /wačəz/; *lodges*, /lajəz/; *wishes*, /wišəz/; *garages*, /gəražəz/.

's POSSESSIVE: Alice's, /ælisəz/; judge's, /ǰəǰəz/; fish's, /fišəz/.

Pronunciation of *d* Ending of Past and Past Participle Forms of Regular Verbs

(1) The *d* ending is pronounced /t/, as in *to*, after voiceless sounds except /t/.

Examples

> *clapped*, /klæpt/; *walked*, /wɔkt/; *coughed*, /kɔft/; *missed*, /mist/; *watched*, /wačt/; *washed*, /wašt/.

(2) The *d* ending is pronounced /d/, as in *do*, after voiced sounds except /d/.

Examples

> *played*, /pleyd/; *rubbed*, /rəbd/; *dragged*, /drægd/; *waved*, /weyvd/; *soothed*, /suwd̄d/; *buzzed*, /bəzd/; *bridged*, /briǰd/.

(3) The *d* ending is pronounced as an unstressed syllable, /əd/, after /t/ and /d/.

Examples

> *heated*, /hiytəd/; *heeded*, /hiydəd/.

APPENDIX B
PRINCIPAL PARTS OF
COMMON IRREGULAR VERBS

NOTE: The *s* (third-person-singular present) and *ing* forms are not included in this appendix because they are formed according to spelling rules. See Chapter 2, Section 2.3.

Base	Past	Past Participle
arise	arose	arisen
awake	awoke (less commonly, *awaked)*	awaked, awoken (principally British English)
be	was	been
bear	bore	born (pertaining to birthdate), borne (carried)
beat	beat	beaten
begin	began	begun
bend	bent	bent
bet	bet	bet
bite	bit	bitten
bleed	bled	bled
blow	blew	blown
break	broke	broken
bring	brought	brought
broadcast	broadcast, broadcasted	broadcast, broadcasted
build	built	built
burst	burst	burst
buy	bought	bought
cast	cast	cast
catch	caught	caught
choose	chose	chosen
come	came	come
cost	cost	cost
cut	cut	cut
deal	dealt	dealt
dig	dug	dug
dive	dived, dove	dived
do	did	done
draw	drew	drawn
dream	dreamed, dreamt	dreamed, dreamt
drink	drank	drunk
drive	drove	driven
eat	ate	eaten
fall	fell	fallen
feed	fed	fed
feel	felt	felt
fight	fought	fought
find	found	found
flee	fled	fled
fly	flew	flown
forbid	forbade	forbidden
forget	forgot	forgotten
forgive	forgave	forgiven
freeze	froze	frozen
get	got	got, gotten (American English)
give	gave	given
go	went	gone
grind	ground	ground
grow	grew	grown
hang		
intransitive:	hung	hung
transitive:	hanged	hanged

Base	Past	Past Participle
have	had	had
hear	heard	heard
hide	hid	hidden
hit	hit	hit
hold	held	held
hurt	hurt	hurt
keep	kept	kept
kneel	kneeled, knelt	kneeled, knelt
knit	knitted, knit	knitted, knit
know	knew	known
lay	laid	laid
lead	led	led
leap	leaped, leapt	leaped, leapt
leave	left	left
lend	lent	lent
let	let	let
lie (recline)[1]	lay	lain
light	lighted, lit	lighted, lit
lose	lost	lost
make	made	made
mean	meant	meant
meet	met	met
mistake	mistook	mistaken
overcome	overcame	overcome
pay	paid	paid
put	put	put
read[2]	read	read
ride	rode	ridden
ring	rang	rung
rise	rose	risen
run	ran	run
say	said	said
see	saw	seen
seek	sought	sought
sell	sold	sold
send	sent	sent
set	set	set
sew	sewed	sewn
shake	shook	shaken
shine		
intransitive:	shone	shone
transitive:	shined	shined
shoot	shot	shot
show	showed	shown, showed
shrink	shrank, shrunk	shrunk[3]
shut	shut	shut
sing	sang	sung
sink	sank, sunk	sunk[4]
sit	sat	sat
sleep	slept	slept
slide	slid	slid
speak	spoke	spoken
speed	speeded, sped	speeded, sped
spend	spent	spent
spin	spun	spun
spit	spit, spat	spit, spat
split	split	split
spread	spread	spread
spring	sprang, sprung	sprung
stand	stood	stood
steal	stole	stolen
stick	stuck	stuck

[1] lie (regular verb); with meaning of not tell the truth: lied, lied.
[2] Pronunciation: base, read /riyd/; past and past participle, read /red/.
[3] Also shrunken when used adjectivally: a shrunken dress.
[4] Also sunken when used adjectivally: a sunken ship.

Base	Past	Past Participle
sting	stung	stung
strike	struck	struck
swear	sworn	sworn
sweep	swept	swept
swim	swam	swum
swing	swung	swung
take	took	taken
teach	taught	taught
tear	tore	torn
tell	told	told
think	thought	thought
throw	threw	thrown
understand	understood	understood
wake	woke	waked, woken
	(less commonly, *waked*)	(British English)
wear	wore	worn
weave	wove	woven
weep	wept	wept
win	won	won
withdraw	withdrew	withdrawn
withhold	withheld	withheld
wring	wrung	wrung
write	wrote	written

TABLE C:

The Present and Past Systems of Verb Forms

Present System (present and all other verb forms with auxiliary in present)

Tense	Voice	Noncontinuous	Continuous
present	active	grow/grows	am/is/are growing
	passive	am/is/are grown	and/is/are being grown
future	active	will grow	will be growing
	passive	will be grown	will be being grown
present perfect	active	have/has grown	have/has been grown
	passive	have/has been grown	*have/has been being grown
future perfect	active	will have grown	will have been growing
	passive	will have been grown	*will have been being grown

Past System (past and all other verb forms with auxiliary in past)

Tense	Voice	Noncontinuous	Continuous
past	active	grew	was/were growing
	passive	was/were grown	was/were being grown
conditional	active	would grow	would be growing
	passive	would be grown	would be being grown
past perfect	active	had grown	had been growing
	passive	had been grown	*had been being grown
past conditional	active	would have grown	would have been growing
	passive	would have been grown	*would have been being grown

*Forms marked with an asterisk (*) are extremely rare and are included only to illustrate the structures of the verb forms.

Indicative and subjunctive forms of verbs in present-day English are alike with only these exceptions:

(1) the present subjunctive of all verb forms is the same as the base form for all subjects;

(2) the past subjunctive of *be* is *were* for all subjects.

Thus all subjunctive forms are the same for all subjects.

INDEX

Items marked by a dagger (†) also have an entry in the index to Volume II.

with past contrary-to-fact (unreal)
    condition, 129–30
with past real condition, 127
with present contrary-to-fact (unreal)
    condition, 127–29
with present real condition, 124–26, 127
conjunction
    coordinate, 7
    subordinate, 7
†conjunctive adverb, 6
continuous aspect, 23
continuous forms, 23
    conditional, 129
    future, 113–14
    future perfect, 114 (Note)
    past, 109–11
    past conditional, 129–30 (Note 1)
    past perfect, 129–30 (Note 1)
    past subjunctive, 129
    present, 87–91
    verbs that do not usually occur in, 89
contractions, of form auxiliaries, modals,
    and *not*, 27–28
contrary-to-fact (unreal) condition, 127–30
coordinate conjunction, 7
could
    ability expressed with, 60–61
    permission expressed with, 57–60
    possibility expressed with, 61–62
could have, ability expressed with, 60–61

d

-d, for past and past-participle forms of
    regular verbs
    pronunciation of, Appendix A
    spelling rules for adding, 19
dare (to), 70 (Note)
demand/be necessary expressions, 135–36
    patterns with, 135–36
dependent clause, 7–9. *See also*
    subordinate clause; *wh*-N clause
†dependent interrogative clause (indirect
    question), 8–9, 136–43
†determiner, 8–9, 33. *See also* indefinite
    relative adjective; interrogative
    adjective; relative adjective
†direct address, words of, 6
†direct object, 1, 2, 3
    phrasal verb and, 199–201, 203–206
    †*wh*-N form as, 9
do/does/did
    as auxiliaries in negative and
        interrogative patterns, 22
    contractions of *not* and, 27–28
    "emphatic *do*," 29 (Note)

e

†elliptical clause, *if*-clause as, 130–31
elliptical construction of verb + *to* + Verb,
    176
exclamatory sentence, *if*-condition as, 130
†expletive-*there* sentence patterns, 34

f

finite verb, 3
form, of verb, distinguished from tense, 18
form auxiliary, 21
    contractions of *not* and, 27–28
†formal usage, 12
†function (sentence function), 1–3
future continuous form, 113
future form, 21–22
    am/is/are + *going to* + Verb compared
        with, 90
future perfect continuous form, 114 (Note)
future perfect form, 24, 113–14
future time
    am/is/are + *going to* + Verb used to
        express, 90
    be about to + Verb used to express,
        90–91
    be + *to* + Verb used to express, 90
    expressions of command that imply, 91
    modals (modal auxiliaries) used to
        express, 91
    present form used to express in
        subordinate clause with adverbial
        function, 133–34
    present or present continuous form
        used to express, 90–91
    verbs with meanings that imply, 91

g

gerund, 167, 168–69. *See also* verb + verbal
    combinations
    forms of, 168–69
    spelling rules for adding *ing*, 19–20
    usage of perfect forms of, 112, 113 (Note,
        top), 170
    verb (± possessive) +, 172
    verb + to +, 178
    verbs that are followed by *to* + Verb or
        be, 173–74.

h

had better (have), 68–69
have
    auxiliary, 23–24
    pattern following, 176–77
have to, necessity or compulsion
    expressed with, 62–63

i

if-clause, 124–25. *See also* conditional
    sentence
    as elliptical clause, 130–31
    expressed without *if*, 8 (Note)
    used to express a wish, 130
imperative form, 26–27
    in present real condition, 126
†indefinite relative adjective, 8–9
†indefinite relative pronoun, 8–9
independent clause. *See* main clause
indicative mood, 25–26
indirect discourse, 136–43
    in reporting printed and written
        material, 142
†indirect object, 1, 2, 3
†indirect question (dependent
    interrogative clause), 8–9, 136–43
    punctuation in, 141
    verb forms used in, 139–43
    †information, with interrogative
        pronoun or interrogative adjective +
        noun phrase (*wh*-N form), 138–39
    information, with *when, where, why,*
        how, or adverbial expression (*wh*-Adv),
        137–38
    yes/no, 137
indirect statement, 136–43
    request in, 59–60
    verb forms used in, 139–43
    word order (patterns) in, 137
infinitive, 18, 167. *See also* bare infinitive;
    base form; *to* + Verb; verb + verbal
    combinations
infinitive phrase, 167
†informal usage, 12
†information question, 32–33. *See also*
    indirect question; questions
-ing, spelling rules for adding to base
instrument, *with* used for, 47
†interjection, 6
†interrogative adjective, 8–9, 32–33, 138–39
†interrogative pronoun, 8–9, 32–33, 138–39
intransitive two-word verb, 202–206. *See*
    also phrasal verb
intransitive verb, 3

l

let, 176–77
let's + Verb, 126
†levels of usage, 12
lexical verb, 17–18
    passive form of, following modal, 70–71
linking verb, 3
logical necessity, modals for expressing,
    64–65

m

main clause (independent clause), 7
make, 176–77
may
    permission expressed with, 57–60
    possibility expressed with, 61–62
†*means, by* used for, 47
"middle voice," 25 (Note)
might
    permission expressed with, 57–60
    possibility expressed with, 61–62
modal (modal auxiliary), 21, 27–28, 55–71.
    See also can; could; may; might; must;
    ought to; shall; should; will; would; and
    have to
    of ability, 60–61
    characteristic features of, 56
    contractions of *not* and, 27–28
    expressions related to, 68–70
    form auxiliary and, 21
    forms of, 55–56
    future meanings expressed with, 91
    future meanings expressed with
        present forms of, 125
    of logical necessity, 64–65
    of necessity or compulsion, 62–63
    of obligation, advisability, and
        expectation, 65–68
    passive forms of lexical verbs with, 70
    of permission, 57–60
    of possibility, 61–62
    in present real condition, 125
    of supposition, 64
    tenses and times expressed by, 55–56
    of willingness and volition, 56–57
modal auxiliary. *See* modal
mood, 25–27
    imperative form, 26–27
    indicative forms, 25–26
    subjunctive forms, 25–26
must
    "logical necessity" expressed with,
        64–65
    necessity or compulsion expressed
        with, 62–63
    supposition expressed with, 64

n

necessity, modals for expressing, 62–63
need (to), 70 (Note)
negative statement
    sentence patterns in, 28–30
    verb forms in, 29–30
negative *yes/no* question, with expected
    answer suggested, 31
†nominal, 2–3, 171
    verbs followed by, + *to* + Verb, 174–75
†nominal function, of verbals, 167–69
nonbasic sentence patterns, 4
nonpassive verb forms, 25
not, contractions of form auxiliaries,
    modals, and, 27–28
†noun
    †noun headword, 8
    †noun phrase, 8
    †noun clause, 8, 9, 136 (Footnote 5)

o

†object complement, 1, 2, 3
†object of preposition
    with phrasal verb, 195, 197–99, 207–208
    preposition and gerund for subordinate
        clause, 112, 113 (Note, top)
    †*wh*-N form as, 9, 139
†objective complement, 1, 2, 3
offers of assistance, 59
ought to, obligation, advisability, and
    expectation expressed with, 65–68

p

†parenthetic expression, 6
participial phrase, 167
participle, 18, 167, 169–70. *See also* verbal
    past. *See* past participle
    present. *See* present participle
particle, in phrasal verb, 195. *See also*
    phrasal verb
†passive voice, 24–25, 45–48
    active voice compared with, 46
    forms following *make, help*, and verbs of
        perception in, 178
    forms of lexical verbs with modals,
        70–71
    order of subject and auxiliary in, 45
    †prepositions used for agent, 46–48
    statal, 48 (Note)
    use of, 48
past conditional form, in past contrary-to-
    fact (unreal) condition, 129–30. *See also*
    past contrary-to-fact (unreal) condition;
    would
past continuous form, 109–11
past continuous subjunctive form, 129

past contrary-to-fact (unreal) condition,
    129–30
past form, 18, 21–22, 92–93
    adding *d* for, 19
    of common irregular verbs, Appendix B
    pronunciation of *d* ending of, Appendix
        A
    usage of, compared with usage of
        present perfect form, 92–96
    used instead of past perfect form, 112
        (Note)
past participle, 18, 169
    adding *d* for, 19
    of common irregular verbs, Appendix B
    in passive voice, 24–25
    in perfect forms, 23–24
    pronunciation of *d* ending of, Appendix
        A
    usage of, compared with usage of
        present participle (Verb-*ing*), 171
past perfect continuous form, 113 (Note),
    129–30 (Note)
past perfect form, 24, 111–13
past subjunctive form
    of *be*, 26, 128 (Note 1), 131–32
    following *wish*, 131–32
    in present contrary-to-fact (unreal)
        condition, 128
past system, verb forms following a
    say/ask verb in, 140–41, 142–43
perception, verbs of + verbal, 177–78
perfect forms (perfect tenses), 23–24
permission, modals for expressing, 57–60
"personal verb," 89
phrasal verb, 195–208
    and two-word verb, 195
    inseparable (meaning of term), 195
    noun derivatives of, 196–97 (Note)
    particle in, 195
    separable (meaning of term), 196
    types of, 195–96
    usage of, 196–97
    verb + adverb combinations, 196,
        199–208
    verb + adverb (± preposition)
        combinations, 207–208
    verb + preposition combinations, 195,
        197–99
please, 58, 126
positive statement
    sentence patterns in, 28–30
    verb forms in, 29–30
possibility, modals for expressing, 61–62
†predicate adjective, 1
†preposition
    for agent, means, and instrument,
        46–48
    object of. *See* object of preposition
    in phrasal verb. *See* phrasal verb
prepositional phrase, phrasal verb and,
    198 (Note 2)
present continuous form, 87–91
    continuing activity expressed with,
        87–88

future time expressed with, 90–91
in *if*-clause, 125
usage of, compared with usage of
present form, 86–89
present contrary-to-fact (unreal)
condition, 127–29
present form, 21–22, 86–89
ability expressed with, 88–89
future time expressed with, 90–91
future time expressed with, in
subordinate clause with adverbial
function, 133–34
professional or characteristic activity
described with, 88
repeated or habitual activity expressed
with, 87–88
usage of, compared with usage of
present continuous form, 86–89
present participle (Verb-*ing*), 18, 169
spelling rules for adding *ing*, 19–20
usage of, compared with usage of past
participle, 171
present perfect continuous form
in *if*-clause, 125
usage of, 96 (Note 2)
present perfect form, 23–24, 94–96
in *if*-clause, 125
usage of, compared with usage of past
form, 92–96
present real condition, 124–26
present subjunctive form, 26
following *demand/be necessary*
expression, 135–36
present system, verb forms following a
say/ask verb in, 139–42
principal parts of verbs, 18, Appendix B
process verb, 89 (Note), 132 (Note)
†pronoun, indefinite relative, interrogative,
and relative, 8–9
pronunciation of *s* and *d* endings,
Appendix A
punctual aspect, 23
†punctuation
in complex sentences, 11, 124
in compound sentences, 10
in indirect questions, 141

q

questions
indirect. *See* indirect question
information, with interrogative pronoun
or interrogative adjective + noun
phrase (*wh*-N form), 32–33, 138–39
information, with *when, where, why,
how,* or other adverbial expression
(*wh*-Adv), 32, 138
about obligation, advisability, and
expectation, 67–68
tag, with *yes/no* answers, 31–32
yes/no. See yes/no question

r

real condition, 124–27
†relative adjective, 8–9
†relative clause, 8–9
†relative pronoun, 8–9
remainder, the, 1
reporting *(say/ask)* expressions, 136–37
reporting printed and written material,
142
requests
in indirect discourse, 59–60
for information about whether or not an
activity is permitted, 58
for permission, 58

s

say/ask (reporting) expressions, 136–37
say/ask verbs, 136–43
in reporting printed and written
material, 142
say-words, 136–37
sentence functions, 1–3
sentence patterns. *See also* word order
basic, 2–3
definition, 2, 7
nonbasic, 4
†sentence types, 10–11
sequence of tenses, 86. *See also* verb
forms, in sentence patterns that require
special usage of
-*s*, for third-person-singular present
form, 18
pronunciation of, Appendix A
spelling rules for adding, 20
s-form (third-person-singular present
form). See -*s*
shall, 21, 22, 55, 55 (Footnote 1)
usage of *shall* and *will* for future forms,
90 (Note)
should
obligation, advisability, and expectation
expressed with, 65–68
usage of *should* and *would* for
conditional forms, 128 (Note 2)
simple sentence, 10
simple verb forms, auxiliaries and, 21–22
spelling rules for adding *d, ing,* and *s* to
verb forms, 19–20
†standard usage, 12
statal passive, 48
status verb, 89 (Note), 132 (Note)
stylistic usage, 12
†subject, 1, 2, 3
in basic sentence patterns, 2
grammatical subject, 24–25
†*wh*-N form as, 9
†subject complement, 1, 2, 3
†subjective complement, 1, 2, 3

subjunctive mood, 25–26. *See also* past
    continuous subjunctive form; past
    subjunctive form; present subjunctive
    form
†subordinate clause, 7–8. *See also*
    conditional sentence; *demand/be*
    necessary expression; elliptical clause;
    if-clause; indirect discourse; *wish*
    with adverbial function, present form to
        express future time in, 133–34
†subordinate conjunction, 7
substantive, 2
supposition, modals for expressing, 64

t

tag question, with *yes/no* answers, 31–32
tense, 18. *See also* verb forms
    form distinguished from, 18
    sequence of tenses, 86, 123–43
    time distinguished from, 25 (Note)
†*there*, expletive-*there* sentence patterns,
    34
third-person-singular present form
    (*s*-form), 18. *See also* -*s*
time
    of modals, 55–56
    tense distinguished from, 25
†time expression
    past continuous form with, 110
    past perfect form with, 113
to, in elliptical constructions following
    verbs, 176
to + Verb (infinitive), 18
transitive two-word verb, word order for,
    199–200, 203, 204, 205, 206. *See also*
    phrasal verb
transitive verb, 3
two-word verb. *See* phrasal verb

u

unreal (contrary-to-fact) condition, 127–30
†usage, levels of, 12
used to + Verb, 93

v

verb. *See also* auxiliary; modal (modal
    auxiliary)
    causative, 175
    finite, 3
    intransitive, 3
    lexical, 17–18
    linking, 3
    of perception + verbal, 177–78

"personal," 89
phrasal. *See* phrasal verb
process, 89 (Note), 132 (Note)
say/ask, 139–42
status, 89 (Note), 132 (Note)
transitive, 3
two-word. *See* phrasal verb
+ verbal combinations, 171–76
verb forms. *See also* specific forms; verb
    forms, in sentence patterns that require
    special usage of (sequence of tenses);
    and Appendix C
    active voice, 24–25
    aspect, 23–24
    continuous, 23
    form, use of term, 18
    imperative mood, 26–27, 27 (Note)
    independent usage of, 85–96
    mood, 25–27
    nonindependent, 109–14
    passive voice, 24–25, 45–48
    perfect, 23–24
    principal parts, 18-20, Appendix B
        (Principal Parts of Common Irregular
        Verbs)
    pronunciation of *d*-ending of regular
        past and past participle, Appendix A
    pronunciation of *s*-ending of third-
        person-singular present form,
        Appendix A
    properties of, 21–27
    spelling rules for adding *d, ing,* and *s,*
        19–20
    simple, 21–22
    subjunctive mood, 25–26
    tense, 18, 25 (Note)
    voice, 24–25
verb forms, in sentence patterns that
    require special usage of (sequence of
    tenses), 86, 123–43
    in clauses following *wish*, 131–33
    in conditional sentences, 123–31
    in indirect discourse, 136–43
    pattern with *demand/be necessary*
        expressions, 135–36
    present form to express future time in
        subordinate clauses with adverbial
        function, 133–34
verb + verbal combinations, 171–78
    have, let, make, help and verbs of
        perception + verbal, 176–78
    to, in elliptical forms of verb + *to* +
        Verb, 176
    verb + nominal + *to* + Verb, 174
    verb (± possessive) + Verb-*ing*, 172
    verb + *to* + Verb 172–73
    verb + *to* + Verb or *(for)* nominal + *to*
        + Verb, 175
    verb + *to* + Verb or Verb-*ing*, 173–74
    verb + *to* + Verb-*ing*, 178
verbal. *See also* gerund; infinitive; past
    participle; present participle; *to*, in
    elliptical constructions following verbs;
    to + Verb

tense and time of, 170
types and forms of, 167–170
usage of Verb-*ing* (present participle)
   compared with usage of past
   participle, 171
Verb-*ing*. *See* gerund; present participle
voice, 24–25. *See also* passive voice

W

wh-Adv, interrogative adverbial words and
   expressions, 32
   indirect questions with, 138
   in information questions, 32, 138
†*wh*-N clause, 8–9, 138–43
†*wh*-N form, 8–9
   indirect questions with, 138–39
   in information questions, 32–33, 138–39
will, 21, 22, 55, 55 (Footnote 1)
   modal use of, 56–57, 124 (Note)
   usage of *will* and *shall* for future forms,
      90 (Note)
wish, verb forms in clauses, following,
   131–33
   use of *if*-clause to express a wish, 130
†word order, 1–9. *See also* sentence
   patterns and specific types of sentences
   and clauses
   of absolutes, 6

†of adverbials of place, manner,
   frequency, and time, 4–5
†of *always*-words (adverbs of indefinite
   time), 7
of prepositional phrases expressing
   agent, 47–58
of verb + adverb in phrasal verbs, 196,
   199–200
of verb + preposition in phrasal verbs,
   195–96, 197–98
would
   in conditional form, 127, 128 (Note 2)
   in conditional form to express past
      time, 93–94
   modal use of, 56–57, 124 (Note)
   past conditional form, 129
   usage of *would* and *should* as
      conditional auxiliaries, 128 (Note 2)
would rather (have), 69–70

Y

yes/no answer, tag question with, 31–32
yes/no question
   indirect, word order in, 137
   negative, with expected answer
      suggested, 31
   sentence patterns in, 28–32
   verb forms in, 29–30

```
A  3
B  4
C  5
D  6
E  7
F  8
G  9
H  0
I  1
J  2
```